Mario Batali Simple Italian Food

Mario Batali

Simple Italian Food

Recipes from My Two Villages

PHOTOGRAPHS BY **MARK FERRI**

CLARKSON POTTER PUBLISHERS **NEW YORK**

To Susi, Benno, and Leo

Some recipes have previously appeared on Food Network's website.

Copyright © 1998 by Mario Batali
Photographs copyright © 1998 by Mark Ferri
Additional photography copyright © 1998 by Melanie Acevedo

Published by Clarkson N. Potter, Inc., 201 East 50th Street, New York, New York 10022. Member of the Crown Publishing Group.

Random House, Inc. New York, Toronto, London, Sydney, Auckland
www.randomhouse.com

CLARKSON N. POTTER, POTTER, and colophon are trademarks of Clarkson N. Potter, Inc.
Printed in the United States of America

Design: Memo Productions; Douglas Riccardi, Kate Johnson, Lisa Eaton

Library of Congress Cataloging-in-Publication Data
Batali, Mario.
   [Simple Italian food]
   Mario Batali simple Italian food : recipes from my two villages
/ color photographs by Mark Ferri. — 1st ed.
      p.   cm.
   Includes index.
   1. Cookery, Italian. I. Title.
TX723.B327   1998
641.5945—dc21   98-35508
                                                         CIP

ISBN 0-609-60300-0
10 9 8 7

Acknowledgments

Special thanks to the community of restaurateurs and chefs in NYC who make it fun to cook and hang in a big city.

To the farmers and suppliers who bring the best ingredients to my two restaurants;

To the regular and irregular customers at Pó and Babbo who have supported us from day one;

To everyone at Food Network for giving me a soapbox;

To Tom Waits for rhythm and inspiration;

To my agent, Marcy Posner;

To my editor, Pam Krauss, for making sense of everything;

To my entire family for eating so well;

To Douglas and Lisa for making this book look like it does, and Marcia and Sabrina for the recipe affirmations;

To Dean and Deluca, who graciously allowed us to photograph in their store;

To my inner ring of advisors: Shanks, Bobby, Andy, Faith, Ed, and, most of all, Susi;

To my staff at Pó: Jude, Norchy, Jennifer, Puff, Lips, Mike, Nina, Peltz, Peter, Hannah, Frank from Venezia, my partners Steve Crane and Joe Bastianich, and all my past sous chefs, without whom I am, and would have been, nothing;

To all the residents of Borgo Capanne, the Lorenzini family, Bob, Gianni, Betta, and Mara especially;

To this beautiful life, a constant source of joy.

Contents

Simplicity.

An unremarkable word, and one that is perhaps overused today. It is nonetheless one of the most fundamental and at the same time most elusive keys to preparing food well. Certainly it is the absolute cornerstone of the spectacular and glorious regional Italian fare that has so influenced my approach to cooking. It is also the object of my desire, whether I am re-creating a 100-year-old dish from the hill country between Bologna and Firenze, or creating a new dish to demonstrate on television. It is certainly my design when cooking at home for friends and family and what is expected at my restaurants, Pó and Babbo, in New York City.

Perfectly pristine ingredients, combined sensibly and cooked properly, are what make Italian food taste so good, both in Italy and here in the United States. Reducing the distance and time food spends on its journey from the soil to the plate is the modus operandi for all Italian cooks—and those who wish to cook in the Italian style. From the young pizzaiaoli to the savvy homemakers, buying the freshest, peak-of-season produce is a habit that is observed for every meal, every day, always. A special holiday may be celebrated with a complex five-course meal; for other days, an arugula salad with shaved cheese and some spaghetti with hot pepper, garlic, and olive oil may do. But in either case, the rigorous pursuit of incomparable fresh-ness elevates the seemingly banal to the superb.

Many of my favorite dishes are those based on the fewest ingredients. And when there are fewer members in the choir, each element must sing perfectly, or harmony is lost. One dish I love is sliced raw mushrooms, drizzled with new olive oil and showered with some shards of local cheese; if even one of these three components is anything but perfect . . . the dish is anything but great.

This passion for simplicity and purity in the dishes I prepare became deeply ingrained in me during the years I spent in Italy cooking at La Volta, a mountainside trattoria on the border of Emilia-Romagna and Toscana. It was there that I relearned how simple cooking could be infinitely more satisfying to my palate (already excited and educated by six years in professional kitchens), both as a cook and as a diner. I made this important move after a stint with the Four Seasons Hotel Company in both San Francisco and Santa Barbara, when I realized that I was no longer inspired by the smooth efficiency of corporate cooking. I decided to submerge myself into Italian life to refine my cooking and language skills. With the help of my father, I sent out some letters to business contacts requesting an apprenticeship opportunity and eventually chose Trattoria La Volta, as they were the first—and only—to reply.

I arrived in Porretta Terme, the closest "big" town, after a ninety-minute train ride from Bologna, winding along the Reno River past cattle and Parmigiano-Reggiano producers, apple and pear trees, honey bee farms, and beautiful villages. I was met there by the owners, Gianni and Roberto Valdiserri, sons of Armando Valdiserri. They immediately drove me up to the restaurant, perched six hundred meters above Porretta on the border of Toscana, to meet everyone and have lunch.

That day I met Gianni's wife, Betta, and Roberto's wife, Mara, the cooks at the restaurant, who had learned from their mothers as well as from Signora Valdiserri, who had recently passed away. Neither Betta nor Mara had been to cooking school, but they both possessed unerring palates and were able to dissect a dish in one or two bites. I also met Quintiglio, Betta's father and resident truffle hunter, porcini and wild mushroom expert, and general forager for wild greens, berries, and various edibles from the forest floor; Emiliano, Gianni's fifteen-year-old son, home on weekends from pilot school in Forli, who helped Gianni in the dining room and the wine cellar; and Mila, Gianni's four-year-old daughter.

Roberto was the older of the two owners, and the larger, with a belly that betrayed years of tortellini and lambrusco. He worked in heat treatment at Pai Demm and was our original contact as he was an old acquaintance of my dad. Each day he would join us for lunch and return each evening to work service as the expediter. Mara worked at La Volta mostly on weekends and holidays, so she and Roberto ate many of their evening meals at their house, thirty meters down the road, away from the post office. Roberto helped me constantly with the language and cultural nuances and often took me out on field trips to see and taste the traditional Emilian table.

Gianni was actually in charge of all aspects of operating La Volta. He had done odd jobs in food and wine before opening the restaurant in 1984, but he had never really worked in a traditional sense. He worked nightly and daily as a waiter with the orally recited menu and wine list, purchased the food and wine, and was generally considered the cool guy around both the little village and Porretta. He was very fond of gambling on horses and cards and often had big games in the trattoria after dinner was served. We frequently went on overnight field trips to wineries or great restaurants on our days off. We went as far away as Venice and San Remo— trips that often included visits to the local casino for a few games of cards. Gianni had built a name for himself as a savvy wine buyer and knew many of Italy's great winemakers personally. In retrospect, the opportunity to live among such an extraordinary group of people and have them as friends and guides added a richness and intensity to my three-year experience in Italy that I could never have found had I looked for it.

La Volta was a twenty-five-seat restaurant with the finest crystal stemware, exquisite linens, solid oak tables, and a rustic elegance that whispered comfort as soon as a guest was seated. Like most restaurants in Italy it opened for dinner at 7:45 each evening, right after the staff meal. The room would fill up between 8:00 and 9:00 and that was the service. Italians would never go out to eat for a simple plate of pasta. At La Volta they came to eat, and eat, and eat. Often a meal would start with one or two different antipasti and continue with three courses of pasta. This was followed by a main course, a selection of local pecorino cheeses and Parmigiano with local chestnut honey, and then dessert. Such a meal could easily last at least three hours. The Italians have a saying that nobody ages while seated at the dinner table, so most of our customers must have been a lot younger then their passports said!

The menu at La Volta was for the most part orally recited, although on some special occasions we would handwrite five or six copies. Since we were in the lower Apennines and had Quintiglio on our team, we always served wild porcini mushrooms, white truffles, and other exotic foraged foods in season. During the autumn, neighbors would bring in wild boar or venison, or wild game birds like teal or tiny woodcocks. In the late spring, villagers might bring us wild asparagus or succulent wild strawberries in exchange for a bowl of pasta. We made weekly excursions to the larger markets in Bologna or Pistoia to soak up inspiration, but our menus were truly dictated by season.

As Betta and I got more comfortable working together, and Gianni started tasting our collaborative efforts during the family meal, I began to have input into the daily menu. Each morning we would start the day by making pasta dough and rolling it out by hand to form strichetti, pappardelle, tortelloni, and tagliatelle. Then Betta would start to write the menu for the day as I would check the refrigerator and the things that Gianni had purchased. We would discuss the menu a bit and then go to work, preparing and tasting until we were happy with it and/or ready for lunch. After lunch everyone took a nap and then came back to the kitchen around 5:30 to prepare family meal and open again at 7:45. And so it went, life in the mountain town of Borgo Capanne, a tiny little village.

Many people ask me why I ever left such an idyllic life. The truth is I was a bit home-sick for America, and besides it was nearly impossible to obtain legitimate working papers. So, after nearly three years, I decided to return home to find my *own* village, taking back with me as much of the experience of Italy's simple, perfect culinary world as I could carry. While I left behind some of the great ingredients used in many classic dishes, I returned with a refined palate, open eyes, and a greater appreciation for the straightforward, traditional techniques that allow good ingredients to shine without too much competition.

Less than a year later I landed in New York in an old red sauce place owned by the father of a college acquaintance. The restaurant had been poorly managed for years, and my efforts to revive it, although not unnoticed by foodies in New York, were ultimately not enough to save it. It was during this time, however, that I met my future wife, Susi Cahn. I was enjoying a drink on my first day off in New York, and I met Susi when she stopped in to drop off some of her hobby produce for Alan Harding, then chef at Nosmo King. Susi was growing exotic varieties of vegetables in a small corner of her family's Hudson Valley farm, which happened to be the Coach Dairy Goat Farm. It was Susi who introduced me to the Coach Farm goat cheeses,

and I was soon buying the cheeses along with her vegetables. Somewhere in there we also managed to fall in love.

By pure luck, and I've had a lot, but also thanks to Susi and her connections to the New York food world, I came upon a lease for a space in the Village. With Steve Crane, an old buddy from San Francisco, I pooled together loans and favors and opened Pó eight weeks later, two days after Susi's birthday. The bounty of Susi's garden and the plethora of wonderful products from local Greenwich Village artisans became the focal point of my menu and enabled me to create food at Pó that approached the level of quality I had experienced in my little village in Italy. The availability of an incredible variety of cheeses and different olive oils at Murray's Cheese Shop, the handmade soppressata and cacciatorini at Faicco's Pork Store, the psychedelic dream of spices, dried fruits, and herbs at Aphrodisia, and the local breads at Zito's and the Sullivan Street Bakery combined with the personal relationships I developed with each of the shops gave—and continues to give—me an incredible advantage at producing delicious food. It's one you can develop in your own village—wherever it is. I've also nurtured relationships with local farmers and producers, many of whom sell their produce and wares in our local farmer's markets.

As I became more and more inspired by the incredible variety and quality of local produce available to me, new dishes—Italian in sensibility, but made of local ingredients—some never used in classical Italian cooking—began to pop up on my menus. Today I would describe my cooking style as filled with Italian spirit and exuberance but equally Italian and American in its flavors. It's based more on superior ingredients than it is on fancy techniques, which is why most of these recipes are very easy to re-create in a home kitchen, just as they would be made by good home cooks in Toscana, Piemonte, or Venezia.

In the pages that follow you will find recipes originating from both of the villages that have left their stamp on my cooking style. Those with the recipe titles in the darker typeface are the resolutely traditional dishes that I never seem to tire of making and that my family and customers love as much as I do. Some of these have been slightly modified to meet the needs of my marketplace and customers, but essentially they are as authentic as I could make them. Those with the lighter titles are the ones I've created for Pó, and while they may never be encountered on the menu of a traditional Italian trattoria like La Volta, I like to think they honor and preserve the spirit of Italian regional cooking so integral to the foods I ate and cooked there. But old or new, all these recipes are, in their own ways, paradigms of the perfection I strive for in every dish I prepare.

What I hope you'll learn from this book is that Italian food is all about style and good ingredients—not necessarily the ingredients in Rome or Venice but the ingredients native to *your* village, where you are cooking, where you are eating. And that is cooking and living and loving in Italy, where the day's offerings from the market or the garden changes from region to region, from city to city, from gardener to gardener, from tiny little town to tiny little town, and hopefully from my two villages to yours.

What was most evident during my stay in Italy was that simplicity and purity reign over all. Traveling and eating with the Valdisseri family, and watching and learning from great cooks all over Italy, the single most important discovery I made was how simply they all combined their local seasonal ingredients.

Living among the hunters, the oven builders, the grandmas, and the winemakers of Emilia-Romagna I was also struck by how the Italians chose their daily meals. Rather than deciding in our heads we wanted spaghetti with eggplant followed by veal with mushrooms, we assessed our appetites in terms of quantity: Should we have antipasto, pasta, and main course today, or should we simply have pasta and a few contorni? That decided, we would head to the market to see what looked good. If there were great porcini, they would be purchased and worked into the menu somewhere. If the eggplant looked a little tired, we would leave it for someone else. The market and the season determined the menu. Rarely did cooks in Bologna try to cook ingredients from Bergamo or Sardegna. Seafood and meat excluded, the cooks in each region used what was available in the local markets or from their own gardens and fields.

Regional variation in the market is what distinguishes cooking within Italy. The variety of citrus in and around the Amalfi coast has led to a an abundance of dishes made with oranges and lemons, but there are few, if any, apple trees south of Napoli. In Trieste, there are no lemon trees; there are, however, hundreds of apple orchards and apples are evident in many Friulian recipes. The whole point here is that Italian cooks use what is available to them, and only the best of that.

Many Americans consider Italian cooking a single, homogeneous cuisine based on spaghetti with tomato and basil. In fact, the variation from region to region is astounding. Each region or town offers cooks different ingredients. My experiences in the town of Borgo Capanne in Emilia-Romagna are evident in the traditional dishes in this book. Living close to gardens, chestnut groves, the grapevines, and the abundant forest floor taught me a respect for the natural ingredients available to cooks in that specific region. And it was proximity to these ingredients as building blocks that essentially designed the dishes considered the jewels of all Italian cooking. In the north, the prevalence of cattle and pigs provides cooks with a rich supply of butter, lard, and pork products from which to create their masterpieces. In the south, where these animals are scarce, the cooks rely on olive oil and vegetables supplemented by goat and sheep products as the cornerstones of their exquisite dishes.

But, like all art forms, Italian cooking is not fixed in one place, silently resisting new ingredients or changes in taste. An Italian chef living in the United States would cook with the ingredients available here. In many of the recipes that follow ingredients can be readily substituted, but there are some ingredients for which there are no substitutes. The four most important of these are a great extra-virgin olive oil (plus a less expensive extra virgin oil), Parmigiano-Reggiano, good balsamic vinegar, and prosciutto. These national treasures form the backbone of cooking where I lived, and you'll find them indispensable for preparing both the traditional and nontraditional recipes in this book. Find a good source for these products and taste several brands to see which you like the best.

Glossary

Almonds — Two varieties are available in Italy: bitter almonds, which, when raw contain toxic hydrocyanic acid but when cooked can be used to make almond extract and amaretto; and sweet almonds, generally available raw and dried, sliced, blanched, salted, smoked, or ground into almond paste. In America only the sweet almonds are available. These should be purchased in their shells if possible; otherwise choose those packed in sealed cans or jars.

Anchovies — Those small, flavorful fish from the Mediterranean and southern Atlantic are used in both their fresh and preserved forms. In this country we most often use the latter. The best are packed whole in salt and must be rinsed and filleted before using, the worst are made into a paste. Those packed in oil can be acceptable, but check carefully before using to be certain they are not rancid.

Balsamic vinegar — A deep, intense vinegar made from the unfermented juice of white Trebbiano grapes. The juice is cooked slowly to form a thick sweet syrup called *mosto*, which is aged in progressively smaller barrels of different woods over a period of twelve years or more to achieve incredible depth of flavor. The finished product is then placed in a bottle whose shape indicates its place of origin, one for Modena, and another for Reggio, the only two areas that can legitimately produce the real thing. True balsamic vinegar will cost upwards of forty dollars for a four-ounce bottle. Alternatively you can buy a commercially produced product at one-tenth the price and cook it down until reduced by half or more to achieve a modicum of intensity. This by no means replaces the real article, but it produces something far better than the unreduced swill.

Butter — Always buy unsalted butter and keep it wrapped in plastic to prevent it from absorbing any strong flavors or odors from its neighbors in the fridge.

Capers — Flower buds produced by a crawling shrub that resembles something from an exotic nursery in an expensive neighborhood, these buds are picked during a very short season. When packed in vinegar brine they lose much of their subtle flavor; those packed in salt retain their character but need a modicum of attention prior to use. Search out the Maseratis of the species, which come from the island of Pantelleria.

Caper berries – While capers are the buds that will eventually become flowers on this fernlike shrub, caper berries are the seed-bearing fruit that appear later in the season. Like capers, they generally come packed in salt or brine, but are larger and usually sold with their stems. If you can find them they are a sexy substitute for capers in any recipe and a very cool martini garnish.

Chestnuts – Sweet and intense, these nuts are available both fresh in the autumn and winter and canned throughout the year. Always choose the largest possible and avoid any with broken skins or discolored shells. Chestnut flour and dried chestnuts are also available in specialty shops.

Garlic – This member of the lily family (along with onions, leeks, and shallots) varies immensely in flavor and intensity. Always check for softened edges or sunken or dried cloves and avoid those with green sprouts emerging from the tops of the cloves. Store in a cool, dry, and dark place and use quickly once you've broken the head.

Grana Padana – The variety of cheese of which Parmigiano-Reggiano is the king. An aged cow's milk cheese from the plains of the Pó River valley, it can be exquisite at best, pedestrian at worst. Choose carefully.

Olive oil – The pressed and centrifuged extract of the fruit of the olive tree, made in nearly every province of Italy. Each region produces its own style and flavor of oil which in turn defines the style and flavor of much of that region's cooking. I recommend having two kinds of olive oil in the pantry: a boutique Tuscan or Ligurian extra-virgin oil for anointing both raw and cooked foods at the moment they are served; and a less expensive oil from a larger producer (referred to in this book as extra-virgin olive oil), whose production volume creates a less distinct but still high-quality oil at a much lower price, for everything else, including frying. In my opinion you simply can not scrimp on extra-virgin olive oil. Choose one that you like and stick with it for general uses, occasionally trying bottles from other areas, particularly when cooking dishes from those regions. My personal favorites are Tenuta di Capezzana (West Tuscan), San Giuliano di Alghero (Sardegnan), Castello di Ama (Chianti Tuscan), and Da Vero, produced by my friends Ridgely Evers and Colleen McGlynn, in California's Dry Creek Valley, from the fruit of trees transplanted from my grandfather's hometown of Segriminio near Lucca. It has a rich and peppery intensity.

Olives – The whole fruit of the olive tree, cured and preserved for eating with salt, water, lye, oil, or a combination of the four. Unprocessed olives contain a bitter component called glycosides that render them inedible. All olives start green and eventually ripen to black or purple. Each olive-growing region in the world has its own specific varietal and processing style;

my favorites include Gaeta, Kalamata, and Nyons, but I love almost all olives and cure my own each year for gifts and for the restaurant.

Olive paste – A great convenience product that can be stirred into sauces and vinaigrettes, spread on crostini, and more. Find it at specialty food shops.

Pancetta – A leaner version of American bacon, widely available. Regular slab bacon is an acceptable substitute. Pancetta (or bacon) can also be used as a substitute for *guanciale*, a flavorful bacon made from the jowls of pigs.

Parmigiano-Reggiano – The undisputed king of cheeses is produced from cow's milk in a geographically defined area and controlled by the Consortium of Parmigiano producers. Each wheel is stamped with a black brand bearing its age and the cheesemaker's name. A master cheesemaker will prepare cheese daily, blending skimmed milk from the evening prior and whole from that morning and heating them slowly in a large copper pot. After the addition of rennet the mixture forms curds which are broken and stirred and then allowed to settle to the bottom of the pot. The curds are lifted out in a cheesecloth and placed into round wooden frames and allowed to set up for two days, then dropped into a salt water brine and allowed to float freely for three weeks. From there the cheese is placed on racks in huge drying rooms and allowed to rest under constant supervision for up to

two years. Choose younger softer cheeses for table eating and older cheeses for grating over anything except pasta with seafood sauces.

Pine nuts – The nuts of several kinds of pine trees indigenous to both the Mediterranean and the central Americas as well as China. The longer thinner Mediterranean variety is prized for its delicate flavor while the squat triangular Chinese variety is more accessible due to its lower price. Both are particularly susceptible to rancidity due to their high fat content so buy only as much as you need and keep them refrigerated in an airtight container.

Polenta – Historically this term applied to any grain mush but today polenta is used almost exclusively to describe the cooked mush of finely ground corn. Polenta was originally a peasant dish made from water and cornmeal, but restaurants in Italy and America now prepare it with milk and even cream, allegedly to upgrade this delicious simple staple. There are many variations in the fineness of the grind and buckwheat polenta is even served in the northernmost regions of Italy, but all the recipes I use in this book use finely ground, quick-cooking cornmeal from Italy. A good brand is Beretta.

Prosciutto di Parma, San Daniele and Carpegna – All of these are salt-cured raw hams from different regions in Italy and represent the pinnacle of the worlds of pork products. Arguably, the best come from the Langhirano, around Parma, and are produced according to rules governed by the Consortium of prosciutto di Parma producers. The raw hind legs of local pigs raised under careful dietary regulation are chosen by size, then cured with salt and nothing else. They are first rubbed with sea salt and cooled for three weeks. They are then hung for two months in a refrigerated room carefully regulated for humidity to control the salt's absorption into the meat. They are then trimmed near the hip joint and rehung for up to four months. Fat is applied to the cut joint to moisten the meat, which is hung again for four to six months in covered buildings with huge moveable walls that allow the natural air and breeze of the Parma plains to slowly dry and perfume the delicate flesh. At this point they are taken down, inspected internally for rancidity, and branded with the traditional five-point crown. Domestically produced prosciutto is nothing compared to the real thing so avoid substitutions, unless specified.

Ricotta — A by-product of the mozzarella-making process. After the curd is separated in handfuls from the floating mass, what remains is a cloudy, semi-thick liquid that is re-cooked (*ricotta* in Italian). What forms from the second cooking is the creamy soft cheese called ricotta. Many recipes call for sheep's milk ricotta as it is quite popular throughout Italy, but as far as I know, only Sini Fulvi imports this product fresh and not in huge quanti-

ties. Your best bet is to find a source for fresh cow's milk ricotta from an artisanal dairy farm or farmer's market near you. My preferred substitute is the soft curd goat ricotta from Coach Farm—but you could also use any soft fresh goat cheese.

Salt — This is an essential ingredient in many facets of cooking and I abide by only two rules. In the kitchen I always use *kosher* salt, due to its milder salinity and to its reduced tendency to stick to my fingers, important when I'm working quickly. For salting the water in which pasta or vegetables are to be cooked I always use sea salt, usually from Sicily. Salt is a matter of personal taste and that rule above all should define both your needs and use.

Semolina — A winter wheat flour, hard and resilient, one of the two ingredients, with water, in hard pasta.

Tomatoes (canned Italian plum) — One of the most inconsistent products available to cooks are canned tomatoes. It is therefore very important to taste them, for acidity and sweetness, each time you use them, particularly as part of a basic building block like Basic Tomato Sauce (page 84). If the tomatoes are lacking acidity, do not be afraid to adjust your finished dish with just a drop or two of good vinegar.

asti

First Courses

ANTIPASTI

Antipasto in Emilia-Romagna has been based traditionally on the region's out-standing pork products, namely prosciutto di Parma and other *salume*, or cured meats, such as salami, culatello, and capicola. Parmigiano-Reggiano also is served in a variety of straightforward but delicious preparations as a way to pique the appetite at the beginning of a meal.

Historically, the presence of an *antipasto* on a home menu was a sign of prosperity, as the poor generally ate only pasta (an inexpensive way to fill up), sometimes followed by *secondo* based on meat or fish. The portions were hearty and the dishes substantial, because after working in the fields or fishing the whole day on the sea the family ate to satisfy physical hunger, not intellectual appetite; obviously a large plate of pasta can assuage hunger pangs more quickly and efficiently than a plate of olives and a few slices of salami. In mod-ern times, our daily work is not nearly so physical, and our appetites are more refined. Thus, an *aperitivo* of a glass of prosecco with a slice or two of prosciutto di Parma makes a nice way to start an evening of entertaining.

Restaurants in Italy and America now offer vast assortments of *antipasti*, and offering three or four of these dishes in succession or all at once can be an enjoyable and more casual way of dining. Since many of these dishes can be pre-pared in advance and served at room temperature or finished at the last minute, the antipasto course makes a lot of sense for the home entertainer. Of course a certain amount of Italian food sense is essential to creating a harmonious meal of even small dishes.

One of the main points that distinguishes cooking in Italy from cooking in America is the level of intensity that is maintained throughout a meal. Italians tend to expect a series of plates of equal size, including at least one, if not sev-eral, pasta courses on the road to a full repast that includes a significant *secondo*, or entree. Americans take the structure of their meals less seriously, so at Pó I have created a menu of slightly more substantial appetizers, fully expecting some of my customers to order antipasto and pasta and nothing more. For that reason I tend to emphasize cheeses and meats as components of the *antipasto* course, though these dishes are quite different from the classic Italian platters of salami or vegetables. I always try to balance protein components with vegetables, and I also like to vary the techniques involved in preparation as well as the color palette to create a visually appealing meal. (You should note that there are many recipes in the *contorni* chapter [page 214] that could easily be served as *antipasti*.)

The most important thing to remember when making and serving *antipasti*, or any of the dishes from the following chapters, is to enjoy the process from the shopping through to the cleanup. It is like a dance, joyful, sometimes repetitive, yet always satisfying, nourishing the body as well as the soul. Assessing the tastes and needs of your guests and meeting them with style is what great hospitality is all about, and it's ultimately what distinguishes your table from mine.

APERITIVI

In Italy, these light predinner cocktails take a thousand forms, from a simple glass of Prosecco to an elaborate cocktail that combines several types of fruit juice. The Bellini, made famous at Harry's bar in Venice, is equal parts fresh peach puree and prosecco, served in a Champagne flute. My favorite base for *aperitivi* is sweet white vermouth, which I mix with pureed fresh seasonal fruit. In the spring, I use strawberries or early melons; in the summer, juicy plums or watermelon; in the fall, late peaches, apples, and quince; and in the winter, fresh persimmon pulp or blood orange juice from Sicily. The trick is to mix equal parts of the fruit pulp and vermouth in a cocktail shaker and to shake them vigorously with three ice cubes per person. Pour the cocktail into a martini glass and garnish with a twist of orange.

Grilled Stuffed Grape Leaves with Goat Cheese and Black Pepper

serves 4

You'll find pickled grape leaves in Middle Eastern specialty shops or fresh leaves at any winery in October. These packets work as a passed *antipasto* and make a terrific first course if you serve them with a small salad of roasted peppers and olives.

12 bottled **GRAPE LEAVES**, rinsed and dried

1 pound soft, fresh **GOAT CHEESE**, preferably Coach Farm

2 tablespoons freshly grated black **PEPPER**

¼ cup extra-virgin **OLIVE OIL**

4 tablespoons **BALSAMIC VINEGAR**

1 tablespoon chopped fresh **THYME** leaves

Spread 12 grape leaves on the countertop. In a mixing bowl, blend the goat cheese and black pepper until homogeneous. Place a generous tablespoon of goat cheese in the center of each leaf. Fold in the sides of each leaf, then roll up burrito fashion and tie with kitchen string. Drizzle 1 teaspoon olive oil over each and refrigerate for 1 hour.

Preheat the grill or light a charcoal fire.

Place the chilled packets over the medium-hot part of the grill and cook until the leaves are just starting to char all over, 1 to 2 minutes per side. Place 3 packets on each plate, drizzle with a teaspoonful of balsamic vinegar and a dusting of fresh thyme, and serve immediately. (You may remove the strings before serving if you wish, but in Italy they'd probably leave them on.)

Stuffed Olives

Olive all'Ascolana

serves 4 as a snack or 1 as a lunch entrée

For an olive lover like me, this dish is absolute heaven. Big plates of these exquisite bar snacks adorn the counters of bars in the seaside town of Ancona, where I first tried them. Use olives from Ascoli if you can find them, otherwise, any tangy, colossal olive such as Alfonso or Sicilian will work well.

20 jumbo Italian **OLIVES**

8 ounces Italian fennel **SALAMI**, or other good pork salami

2 cups extra-virgin **OLIVE OIL**, for frying

2 **EGGS**, lightly beaten

½ cup all-purpose **FLOUR**

½ cup dry **BREAD CRUMBS**

Using a cherry pitter, pit the olives carefully, leaving them whole with a hole at either end.

Chop the salami and then crumble with your fingers, or chop quite finely in the food processor. Stuff each olive with 1 teaspoon of chopped salami.

In a 10- to 12-inch skillet, heat the olive oil to 375°F.

Place beaten eggs on a plate, the flour on a second plate, and the bread crumbs on a third. Roll the stuffed olives in the egg, then flour, then bread crumbs. Fry the olives until golden brown, about 3 to 4 minutes. Serve warm.

Grilled Linguica Crostini with Red Onion Marmalade

serves 4

Although historically these garlic sausages are a product of Portugal, I buy linguica from Faicco's Italian pork store on the corner of Cornelia and Bleecker, where it is made fresh every day. The combination of sweet marmalade and salty, garlicky sausage is a natural for this simple, quick-to-finish appetizer. The marmalade will hold for up to two weeks, covered in the refrigerator, and is also good for tortellini in chicken broth or on sandwiches.

2 medium **RED ONIONS**, cut into ¼-inch dice

2 cups fresh **ORANGE JUICE**

1 cup **PORT** wine

1 cup **WATER**

1 teaspoon **SALT**

1 tablespoon **SUGAR**

8 ounces **LINGUICA** sausages

12 1-inch-thick slices Italian peasant **BREAD**

Grated zest of 1 **ORANGE**

Preheat the grill or broiler.

In a saucepan, combine the onions, orange juice, wine, water, salt, and sugar. Bring to a boil; reduce this mixture to a thick marmalade consistency, about 20 minutes. Set aside.

Place the sausage on the grill or under the broiler and cook thoroughly, 5 to 7 minutes per side, turning frequently. Remove from the grill and slice into ¼-inch-thick rounds.

Grill the bread until lightly toasted on both sides. Smear each slice with about 2 tablespoons of the onion mixture, then arrange 4 or 5 slices of sausage on top. Garnish with the orange zest and serve.

Broccoli Rabe Crostini with Crotonese and Black Pepper–Oregano Oil

serves 4

There are more Italian-American lovers of broccoli rabe in New York City than in the entire city of Bologna, so I am always thinking of new ways to use this pleasantly bitter cruciferous green. Sheep's milk cheese really smoothes out the flavors here, but you could substitute fontina or Asiago.

8 ounces **BROCCOLI RABE**, trimmed,
   rinsed, and dried

4 **GARLIC** cloves, sliced paper-thin

¼ cup extra-virgin **OLIVE OIL**

¼ cup red wine **VINEGAR**

½ teaspoon dried **OREGANO**

SALT and **PEPPER**

12 slices Italian peasant **BREAD**

2 tablespoons **BLACK PEPPER–OREGANO OIL**

8 ounces **CROTONESE** cheese or other
   semi-soft sheep's milk cheese

Black Pepper–Oregano Oil

¼ cup fresh **OREGANO** leaves

2 tablespoons freshly ground black
   PEPPER

½ cup extra-virgin **OLIVE OIL**

In a blender, mix the oregano leaves, black pepper, and olive oil until smooth and dark green. Makes ½ cup.

Bring about 6 quarts of water to a boil. Make an ice bath by combining 4 cups water and 4 cups ice in a large mixing bowl.

Submerge the broccoli rabe in the boiling water and cook for 3 minutes, until bright green and fork-tender. Remove from the boiling water, plunge into the ice bath, and allow to cool, about 5 minutes.

Drain the broccoli rabe well. Remove the florets and cut the remaining stalks into ½-inch pieces. Place the florets and chopped stalks in a mixing bowl and add the garlic, ¼ cup olive oil, the vinegar, and oregano. Season to taste with salt and pepper and set aside.

Preheat the grill or broiler.

Grill or toast the bread on both sides. Spoon 2 tablespoons broccoli rabe over each piece of bread and drizzle with ½ teaspoon of the black pepper–oregano oil. Shave a piece of crotonese over each with a vegetable peeler and serve warm.

Duck Liver Crostini Toscane with Spicy Cucumber Salad

serves 6–8

Cucumber Salad

1 large English **CUCUMBER**

2 tablespoons extra-virgin **OLIVE OIL**

2 tablespoons **RED WINE VINEGAR**

½ teaspoon **SUGAR**

1 tablespoon hot red **PEPPER FLAKES**

SALT and **PEPPER**

Peel the cucumber, halve lengthwise, and use a teaspoon to remove seeds. Slice into ⅛-inch-thick half-moons and place in a medium bowl. Dress with olive oil, vinegar, sugar, and red pepper flakes and season to taste with salt and pepper, tossing well to coat. Makes 2 cups.

When cooking duck at the restaurant, I save the livers, a frugal business practice that results in this great *antipasto* but it tastes nearly as good made with chicken livers, which is a more traditional version. The spicy cucumbers are definitely not traditional, but work well to cut the richness of the crostini.

¼ cup extra-virgin **OLIVE OIL**

1 medium **RED ONION**, thinly sliced

1 pound duck or chicken **LIVERS**

2 tablespoons **CAPERS**, rinsed and drained

2 **ANCHOVY** fillets, rinsed and patted dry

1 tablespoon hot red **PEPPER FLAKES**

1 cup dry **RED WINE**

SALT and **PEPPER**

12 slices Italian peasant **BREAD**, cut ¾ inch thick

1 recipe **CUCUMBER SALAD**

Preheat the grill or broiler.

In a 10- to 12-inch sauté pan, heat the olive oil slowly over medium heat. Add the onion and cook slowly until soft but not brown, about 10 minutes. Add the livers, capers, anchovies, and red pepper flakes and cook until lightly browned, about 8 minutes. Add the wine and cook until only 3 to 4 tablespoons of liquid remain, about 8 minutes.

Transfer the liver mixture to a food processor and pulse on and off until blended but still lumpy—it should not be smooth like a puree. Season to taste with salt and pepper and remove to a small mixing bowl.

Grill or toast the bread on both sides and spread each piece with 1 heaping tablespoon of duck liver mixture. Divide among 4 plates. Place 2 tablespoons of cucumber salad on each plate and serve immediately.

Salmon Tartare on Green Olive Crostini

serves 4

Raw fish is not very popular in Italy, although seared rare tuna sold well at La Volta, and raw crustaceans and cephalopods are eaten regularly in Puglia. When I served this at La Volta, it got mixed reviews, as most patrons found the mustard too aggressive for the farm-raised salmon available in Europe. The wild King salmon I use in the United States stands up to it beautifully, however, making this a particularly interesting seasonal treat.

1 tablespoon **CAPERS**, rinsed and drained

juice and finely grated zest of 1 **LEMON**

¼ cup extra-virgin **OLIVE OIL**

1 tablespoon Dijon **MUSTARD**

2 tablespoons black **MUSTARD SEEDS**

8 ounces **SALMON** fillet, skin and bones removed

SALT and **PEPPER**

8 ¼-inch-thick slices of **BAGUETTE**, toasted in
    400°F. oven for 2 minutes

¼ cup **GREEN OLIVE PESTO**

2 **SCALLIONS**, thinly sliced on the diagonal

In a blender, combine the capers, lemon juice and zest, olive oil, mustard, and 1 tablespoon of the mustard seeds until smooth, about 1 minute.

With a sharp knife, cut the salmon into ¼-inch dice and place in a large mixing bowl. Add the caper mixture and stir to mix well. Season to taste with salt and pepper.

Spread each piece of toasted bread with 1½ teaspoons of pesto and top with 2 heaping tablespoons of salmon mixture. Sprinkle with the remaining mustard seeds and scallion slices and serve immediately.

Green Olive Pesto

1½ cups large or jumbo green **OLIVES**,
    such as ascolane, pitted

½ **RED ONION**, chopped

¼ cup **PINE NUTS**

1 clove **GARLIC**, thinly sliced

½ cup extra-virgin **OLIVE OIL**,
    approximately

In a food processor, combine the olives, onion, pine nuts, and garlic and blend for 1 minute. With the motor running, slowly add the olive oil until it forms a thick, smooth paste. Allow to stand ½ hour before using. Makes 2½ cups.

White Bean Bruschetta with Grilled Radicchio Salad

serves 4

White bean bruschetta has become a signature dish at Pó; it captures the simplicity that defines the *mangia fagioli* Tuscan kitchen. This is not, however, a dish I'd seen in Italy, but one I developed for Pó as a substitute for the banal tomato bruschetta given away in so many restaurants.

1 cup cooked **CANNELLINI BEANS**
　(see page 65)
6 tablespoons extra-virgin **OLIVE OIL**
6 tablespoons **BALSAMIC VINEGAR**
½ teaspoon hot red **PEPPER FLAKES**
2 tablespoons **BASIL** leaves, cut in narrow
　ribbons (chiffonade)
1 **GARLIC** clove, thinly sliced
SALT and **PEPPER**
2 large heads **RADICCHIO** di Treviso
4 1-inch-thick slices Italian peasant
　BREAD, grilled

Preheat the grill or broiler.

In a mixing bowl, gently stir together the beans, 2 tablespoons of the olive oil, 2 tablespoons of the balsamic vinegar, the red pepper flakes, basil, and garlic. Season lightly with salt and pepper.

Halve the radicchio top to bottom and place on an unoiled grill or under the broiler. Cook until wilted, about 3 minutes per side. Cut each half in half again to form wedges. Cut the core out and separate the leaves. Toss the leaves in a bowl with the remaining 4 tablespoons oil and 4 tablespoons vinegar, then season to taste with salt and pepper.

Arrange the radicchio leaves on 4 plates like the fingers of a hand. Spoon the bean mixture onto 4 freshly grilled bread slices, place 1 slice in the middle of each salad, and serve.

Pugliese Mushroom Hodge-Podge with Green Olive Crostini

serves 4

I was taught to make this dish by an incredible natural cook from Lecce. She used plain button mushrooms, and I was surprised to taste how much flavor this cooking process develops in the mildly flavored mushrooms. I've gussied the dish up a bit with exotic mushrooms, but you could easily go back to the buttons or use a mix of whatever is in season.

4 ounces **CHANTERELLE** mushrooms, brushed clean

4 ounces **CREMINI** mushrooms, brushed clean

4 ounces **OYSTER** mushrooms, brushed clean

4 ounces **YELLOW FOOT** mushrooms, brushed clean

½ medium **RED ONION**, thinly sliced

1 tablespoon hot red **PEPPER FLAKES** (optional)

4 **SCALLIONS**, green and white parts, cut into 1-inch pieces (about ⅔ cup)

2 **GARLIC** cloves, thinly sliced

1 cup dry **WHITE WINE**

4 ripe plum **TOMATOES**, halved

1 cup **BASIC TOMATO SAUCE** (page 84)

SALT and **PEPPER**

4 1-inch-thick slices Italian peasant **BREAD**

1 cup **GREEN OLIVE PESTO** (page 29)

In a heavy 4-quart saucepan, combine the mushrooms, red onion, red pepper flakes, scallions, garlic, wine, tomatoes, and tomato sauce and bring to a boil. Lower the heat and simmer, partially covered, for 20 minutes. The mixture should be thick like a ragu. Season to taste with salt and pepper and pour into a large, shallow serving bowl.

Toast the bread and smear with green olive pesto. Stand the crostini at fun angles in the bowl of mushroom hodge-podge and serve immediately in the center of the table.

Bruschetta with Bresaola, Eggplant, and Mozzarella

serves 4

Served with a salad and a couple of olives, this simple, satisfying dish can easily make a light lunch.

3 tablespoons extra-virgin **OLIVE OIL**

½ medium **RED ONION**, thinly sliced

2 small Japanese **EGGPLANTS**

2 tablespoons red wine **VINEGAR**

8 ounces fresh **MOZZARELLA** cheese

8 **BASIL** leaves, cut in narrow ribbons (chiffonade)

SALT and **PEPPER**

4 large slices Italian peasant **BREAD**

4 ounces **BRESAOLA**, sliced paper-thin
   (12–15 slices; see Note)

In a 10- to 12-inch sauté pan, heat the olive oil until smoking over medium heat. Add the onion and cook until soft, 9 to 10 minutes. Meanwhile, cut the eggplant into ¼-inch-thick rounds. When the onion is softened, add the eggplant to the pan and cook, stirring regularly, until the eggplant has darkened and is soft, about 7 to 8 minutes. Add the vinegar and remove from the heat to cool.

Cut the mozzarella into ¼-inch cubes and add to the cooled eggplant mixture. Add the basil and season to taste with salt and pepper.

Preheat the grill or broiler.

Grill or toast the bread on both sides and spoon a generous amount of eggplant over each slice of bread. Top each with 3 slices of bresaola and serve.

Note: Prosciutto or capicola may be substituted for the bresaola.

BRUSCHETTA

The terms *bruschetta* and *crostini* are often used interchangeably in America, but there are differences in preparation. Derived from *bruscare*, the verb meaning to char over hot coals, bruschetta is grilled bread that is invariably served warm, often with nothing more than a drizzle of good oil and the rub of a raw garlic clove. (If you do not have hot coals ready to grill your bread, a broiler works as well.) This is also referred to as *fett'unta*, or greased slice, and is served in the time of new oil to showcase the intense flavor of the fall crop. Crostini, on the other hand, are often fried or toasted and can be served cool or at room temperature, usually smeared with some chicken liver paste (for Crostini Toscane) or with a pâté of olives. The variations are endless for either, but I return again and again to these bruschetta toppings, as they are quick to make yet large on flavor.

— White beans and rosemary
— Sautéed summer squash with garlic and marjoram
— Shrimp sautéed with garlic and lemon zest
— Eggplant cooked *al fungo* (see page 37)
— Sautéed turnips with prosciutto and sage

MOZZARELLA

Fresh mozzarella is a creamy white cheese that bears little resemblance to the packaged stuff found next to the Velveeta in American grocery stores. It is best eaten the day it is made. Search out tennis ball–size orbs wrapped in paper, partially submerged in lightly salted, milky whey. Though it was originally produced only from water buffalo milk in Campania, there are now good producers in Basilicata, Calabria, and even Texas and California, some of which use regular cow's milk with slightly different yet highly successful results.

Mozzarella is made by heating whole milk with a natural animal rennet found in cows' stomachs, which causes curds to form and separate from the whey. The cheesemaker then stirs the curds to stretch and form them into long bands. At exactly the right moment, the cheesemaker forms the balls by ripping (*mozzando*, from the verb *mozzare*, thus mozzarella) pieces off and forming them into rounds much as a baker shapes balls of dough. Eaten at room temperature with just a drizzle of good oil, fresh mozzarella makes a great light meal with a slice or two of bruschetta or a couple of slices of a great tomato. This is not a cheese to eat after dinner, but one to caress the appetite at the beginning of a meal.

Shrimp Bruschetta from "da Zaccaria"

serves 4

I could wax poetic for days about the cooking of the Amalfi coast, and in particular about my love of one perfect seafood *trattoria* in Atrani called da Zaccaria. Try this recipe and you'll see why. The success of this deceptively simple appetizer depends entirely on the quality of the shrimp. Limoncello is a sweet lemon-flavored liqueur made all over Amalfi, and it's actually quite a hangover producer. Though the alcohol cooks out, a deliciously pungent fragrance remains.

¼ cup extra-virgin **OLIVE OIL**

2 **GARLIC** cloves, thinly sliced

12 large **SHRIMP**, peeled and deveined

juice and finely grated zest of 1 **LEMON**

2 ounces **LIMONCELLO** liqueur

½ cup dry **WHITE WINE**

4 ¾-inch-thick slices Italian peasant
    BREAD

1 bunch **CHIVES**, snipped into
    ¼-inch lengths

SALT and **PEPPER**

Preheat the grill or broiler.

In a 12- to 14-inch sauté pan, heat the olive oil over medium heat until just smoking. Add the garlic and cook until it turns light brown. Add the shrimp and cook without turning for 2 to 3 minutes, until bright red. Turn the shrimp over and cook for 1 minute. Transfer the shrimp to a plate and add to the pan the lemon juice, Limoncello, and wine. Boil the sauce for 3 minutes.

Grill or toast the bread and place 1 slice on each plate. With tongs, transfer 3 of the shrimp to each piece of bread. Stir the chives into the sauce in the pan and season with salt and pepper. Spoon the sauce over the shrimp, sprinkle with the lemon zest, and serve immediately.

Morel and Asparagus Bruschetta

serves 4

I first prepared a version of this recipe at Arlene Feltman Sailhac's very cool cooking school in New York City, Degustibus at Macy's. It was the first live demo I had ever done, and I remember being so nervous about it that I rehearsed at home in front of my wife, Susi, and some of her friends for weeks in advance. Since then I return at least once a year.

To make the recipe up to a day in advance, omit the vinegar and then add it at the very last minute.

1 pound fresh **MORELS**, cleaned and trimmed

4 tablespoons extra-virgin **OLIVE OIL**

2 tablespoons **BALSAMIC VINEGAR**

½ teaspoon hot red **PEPPER FLAKES**

2 tablespoons **BASIL** leaves, cut in thin strips (chiffonade)

1 **GARLIC** clove, thinly sliced

SALT and **PEPPER**

8 ounces medium **ASPARAGUS** spears

8 1-inch-thick slices Italian peasant

   BREAD, grilled

Preheat the grill or broiler. Fill a mixing bowl with ice water.

Sauté the mushrooms in 2 tablespoons of the olive oil for about 2 minutes, or until wilted.

In a mixing bowl, gently stir together the morels, remaining 2 tablespoons of olive oil, balsamic vinegar, red pepper flakes, basil, and garlic. Season lightly with salt and pepper.

Bring a saucepan of water to a boil and blanch the asparagus for 1 minute. Refresh in the ice bath until chilled (about 1 minute), then drain well and slice into ½-inch pieces. Gently mix the asparagus with the morels. Grill or toast the bread slices and arrange 2 on each plate. Divide the morel mixture evenly among the bread slices and serve.

Turnip and Prosciutto Bruschetta

serves 4

Faced with a bag of turnips delivered in error to Pó, I decided to find a use for them and came up with two new turnip recipes a day for a week. This simple bruschetta recipe emerged the winner.

¼ cup extra-virgin **OLIVE OIL**

1 medium **RED ONION**, cut into ¼-inch cubes

2 medium **TURNIPS**, cut into ¼-inch cubes

1 teaspoon fresh **ROSEMARY** leaves

1 tablespoon **BALSAMIC VINEGAR**

4-ounce piece **PROSCIUTTO** di Parma, cut into ¼-inch cubes

SALT and **PEPPER**

8 slices Italian peasant **BREAD**

In a 12- to 14-inch sauté pan, heat the olive oil until smoking. Add the onion and turnips and cook over low heat, stirring regularly, until softened and golden brown, 8 to 10 minutes. Remove to a mixing bowl and, while still warm, stir in the rosemary, balsamic vinegar, and prosciutto cubes. Season to taste with salt and pepper and set aside.

Preheat the grill or broiler.

Toast the bread on the grill or under the broiler until brown. Spoon equal amounts of the turnip mixture over each piece of bread and serve.

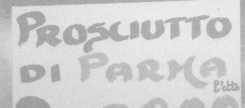

Bruschetta with Melanzane al Fungo

serves 4

Preparing eggplant to mimic mushrooms (*al fungo*) is common in many regions of Italy. I first encountered this variation, in all its simplicity, at La Volta when Mara prepared it for a summer dinner we served to Andrea Trinci, a famous coffee roaster and a regular at the restaurant.

6 tablespoons extra-virgin **OLIVE OIL**

1 medium **RED ONION**, cut into ¼-inch dice

2 **GARLIC** cloves, thinly sliced

4 medium Italian **EGGPLANTS**, long and thin, halved lengthwise
    and cut into ¼-inch-thick half-moons

SALT and **PEPPER**

½ cup finely chopped Italian **PARSLEY**

8 slices Italian peasant **BREAD**

Preheat the grill or broiler.

In a 10- to 12-inch sauté pan, heat the olive oil until smoking over medium-high heat. Add the onion and cook until lightly browned and softened, 7 to 8 minutes. Add the garlic and cook until soft, about 2 minutes. Add the eggplant and cook, stirring frequently, until it is golden brown and soft, resembling sautéed mushrooms. Remove from the heat, season to taste with salt and pepper, and allow to cool. Add the parsley and mix well.

Grill or toast the bread on both sides. Divide the eggplant mixture among the bread slices and serve, 2 per person.

Black Olive Polenta with Shiitakes, Garlic, and Rosemary

serves 8

Tapenade

6 **ANCHOVY** fillets, soaked in milk
   overnight, drained, and patted dry

2 tablespoons **ANCHOVY PASTE**

1 cup pitted black **OLIVES** (such as
   Gaeta or Kalamata)

¼ cup **CAPERS**, roughly chopped

3 tablespoons Dijon **MUSTARD**

3 tablespoons **RED WINE VINEGAR**

½ cup extra-virgin **OLIVE OIL**

½ small **RED ONION**, roughly chopped

Combine all the ingredients in a food processor and blend until a smooth, homogeneous paste is formed, about 2 minutes. Transfer to a jar, cover tightly, and store in the refrigerator up to 2 weeks. Makes 2 cups.

I had never considered polenta a strong selling point for a dish, assuming people would prefer to spend their calories on something more sexy than cornmeal mush. But obviously they knew more than I; as a winter lunch entrée it became a surprise hit and is still on the menu today. It is substantial enough to serve as an entrée in larger portions.

1 cup quick-cooking **POLENTA** or yellow cornmeal

½ cup **TAPENADE**

½ teaspoon **SALT**

½ cup extra-virgin **OLIVE OIL**

6 **GARLIC** cloves, peeled and left whole

2 pounds **SHIITAKE** mushrooms, cleaned, stems
   removed, and cut in half

1 cup dry **WHITE WINE**

1 to 2 tablespoons finely chopped **ROSEMARY**

¼ cup finely chopped **PARSLEY**

SALT and **PEPPER**

Bring 4 cups of water to a boil in a large pot. Add the polenta in a thin stream, stirring constantly, then lower the heat to a simmer. Stir in the tapenade and salt and cook 5 to 7 minutes, stirring continuously, until very thick or the consistency of thick oatmeal.

Pour the polenta into an ungreased 8 × 12-inch baking pan, spreading to an even thickness with the back of a spoon. Set aside to cool for ½ hour. When cool, cut into quarters and cut each quarter into triangles. Remove from pan.

Preheat the broiler.

In a 12- to 14-inch sauté pan, heat the olive oil over moderate heat. Add the garlic and sauté until just lightly browned.

Add the shiitakes and, stirring quickly to move the garlic off the pan bottom, sauté 3 to 4 minutes until lightly browned, stirring often.

Add the wine and rosemary and cook until reduced by one-half, about 5 minutes. The mixture should be loose but not thin like a sauce. Remove from the heat. Add parsley and season with salt and pepper.

Place the polenta wedges under the broiler and broil, turning once, until hot but not darkened, about 3 minutes per side. Reheat the shiitake mixture if necessary over moderate heat. Place 1 wedge of polenta on each of 8 plates and spoon the shiitake mixture over each serving. Serve immediately.

OLIVES

Olives have been cultivated in Mesopotamia for both fruit and oil since the dawn of civilization, and their cultivation initiated the rise of agriculture in the Mediterranean and Near East. The people of the Mediterranean define much of their cooking by the way they treat, cure, prepare, or crush the olive. Inedibly bitter when picked off the tree, whether green, unripe, mottled reddish, and partially ripened, or black, when mature, the fruit must be processed to remove the bitter glycosides that are naturally present in the fruit. Most olives are cured in water, salt, or lye, or a combination of the three, and it can take up to a year to achieve an edible or desirable state. My favorite method is to soak raw green olives in six parts water and one part salt, changing the solution weekly for six weeks. At that point, they are still slightly bitter, crunchy, and badly in need of dressing. I like to add olive oil with oregano, garlic, orange peel, hot peppers, and red wine vinegar. In most of Tuscany, olives are harvested right after the grapes, around the beginning of November, and huge parties sloshing the fresh "new" oil all over everything are the norm.

Warm Terrine of Sausage, Peppers, Polenta, and Mozzarella

serves 6

After I demonstrated this recipe on television, it became one of my most requested ever. It is definitely best made a day ahead and lends itself to myriad variations. At Pó, we often use soft goat cheese in place of the mozzarella and also add pitted Gaeta olives and chopped fresh thyme leaves to different layers.

8 ounces sweet **SAUSAGE**

2 tablespoons extra-virgin **OLIVE OIL**

12 **GARLIC** cloves, peeled and left whole

1 large red **BELL PEPPER**, cored, seeded, and cut into ½-inch-wide strips

1 large green **BELL PEPPER**, cored, seeded, and cut into ½-inch-wide strips

8 ounces fresh **MOZZARELLA** cheese, cut into strips 3 inches by ¼ inch
   by ¼ inch

6 cups **WATER**

1 teaspoon **SALT**

1 teaspoon **SUGAR**

2 cups quick-cooking **POLENTA** or yellow cornmeal

¼ cup grated **PARMIGIANO-REGGIANO** cheese

Preheat the oven to 350°F.

Arrange the sausage in a baking pan and cook in the oven for 20 minutes. Drain off the fat, then crumble the cooked sausage to resemble rough bread crumbs. Set aside.

In a medium sauté pan, heat the olive oil over medium-low heat. Gently sauté the garlic until golden brown on all sides, 8 to 10 minutes. Add the bell peppers and sauté until soft but not browned, 7 to 8 minutes longer. Remove from heat, transfer the garlic and peppers to a bowl, and let cool.

Bring the mozzarella to room temperature. Arrange the sausage, peppers, garlic, and mozzarella in separate bowls. Set out a terrine, 13 × 4 × 4 inches.

Bring the water to a boil, adding the salt and sugar. Slowly add the polenta to the boiling water in a thin stream, whisking continuously. Lower the heat and cook until the polenta resembles the texture of hot cereal, 2 to 3 minutes. Remove the pot from heat. The polenta will begin to thicken immediately, so time here is of the essence.

Moving quickly, pour a 3/4-inch layer of polenta into the prepared terrine. Sprinkle all the crumbled sausage over the polenta. Cover the sausage with about 1 1/2 cups more polenta, using a spatula to smooth the top. Next, make a layer with the peppers and garlic cloves and top with another 1 1/2 cups warm polenta. Smooth and flatten the polenta to make a nice, even layer all the way to the edges. Arrange the mozzarella over the polenta (but do not

bring the mozzarella to the edges as it will stick to the sides when it melts). Fill the terrine with a final layer of warm polenta; there may be polenta left over. Smooth the top all the way to the edges. Cover the terrine with plastic wrap and chill overnight.

Preheat the oven to 475°F.

To serve, invert the terrine onto a cutting board. (It should come out quite easily.) Cut the terrine in 3/4-inch-thick slices. Place the slices on a baking sheet and bake for 10 to 12 minutes. Sprinkle with the grated cheese and serve immediately.

Hot Polenta Sandwiches

Rebecchini

serves 4

These groovy hot *antipasti* can be made up to four hours in advance and then reheated in a hot oven for five minutes just before serving. They are generally served during the *aperitivo* phase as an appetite teaser rather than at the table as an *antipasto*.

3 cups **WATER**

1 teaspoon **SALT**

1 cup quick-cooking **POLENTA** or yellow cornmeal

1 tablespoon extra-virgin **OLIVE OIL**, plus more for frying

4 **GARLIC** cloves, thinly sliced

8 **ANCHOVY** fillets

2 tablespoons **CAPERS**, rinsed and drained

½ cup all-purpose **FLOUR**

3 large **EGGS**

Brush a large baking sheet with vegetable oil and set aside.

In a medium saucepan, bring the water to a boil and add the salt. Whisking vigorously, slowly add the polenta in a thin stream and cook until quite thick, about 1 minute, switching to a wooden spoon to stir as the polenta thickens. Pour the polenta onto the baking sheet and spread with a spatula to a ⅛- to ¼-inch thickness, covering the sheet. Allow to cool 1 hour.

In a small saucepan, heat the olive oil over medium heat. Add the garlic and cook until just light brown. Add the anchovies and capers and stir until broken up into paste. Remove from the heat and set aside.

Place the flour on a plate. Break the eggs in a shallow bowl and beat lightly with a fork.

Pour 3 inches of olive oil into a deep pot and heat to 360° F.

While the oil is heating, cut the cooled polenta into 2-inch rounds using a glass or cookie cutter; you will have about 24 pieces. Place ½ teaspoon of anchovy mixture on the smooth side of a polenta disk and create a sandwich by covering with a second polenta disk, smooth side in. Press together.

Dredge the sandwiches in flour, then in egg, and deep-fry 4 or 5 at a time until golden brown, about 1½ minutes on each side. Serve hot.

Asparagus Milanese Style

serves 4

This simple *antipasto* is particularly popular when the asparagus first arrives in April. After a long winter of muted slow-cooked flavors, the first bite of asparagus dripping with a bit of runny yolk is an instant reminder of spring's delicious vitality, nearly forgotten over the long, cold season.

28 medium **ASPARAGUS** spears

½ cup (1 stick) unsalted **BUTTER**

4 large **EGGS**

½ cup freshly grated **PARMIGIANO-REGGIANO** cheese

Bring about 4 quarts of water to a boil and fill a large bowl with ice water. Trim the hard ends of the asparagus spears and drop the spears into the water. Cook 70 seconds. Remove with tongs and refresh in the ice bath. Drain and set aside.

In a 10- to 12-inch sauté pan, slowly heat 4 tablespoons of the butter over medium-low heat until very dark brown. Add the asparagus and toss until heated through.

Divide the asparagus among 4 plates. Wipe out the sauté pan with a paper towel and add the remaining 4 tablespoons butter. When the foam subsides, crack the eggs into the pan and cook sunny side up, about 2 minutes. Place 1 egg over each portion, sprinkle with cheese, and serve.

Shaved Fennel with Blood Oranges, Pomegranate, and Pecorino

serves 4

A classic winter salad to begin with, this dish is made both texturally and visually intriguing by the sweet and sexy addition of pomegranate seeds. The optional addition of paper-thin red onion slices and an oil and lemon dressing makes a lot of sense; the sharpness of onion works well with the sweet combo of fennel and pomegranate and the creamy contrast of sharp cheese.

2 large **FENNEL** bulbs, trimmed

juice of 1 **LEMON**

4 tablespoons extra-virgin **OLIVE OIL**

4 large **BLOOD ORANGES**, peeled and segmented

1 cup fresh **POMEGRANATE** seeds

SALT and **PEPPER**

6-ounce piece of hard **PECORINO** (sardo or Tuscan) cheese

Use a mandolin or sharp knife to slice the fennel as thin as possible. Place the fennel slices in a bowl and toss with the lemon juice and olive oil. Add the blood orange segments and pomegranate seeds, season to taste with salt and pepper, and toss gently to mix.

Arrange the fennel salad on 4 individual plates. Shave the pecorino in long shards over the top of each plate and serve.

Shaved Celery Root with Arugula, Parmigiano, and Truffles (or Porcini)

serves 4

Although I had tried truffles several times before my years in Italy, it was always a few shavings at a time. The day after I arrived in Borgo Capanne I sampled this elegant autumn salad, and for the first time exprienced truffles in sufficient abundance to truly appreciate them—it was pure heaven. If you do splurge on truffles, I recommend using them liberally on one course.

2 large **CELERY ROOTS** (celeriac)

2 bunches **ARUGULA**, washed and spun dry

½ cup extra-virgin **OLIVE OIL**

juice of ½ **LEMON**

SALT

1 pound **PARMIGIANO-REGGIANO** cheese

1 ounce fresh white **TRUFFLES** or 8 ounces fresh **PORCINI**

Use a paring knife to peel the celery roots, cutting out any blemishes. Slice paper-thin on a mandolin, or as thin as possible using a sharp knife. Place 5 or 6 slices on each plate.

In a mixing bowl, dress the arugula with ¼ cup of the olive oil, lemon juice, and salt and divide among the plates. Shave the Parmigiano-Reggiano over each plate and then blanket with paper-thin slices of truffle or porcini. Drizzle a tablespoon of the remaining oil over each salad and serve.

CELERY ROOT

Celery root, celeriac, and knob celery are all names for the white bulbous root often mistaken for the root of the common celery stalk. In fact, the foliage-bearing stalks of the celery root plant are much more leafy and fibrous than their Waldorf salad cousins. Celery root is harvested from late summer through early winter and is prized in Emilia-Romagna and Tuscany for its earthy but neutral flavor that combines readily with Parmigiano-Reggiano and/or spicy newly pressed Tuscan extra-virgin olive oil. To use, remove the stalks if any, reserving the leaves for frying as a garnish or for augmenting the soup pot. Peel the knob carefully with a paring knife and remove all of the potatolike eyes. Slice the root thin and serve raw in salads, or cube it and cook slowly over low heat until caramelized to use as a *contorno* or as a simple, delicious *antipasto*.

Grilled Chanterelles with Lemon, Sweet Chiles, and Wild Greens

serves 4

Chanterelles are a lot more plentiful and less expensive than the porcini we traditionally used in this La Volta classic. If you have a choice, select small to medium mushrooms, less than four inches long. If they are large, halve the chanterelles lengthwise before broiling.

1 pound **CHANTERELLE** mushrooms, cleaned with a brush

7 tablespoons extra-virgin **OLIVE OIL**

1 tablespoon freshly ground black **PEPPER**

grated zest and juice of 1 **LEMON**

½ medium **RED ONION**, thinly sliced

5 large yellow or green Anaheim **CHILES**, seeded, ribbed,
    and sliced ⅛ inch thick

4 cups **BABY GREENS** like mizuna, field cress, or young
    spinach, cleaned, washed, and spun dry

SALT

Preheat the grill or broiler.

In a large mixing bowl, toss the chanterelles, 3 tablespoons of the olive oil, and the black pepper to coat thoroughly. Arrange over the grill or on a broiler pan and cook, turning every minute or so, until softened and lightly browned, 8 to 10 minutes.

Heat the remaining 4 tablespoons oil in a 12- to 14-inch skillet and add the lemon zest and onion. Cook over medium heat until the onion is soft and translucent, 6 to 7 minutes. Add the chiles and sauté 1 minute longer. Add the greens and lemon juice and remove from the heat.

Place the grilled chanterelles on top of the greens and return the skillet to high heat. Stir gently with tongs until the greens are wilted. Season to taste with a dash of salt, transfer to a large serving bowl, and serve immediately.

Grilled Portobellos with Pea Sprouts, Cacio di Roma, and Shaved Field Mushrooms

serves 4

Here's a great example of bi-village cooking. Portobellos are available in Italy, but they are not nearly as popular as they are in the United States, especially at Pó. I find pea sprouts in Chinatown, but they can be successfully replaced by alfalfa sprouts or even spicy young watercress. The tangy shards of cheese elevate the quartet to a harmonious level of earthy Zen perfection.

4 large **PORTOBELLO** mushrooms, stems removed

4 domestic white **MUSHROOMS**

8 ounces fresh **PEA SPROUTS** or other tender young sprouts

4 tablespoons extra-virgin **OLIVE OIL**

2 tablespoons fresh **LEMON JUICE**

SALT and **PEPPER**

8 ounces **CACIO DI ROMA** or other semi-soft sheep's milk cheese

Preheat the grill or broiler.

Arrange the portobello mushrooms on the grill or in a broiler pan and cook until soft and barely charred, 3 to 4 minutes per side. Set aside.

Using a mandolin or very sharp knife, slice the domestic mushrooms paper-thin.

Combine the pea sprouts, olive oil, and lemon juice in a mixing bowl and toss to evenly coat the sprouts. Season to taste with salt and pepper and divide among 4 plates in little haystacks.

Using a vegetable peeler, shave the cheese over and around each haystack. Scatter the domestic mushroom slices over and around the salad, place a grilled portobello on each haystack, and serve.

Raw Porcini Salad with Grilled Caps, Arugula, and Grana

serves 4

Of all of the porcini dishes we served at La Volta, this was the true classic. It was the ideal way to prepare the ten kilos Quintiglio presented to us every day in early autumn. Alas, fresh porcini are very dear in this country, but I serve this dish at Pó at least once every fall because it's so evocative of the simple perfection in everything Quintiglio did.

4 large fresh **PORCINI** mushrooms (about 1 pound)

2 bunches **ARUGULA**, washed and spun dry (about 3 loose cups)

½ cup extra-virgin **OLIVE OIL**

juice and julienned zest of 1 **LEMON**

SALT and **PEPPER**

8-ounce piece **GRANA** or Parmigiano-Reggiano cheese

Preheat grill or broiler.

Carefully remove the cap from each mushroom (reserve the stems) and place on the grill or under the broiler. Cook, turning often, until lightly charred and slightly softened, 8 to 10 minutes.

While the mushroom caps cook, clean the mushroom stems and slice lengthwise into ⅛-inch slices. In a large mixing bowl, combine the sliced stems, arugula, 4 tablespoons of the olive oil, and the lemon juice and zest. Season to taste with salt and pepper and toss to mix thoroughly.

Divide the salad among 4 plates. Place a hot mushroom cap in the center of each salad. Using a vegetable peeler, shave the cheese onto each salad. Spoon 1 tablespoon of oil over each cap and serve immediately.

Raw Trumpet Mushrooms with Sun-dried Tomatoes, Balsamic Glazed Onions, and Truffle Oil

serves 4

Farm-raised trumpet mushrooms from Oregon have a delicate earthy flavor and are reasonably priced, considering their weight-to-volume ratio. The balsamic glazed onions, great as a side dish, are also excellent in salads, and work particularly well as a textural anchor here for the superlight fungi and the somewhat chewy sun-dried tomatoes. No need to use your best quality balsamic vinegar here; a reasonably good commercial brand will do fine.

1 recipe **BALSAMIC GLAZED ONIONS** (page 232), cooled

12 ounces fresh **TRUMPET** mushrooms

¼ cup oil-packed **SUN-DRIED TOMATOES**, cut into fine julienne

6 tablespoons **WHITE TRUFFLE OIL** (available at gourmet markets)

julienned zest and juice of 1 **LEMON**

SALT and **PEPPER**

Cut the cooled onion halves into quarters, discarding the skins. Place in a large mixing bowl with the trumpet mushrooms, sun-dried tomatoes, truffle oil, and lemon zest and juice and toss together. Season to taste with salt and pepper, divide among 4 plates, and serve.

Fried Zucchini Flowers with Ricotta and Golden Tomato Oil

serves 4

The trick to this dish is serving the fried flowers as soon as they are cooked; allowing them to sit even for five minutes causes them to become soft and heavy. I love the tangy goat ricotta or soft curd produced by my wife's family farm in upstate New York; it is shipped as quickly as it is made, and its freshness adds immeasurable distinction to delicate flavors such as these. You may, of course, substitute cow's milk ricotta.

12 2-inch **ZUCCHINI FLOWERS**

½ cup fresh **RICOTTA** cheese, preferably goat's milk ricotta

2 tablespoons beaten **EGG**

1 **SCALLION**, thinly sliced

⅛ teaspoon freshly grated **NUTMEG**

SALT and **PEPPER**

2 tablespoons extra-virgin **OLIVE OIL**

½ cup **GOLDEN TOMATO OIL**

Golden Tomato Oil

1 pound fresh **GOLDEN TOMATOES**
    or golden cherry tomatoes

½ cup extra-virgin **OLIVE OIL**

8 **BASIL** leaves

1 teaspoon **SALT**

Roughly chop the tomatoes and place in a blender with the olive oil, basil leaves, and salt and blend until smooth. Pour through a strainer into a bowl. Makes 1 cup.

Gently open up the zucchini flowers to remove the stamens and check for insects. In a medium mixing bowl, stir together the ricotta, egg, scallion, nutmeg, and salt and pepper to taste. Using a teaspoon, stuff each blossom with 1½ teaspoons of filling.

In a 10- to 12-inch nonstick sauté pan, heat the olive oil over medium-high heat until almost smoking. Place 4 of the stuffed flowers into the pan at a time and cook until golden brown on both sides, about 2 minutes per side. Keep warm in a 200° F. oven on a paper towel–lined sheet as you cook the rest.

Arrange 3 blossoms on each plate, drizzle with the golden tomato oil, and serve immediately.

Raw Artichokes with Bresaola and Shiitakes

serves 4

Raw artichokes were never part of my family's cooking repertoire, so when I tasted them for the first time, I was amazed. I've substituted shiitakes here for the ovoli mushrooms we used in Italy, but even raw button mushrooms work quite well.

zest and juice of 1 **LEMON**

¼ cup extra-virgin **OLIVE OIL**

8 **BABY ARTICHOKES**

6 ounces **BRESAOLA** or capicola, sliced paper-thin

4 ounces **SHIITAKE** mushrooms

SALT and **PEPPER**

In a mixing bowl, stir together the zest and lemon juice and olive oil and set aside. Remove the tough outer leaves from each artichoke and trim the stems. Using a sharp knife or mandolin, slice an artichoke lengthwise into paper-thin slices and immediately toss with the lemon juice mixture. Continue with the remaining artichokes.

Arrange the bresaola on 4 cool plates. Remove the stems from the shiitake mushrooms. Slice the shiitakes $1/16$ inch thick and toss with the artichokes. Season the mixture to taste with salt and pepper. Spoon one-fourth of the mushroom mixture over the bresaola on each plate and serve immediately.

Eggplant Portafoglio with Fontina Cheese, Oven-Dried Tomatoes, and Tomato Oil

serves 4

This "wallet" makes a great *antipasto*, but it can also be served as a fancy *contorno* to a simple braised rabbit or grilled meat dish.

1 large **EGGPLANT** (2 pounds)

4 ounces **FONTINA** cheese, grated

16 **OVEN-DRIED TOMATO** halves

½ cup finely chopped Italian **PARSLEY**

6 tablespoons extra-virgin **OLIVE OIL**

SALT and **PEPPER**

¼ cup **TOMATO OIL** (page 169)

Preheat the grill or broiler.

Slice the eggplant crosswise into ½-inch-thick rounds (you need 16 slices altogether). Place on an unoiled grill and toast until light brown and softened, about 1 minute on each side. Remove and set aside on a cookie sheet. Sprinkle 8 of the eggplant slices with the grated fontina. Over the cheese, place 2 pieces of oven-dried tomatoes. Sprinkle the tomatoes with 1 tablespoon of parsley and cover with second eggplant slice. Press down lightly with your fingers to compress somewhat.

In a large nonstick skillet, heat 4 tablespoons of olive oil over medium heat until just smoking. Place 4 "wallets" in the pan and cook until golden brown, about 3 minutes. Turn over carefully and cook until the second side is golden brown and the cheese is soft and melted. Remove to plate to keep warm. Add the remaining 2 tablespoons of oil to the pan and fry the remaining "wallets." Serve immediately with a drizzle of tomato oil.

Oven-Dried Tomatoes

4 pounds ripe plum **TOMATOES**

3 tablespoons **KOSHER SALT**

3 tablespoons **SUGAR**

Preheat the oven to 150° F.

Slice the tomatoes in half lengthwise and place cut side up on baking sheets. Combine the salt and sugar and sprinkle a little bit over each tomato, about ½ teaspoon. Place in the oven and cook slowly for 10 hours. (It works well to put the tomatoes in right before you go to bed and remove them in the morning.) Allow to cool and refrigerate for later use. Makes 6 cups.

Eggplant Preserved in Oil

Melanzane Sott'Olio

makes 40 to 50 slices

This recipe comes from my good friend Mauro Cuppone's mother, who would carry on about her lack of cooking skills every time I was invited over for a five- or six-course lunch. Each dish she made was a symphony of traditional ingredients and subtle flavors, and she often started with a plate of this incredible eggplant. Under a preserving layer of oil, this becomes even better after a week or more in the refrigerator. Be certain to let it stand at room temperature for at least hour before serving so that the solidified oil will liquefy.

3 pounds Japanese **EGGPLANTS**

1 cup **SALT**

1 bunch **MINT**, leaves only

4 **GARLIC** cloves, thinly sliced

1 tablespoon dried **ACACIA FLOWERS** (can substitute dried oregano or thyme)

4 tablespoons **RED WINE VINEGAR**

4 serrano **CHILES**

1 to 2 liters extra-virgin **OLIVE OIL**

2 wide-mouth 1-quart mason **JARS**

Trim the eggplants and cut lengthwise into ¼-inch-thick slices. In a bowl, toss the slices with the salt to coat, then place them on a rack over a roasting pan. Cover with one layer of cheesecloth and place about 4 bricks or other weights on top. Set in a cool place to drain for 12 hours.

Remove the eggplant from the rack and place in a large bowl. Add the mint, garlic, acacia flowers, and 2 tablespoons of the vinegar and toss to coat thoroughly. Layer the eggplant slices in a jar, one on top of another, placing a chile between the layers every so often. When the jar is nearly full, press the eggplant down with your fingers and add the remaining 2 tablespoons of vinegar. Fill the jar with olive oil, cover, and refrigerate until an hour before serving.

The eggplant is now ready to eat, but its flavor will improve after a week of aging. If topped with oil, the eggplant will last 2 months in the back of your refrigerator.

Quail Spiedini with Sage Polenta and Asiago

serves 4

I had this dish at a working farm outside of Venice and will remember it forever. The smoky sweetness of the crisp quail, combined with the abruptly clean corn flavor of the polenta and sage, was almost shocking in its intensity. If you cannot buy boneless quail, the dish is a little trickier to eat, but it is still definitely worth the effort. The single most important step is the marinade, and the quail will be even better if you allow them to sleep overnight in their honey and vinegar beauty bath.

8 **QUAIL**, preferably boneless

MARINADE

4 pieces **PANCETTA**, cut into 1-inch cubes

¼ cup **BALSAMIC VINEGAR**

¼ cup extra-virgin **OLIVE OIL**

2 tablespoons **HONEY**

1 tablespoon black **PEPPER**

1 medium **RED ONION**, cut into ¼-inch dice

4 cups **WATER**

10 fresh **SAGE** leaves, chopped

1 cup quick-cooking **POLENTA** or yellow cornmeal

½ cup freshly grated **ASIAGO** cheese

Soak 4 bamboo skewers in water to cover for several hours.

Check the quail for bones or feathers, and place in a large mixing bowl. Add the marinade ingredients and toss to coat. Set aside for at least 2 hours or cover and refrigerate overnight.

Preheat the grill or broiler.

In a 3-quart saucepan, combine the onion, water, and sage and bring to a boil. On each skewer, thread 1 quail, followed by a piece of pancetta and a second quail. Place on the hottest part of grill and cook 4 to 5 minutes on each side, until just pink at the leg bones.

Meanwhile, pour the polenta slowly into the boiling water in a thin stream, whisking constantly until all is incorporated and the polenta thickens, 1 to 2 minutes. Switch to a wooden spoon, add the Asiago, and cook another minute, until the polenta is as thick as oatmeal. Remove from the heat and pour onto a heatproof platter. Pile the skewers on top of the polenta and serve.

Chicken Livers with Leeks, Balsamic Vinegar, and Dried Apricots

serves 4

This warm salad combines the richness of chicken livers with sweet and sour fruit and vinegar to really nail comfort food in a modern way.

4 tablespoons extra-virgin **OLIVE OIL**

1 pound **CHICKEN LIVERS**, rinsed and dried

½ cup all-purpose **FLOUR,** seasoned with salt and pepper

2 large **LEEKS**, white and tender green parts, rinsed and cut into 2-inch julienne

8 ounces dried **APRICOTS**

½ cup **BALSAMIC VINEGAR**

3 tablespoons unsalted **BUTTER**

2 cups **CURLY ENDIVE**, washed and spun dry

In a 12- to 14-inch sauté pan, heat the olive oil over medium heat until smoking. Dredge the chicken livers in the seasoned flour and shake off the excess. Add the chicken livers to the pan and sauté until crisp and golden brown, 8 to 10 minutes, and remove to a plate. Add the leeks and apricots to the pan and cook until the leeks are softened, 6 to 8 minutes.

Return the chicken livers to the pan, add the vinegar and butter, and cook until the liquid is reduced by half, 3 to 4 minutes. Add the endive, toss to coat, and serve immediately.

Historically, the presence of an *antipasto* on a home menu was a sign of prosperity.

My Favorite Way with the New Olive Oil

serves 4

Around olive harvest time, cookbook author Faith Willinger directs a program at a great working farm called Tenuta di Cappezzana, where owners Ugo and Lisa Contini, and their daughters, Benedetta and Beatrice, represent everything Tuscan and perfect. I often teach classes there on using the new oil. The whole idea of the week-long adventure is to pour the freshly pressed nectar on everything we eat, from toast at breakfast to raw vegetables after the *secondo* at dinner. I include this "nonrecipe" to remind people how great the new oil is every November.

2 large **BELL PEPPERS,** one red, one yellow

1 large **FENNEL** bulb

4 **CELERY** stalks

4 large **SCALLIONS**

1 large **CARROT**

8 large **RADISHES**

4 ounces **HARICOTS VERTS**
 (slender green beans)

1 cup just-pressed extra-virgin **OLIVE OIL**
 from Cappezzana or another great
 Tuscan oil producer

¼ cup **RED WINE VINEGAR**

SEA SALT

Cut the vegetables into fancy shapes. Pour the olive oil, vinegar, and sea salt into small bowls. Arrange the prepared vegetables in a basket with the condiments tucked among them and serve.

Peperonata with Grilled Sardines

serves 6

The smoky sweet flavor of fresh sardines sings in pure harmony with late summer peppers kissed with thyme. I first ate this dish at La Buca in Cesenatico, and have never forgotten its classic simplicity. If you cannot find sardines, anchovies, smelts, or mackerel are equally delicious and full-flavored substitutes.

12 fresh **SARDINES**, gutted, gills removed

⅓ cup extra-virgin **OLIVE OIL**

1 large **RED ONION**, cut into ½-inch slices

2 **GARLIC** cloves, thinly sliced

9 large **BELL PEPPERS** (3 red, 3 yellow, 3 green), halved, with stems, ribs, and seeds removed, cut into ½-inch slices

1 dried hot **CHILE**, crushed

1 tablespoon **SUGAR**

3 sprigs fresh **THYME**, leaves removed (about 1 teaspoon)

1 cup **BASIC TOMATO SAUCE** (page 84)

SALT and **PEPPER**

Preheat the grill or broiler.

Rinse the sardines inside and out with cool water and pat dry with paper towels. Set aside.

Heat the olive oil in a deep casserole. Add the onion and garlic and sauté over medium heat until soft and translucent, 8 to 10 minutes. Add the peppers and cook 5 minutes longer, until softened.

Add the chile, sugar, thyme, and tomato sauce and bring to a boil, then lower the heat and simmer 15 minutes. Season to taste with salt and pepper.

Grill or broil the sardines until they are crisp and the skin is slightly charred, about 2 minutes per side. Divide the peperonata evenly among 6 dishes. Arrange 2 sardines each on top of the peperonata and serve.

Tuma Cheese with Fresh Anchovies in Scapece

serves 4

Like the tuna recipe on page 68, this preparation is reminiscent of the Spanish *escabeche*. Tuma cheese is a fresh cow or goat cheese that is eaten very young and is sometimes difficult to find; you can substitute mozzarella quite successfully. I first tried this dish on the Amalfi coast and was surprised by the combination of flavors; the cheese is so delicate that the briny anchovies become the true emphasis on the palate.

16 fresh **ANCHOVY** fillets, gutted and heads removed

juice and zest of 2 **LEMONS**

SALT and **PEPPER**

¼ cup extra-virgin **OLIVE OIL**

¼ cup finely chopped Italian **PARSLEY**

½ teaspoon hot red **PEPPER FLAKES**

8 ounces **TUMA** cheese or fresh mozzarella

Lay the anchovy fillets out on a jelly roll pan and sprinkle the lemon juice and zest evenly over the anchovies. Cover and refrigerate for 2 hours to "cook" the anchovies.

Remove anchovies from the refrigerator, place in a large mixing bowl, and add salt and pepper, olive oil, parsley, and red pepper flakes. Stir gently to coat, taking care not to break the anchovies. Set aside or refrigerate for up to 24 hours.

Divide the cheese into 4 equal portions. Spoon the anchovies and some of their liquid over and around cheese, and serve.

Barbecued Oysters and Razor Clams with Chile Vinegar Dipping Sauce

serves 4

Italians would be most perplexed by this variation on French *mignonette* for dipping the hot shellfish, but I love the exotic depth chiles add to simple dishes like this one. Try it with any raw or cooked shellfish.

2 dozen **OYSTERS**, scrubbed

2 dozen **RAZOR CLAMS**, scrubbed

ROCK SALT

1 recipe **CHILE VINEGAR DIPPING SAUCE**

Chile Vinegar Dipping Sauce

2 tablespoons chopped fresh **JALAPEÑO** peppers

½ cup **RED WINE VINEGAR**

2 tablespoons **SUGAR**

1 teaspoon **SALT**

2 tablespoons finely chopped **RED ONION**

6 **MINT** leaves, cut in fine strips (chiffonade)

In a small mixing bowl, combine the chopped peppers, vinegar, sugar, salt, onion, and mint and stir. Makes ¾ cup.

Preheat the grill or light a charcoal fire.

Place the shellfish on the grill and cook until the shells open. Remove to a platter lined with a ¾-inch layer of rock salt. Place a small bowl of the dipping sauce in the center and serve the shellfish with cocktail forks.

Marinated Calamari and Artichokes in a Spicy Olive Vinaigrette

serves 4

Fresh calamari, when properly cooked, is truly a perfect canvas on which to paint any of a thousand flavors. Tasting of little more than light sea foam, calamari can be treated aggressively with vinegar, chiles, and powerful herbs or delicately with just lemon and chives and it will sing a beautiful melody each time. Here the raw artichoke's bitter component is tamed by a spicy vinaigrette, while the dressing's heat is soothed by the cool calamari and frisée.

2½ pounds **CALAMARI**

1 recipe **SPICY OLIVE VINAIGRETTE**

16 **BABY ARTICHOKES**, outer leaves removed
   and trimmed

2 cups **FRISÉE**, or mesclun

SALT and **PEPPER**

Spicy Olive Vinaigrette

½ medium **RED ONION**, finely minced

¼ cup **RED WINE VINEGAR**

¼ cup **BLACK OLIVE PASTE**

½ cup extra-virgin **OLIVE OIL**

1 tablespoon hot red **PEPPER FLAKES**

½ cup crushed dried hot **CHILES**

Whisk together the onion, vinegar, olive paste, olive oil, red pepper flakes, and chiles until well combined. Makes 1 cup.

Bring 6 quarts of water to a boil. Fill a large bowl with ice water. Separate the calamari bodies from the tentacles. Cut the bodies into ¼-inch-thick rings and halve the tentacles.

Plunge the sliced calamari into boiling water and cook until just opaque, 1½ to 2 minutes. Drain and plunge into ice water to refresh. Drain again and set aside in a large mixing bowl.

Place the vinaigrette in a large bowl. Using a mandolin, slicer, or sharp knife, slice the artichokes paper-thin and add immediately to the vinaigrette. Toss until well mixed, and refrigerate for ½ hour.

To serve, toss the chilled calamari and artichoke mixture with the frisée, season to taste with salt and pepper, and mix well. Divide among 4 plates and serve.

Spiedini of Sea Scallops with Marinated Onions, Lemon, and Baby Spinach

serves 4

When we offer these skewers as an occasional entrée special at Pó, they are quite popular. The trick to buying scallops is to make sure they are hand harvested and have not been treated with tripolyphosphate, a preservative used to extend their freshness that causes them to swell with water and become flaccid and heinous.

1 large **RED ONION**, thinly sliced

2 large **LEMONS**, halved lengthwise, seeded, and sliced into
   ¼-inch-thick half-moons

2 cups plus 2 tablespoons **RED WINE VINEGAR**

½ cup **WATER**

¼ cup **SUGAR**

¼ cup **SALT**

16 large **SEA SCALLOPS**, about 1½ pounds

SALT and **PEPPER**

2 cups baby **SPINACH** leaves, rinsed and spun dry

10 tablespoons extra-virgin **OLIVE OIL**

Preheat the grill or broiler. Soak 4 bamboo skewers in water.

In a large mixing bowl, stir together the onion, lemons, 2 cups vinegar, the water, sugar, and salt until well mixed and let stand 1 hour.

On each of the skewers, thread 4 scallops alternately with the marinated lemon pieces, beginning and ending with lemon pieces. Season with salt and pepper and grill until just cooked through, about 4 minutes per side.

While the scallops cook, toss the baby spinach in a mixing bowl with 6 tablespoons of the olive oil and the remaining 2 tablespoons vinegar and mix until evenly coated. Divide the spinach among 4 plates.

Strain the onions and place in 4 small piles around the rim of each plate. Place a scallop skewer over the spinach on each pile. Drizzle each with 1 tablespoon of the remaining olive oil and serve.

Stuffed Calamari on the Grill

serves 4

The trick to this dish is insisting on *fresh* calamari. You can stuff the squid in advance and refrigerate them until dinner.

8 small whole **CALAMARI** (about 1 pound)

STUFFING

4 tablespoons extra-virgin **OLIVE OIL**

4 **GARLIC** cloves, thinly sliced

½ cup finely chopped **SUN-DRIED TOMATOES**

1 cup toasted **BREAD CRUMBS**

1 tablespoon fresh **THYME** leaves

4 **SCALLIONS**, thinly sliced

¼ cup roughly chopped Italian **PARSLEY**

SALT and **PEPPER**

4 tablespoons extra-virgin **OLIVE OIL**

4 plum **TOMATOES**, chopped into ¼-inch dice

1 bunch **CHIVES**, chopped

Remove the tentacles and clean the calamari, leaving the bodies whole. Set the tentacles aside. Place the calamari in an 8-quart pot and cover with water. Bring to a boil over high heat. Cook for 1 hour or until quite tender. Drain and cool.

Make the stuffing. Heat the olive oil in a 10- to 12-inch sauté pan until smoking. Add the garlic and sun-dried tomatoes and cook until light golden brown, about 30 seconds. Add the bread crumbs and continue cooking until well mixed. Allow to cool then stir in the thyme, scallions, and parsley.

Preheat the grill or broiler.

Stuff the cooled calamari with the bread crumb mixture and season with salt and pepper. Brush the stuffed calamari and tentacles with 1 tablespoon of the oil and grill or broil until nicely charred, about 10 minutes, turning once.

While the calamari grills, place the tomatoes, remaining 3 tablespoons olive oil, and the chives in a small mixing bowl, and season with salt and pepper. Arrange the calamari on a platter, top with spoonfuls of the tomatoes, and serve.

Barbecued Baby Octopus with Giant Lima Beans in a Spicy Red Wine and Tapenade Vinaigrette

serves 4

Tapenade Vinaigrette

2 **SHALLOTS**, peeled and finely minced

¼ cup **TAPENADE** (page 38)

¼ cup **RED WINE VINEGAR**

2 tablespoons hot red **PEPPER FLAKES**

¼ cup extra-virgin **OLIVE OIL**

Combine the shallots, tapenade, vinegar, and red pepper flakes in a blender and puree until smooth. With the blender running, drizzle in the olive oil until the dressing is smooth and creamy. Makes ¾ cup.

As a child I always hated frozen lima beans' textural wimpiness, and as an adult I still feel much the same. These giant lima beans, introduced to me by Lynn Saathoff, then of Gabriel's restaurant in New York City, are used in many Greek restaurants and are available only dried. Fresh fava beans work just as well and are certainly easier to find.

1½ cups cooked giant **LIMA BEANS**
 (see opposite) or cooked fava beans

1 **GARLIC** clove, thinly sliced

2 **SCALLIONS**, thinly sliced

1 teaspoon fresh **THYME** leaves

¼ cup extra-virgin **OLIVE OIL**

SALT and **PEPPER**

2 pounds baby **OCTOPUS** (16–24 size), cooled (see opposite)

1 recipe **TAPENADE VINAIGRETTE**

1 bunch **CHIVES**, cut into 3-inch lengths

Preheat the grill or broiler.

In a mixing bowl, stir together the cooked limas, garlic, scallions, thyme, and olive oil. Season to taste with salt and pepper and set aside.

Lightly oil and season the octopus and arrange on the grill or broiler pan. Cook until crispy, about 4 minutes per side.

Arrange the lima salad in the center of a large serving plate. Arrange the octopus on and around the beans. Drizzle the platter with vinaigrette, sprinkle with chives, and serve.

Broccoli Rabe Crostini with Crotonese and Black Pepper-Oregano Oil (page 27)

Shaved Fennel with Blood Oranges, Pomegranate, and Pecorino (page 44)

PREVIOUS PAGE: Barbecued Baby Octopus with Giant Lima Beans in a Spicy Red Wine and Tapenade Vinaigrette (page 64)

Grilled Shrimp with White Beans, Rosemary, Mâche,
and Mint Oil (page 66)

Quail Spiedini with Sage Polenta and Asiago (page 54)

Stuffed Calamari on the Grill (page 63)

Spiedini of Sea Scallops with Marinated Onions, Lemon, and
Baby Spinach (page 62)

NEXT PAGE: Crespelle (page 102)

COOKING OCTOPUS

Many cooks disdain octopus as rubbery, an unfortunate reputation reinforced by tourist images of fishermen squatted on the rocks by the sea, flailing away at some poor octopus. I've tried beating them with mallets, puncturing them with tiny fork holes, and marinating them with base or acid—the only thing that makes octopus tender is a cork. Cooking the octopus at a low boil with a common wine cork in the water results in edible flesh in as much as twenty minutes less cooking time and much less of the toughness associated with OPC (other people's cephalopods). I've heard this is the result of an enzymatic reaction between something in the cork and the protein in the flesh, but beyond that I cannot say. Just add a cork to your cooking water and enjoy.

COOKING DRIED BEANS

The dried seedpods of legumes, called pulses or beans, possess an incredible amount of protein as well as vitamins A and C, and for centuries have formed the basis of the poor man's diet in Mediterranean and Middle Eastern societies. Dried beans have a long shelf life, are quite easy to prepare, and are very nutritious. Starting the rehydration process soaking beans overnight reduces the cooking time and allows the complex sugars to begin to break down, thus reducing the flatulence sometimes caused by secondary fermentation and digestion in the lower intestine.

To cook dried beans, I recommend this 3-part process: soak the beans overnight and drain. Add clean, cold water (three times as much as the beans by volume) and bring to a boil. Lower the heat to a high simmer and cook until just tender (time will vary with the beans' age and variety). Drain and refresh with cold water. Do not add salt or acidic ingredients such as lemon juice to the first three steps or the skins may become tough. The drained, cooled beans can be stored in the refrigerator for 2 or 3 days..

Grilled Shrimp with White Beans, Rosemary, Mâche, and Mint Oil

serves 4

Versions of this dish are served all over Italy, often with the shrimp (or prawns) boiled and cooled. I find that grilling the shrimp with the heads on not only creates a more dramatic presentation but also makes sopping up the combined juices of mint, shrimp drippings, and bean dressing totally satisfying. Partially peeling the shrimp but leaving the tail flap intact leaves a convenient "handle" to grab them by.

Mint Oil

½ cup packed fresh **MINT** leaves

¾ cup extra-virgin **OLIVE OIL**

Bring a saucepan of water to a boil. Prepare an ice bath. Plunge the mint leaves into the boiling water for 30 seconds, then remove to the ice bath. Squeeze out the excess liquid and puree in a food processor for 1 minute with the olive oil. Makes 1 cup.

1½ cups cooked **GREAT NORTHERN BEANS** (see page 65)

1 tablespoon chopped fresh **ROSEMARY** leaves

2 tablespoons extra-virgin **OLIVE OIL**

4 tablespoons finely chopped **RED ONION**

1 tablespoon chopped fresh **MARJORAM** leaves

juice and zest of 1 **LEMON**

SALT and **PEPPER**

2 cups fresh **MÂCHE**, washed and spun dry

12 jumbo **SHRIMP** (about 1⅓ pounds), preferably with heads on and partially peeled

¼ cup **MINT OIL**

Preheat the grill or broiler.

In a mixing bowl, stir together the cooked beans, rosemary, olive oil, onion, marjoram, and lemon juice and zest. Season to taste with salt and pepper.

Add the mâche to the beans and toss to combine. Arrange in the centers of 4 plates.

Season the shrimp with salt and pepper, brush with a bit of additional oil, and grill just until cooked through, about 4 minutes per side. Prop 3 shrimp against the mâche and beans, tepee fashion, on each plate.

Drizzle with the mint oil and serve.

Swordfish Paillard with Leeks and Grapefruit

serves 4

A light and flavorful paillard is an excellent *antipasto* in a three- to four-course meal, as it is big on flavor, dramatic in presentation, yet not too filling. Cooking on the plate is a lot easier than trying to sear something so fragile in a pan. Be careful not to overcook the fish; an extra twenty seconds can dry it out.

12 ounces center cut **SWORDFISH**, cut into 4 $\frac{1}{8}$-inch-thick scallops on
   slicer or by fishmonger

2 large **LEEKS,** white part cut into 4-inch julienne strips

1 pink **GRAPEFRUIT**

1 teaspoon Dijon **MUSTARD**

6 tablespoons extra-virgin **OLIVE OIL**

2 teaspoons black **MUSTARD SEEDS**

1 tablespoon fresh **LEMON JUICE**

Preheat the oven to 450° F.

Place the swordfish paillards on 4 individual ovenproof plates, cover with plastic, and refrigerate. Bring about 2 quarts of water to a boil, add about 1 tablespoon salt, and set up a handy ice bath.

Drop the julienned leeks into the boiling water and cook until tender, about 1 minute. Remove the leeks and plunge into the ice bath to cool, about 1 minute. Drain well and set aside.

Remove the zest from the grapefruit with a zester or a sharp knife, then cut off any remaining skin and pith. Holding the grapefruit over a bowl to catch any juice, cut between the membranes to free the individual segments.

In a small mixing bowl, whisk together half the grapefruit zest, the grapefruit juice, mustard, $\frac{1}{4}$ cup of the olive oil, and the mustard seeds.

Remove the swordfish from the refrigerator and uncover. Place in the oven, plates and all, and cook 30 to 45 seconds, until fish is just opaque.

Dress the leeks with the remaining 2 tablespoons oil and the lemon juice and make a pile in the center of paillard. Arrange 3 grapefruit segments on each plate and sprinkle with the remaining zest. Drizzle with the sauce and serve.

Tuna in Scapece with Scallion Frittata

serves 4

Both phonetically and technically, *scapece* is quite close to *escabeche*, the Spanish technique of cooking and preserving fish in an acidic bath. The tuna in this dish picks up most of its rich moistness from the very delicate cooking in the first step. The combination of cool mint and hot chiles is one that I favor in many of my dishes that are inspired by southern Italian cooking.

1 pound fresh **TUNA**

6 tablespoons extra-virgin **OLIVE OIL**

¼ cup **RED WINE VINEGAR**

1 **GARLIC** clove, thinly sliced

2 plum **TOMATOES**, finely chopped

¼ cup fresh **MINT** leaves

1 teaspoon hot red **PEPPER FLAKES**

1 teaspoon dried **OREGANO FLOWERS** or dried oregano

SALT and **PEPPER**

6 **EGGS**, beaten

½ cup finely sliced **SCALLIONS**

½ cup freshly grated **PECORINO** cheese

Bring 2 quarts of water to a boil.

Cut the tuna into ¾-inch cubes and drop into the boiling water. Lower the heat to a simmer and cook for 2 minutes, stirring to separate the cubes. Drain carefully and spread on a serving platter in one layer to cool.

In a large mixing bowl, stir together ¼ cup of the olive oil, the vinegar, garlic, tomatoes, mint, red pepper flakes, oregano flowers, and salt and pepper. When the tuna is cool, pour the dressing over and set aside. In a large mixing bowl, stir together the eggs, scallions, and pecorino.

In a 6- to 8-inch nonstick sauté pan, heat the remaining 2 tablespoons of oil until smoking. Add the egg mixture and cook until set, about 8 minutes. Cool and cut into 8 wedges. Divide the tuna over the omelet and serve 2 wedges to each person.

Tuna Carpaccio with Cucumbers, Sweet Potatoes, and Saffron Vinaigrette

serves 4

Purely New York, this dish is a variation on a familiar theme. The sweet potatoes of early autumn, combined with summer's last cucumbers, make a perfect textural contrast to the Bigeye tuna that run off Long Island in late September.

8 ounces sushi-grade **TUNA**

1 small **SWEET POTATO**, peeled and diced into ¼-inch cubes

1 medium **CUCUMBER**

2 tablespoons extra-virgin **OLIVE OIL**

SALT and **PEPPER**

½ recipe **SAFFRON VINAIGRETTE**

Slice the tuna into 4 equal portions and place each between lightly oiled pieces of aluminum foil. Lightly pat the tuna with a cleaver until paper-thin. Carefully flip each piece onto a chilled plate, cover with plastic wrap, and set aside in the refrigerator until ready to serve.

Bring a large saucepan of water to a boil. Add the sweet potato cubes and cook until tender yet firm, 1 to 4 minutes. Drain, then rinse under running water until cool. Drain again and set aside.

Halve the unpeeled cucumber lengthwise and use a spoon to remove the seeds. Cut into ⅛-inch-thick half-moons. Set aside.

Remove the plated tuna from the refrigerator and season with salt and pepper. In a mixing bowl, dress the cucumber and sweet potato with the olive oil and season with salt and pepper. Spoon some of the sweet potato mixture onto the center of each plate, drizzle with the saffron vinaigrette, and serve immediately.

Saffron Vinaigrette

¼ medium **RED ONION**, finely chopped

1 teaspoon **SAFFRON** threads

¼ cup **WHITE WINE VINEGAR**

2 tablespoons Dijon **MUSTARD**

½ cup extra-virgin **OLIVE OIL**

SALT and **PEPPER**

Combine the onion, saffron, and vinegar in a saucepan and boil until reduced by half. Transfer the mixture to a blender with the mustard and blend until smooth. Drizzle in the olive oil until emulsified and season to taste with salt and pepper. Makes ¾ cup.

Prosciutto di Parma with a
Grilled Fig–Fresh Fig Salad

serves 4

This recipe, and the following two, are all about summer, when figs are exploding with complex sweetness and easy to find. True Italians would just serve them raw with the prosciutto, so this recipe is probably the result of having too much free time on my hands (and perhaps one too many boxes of ripe figs in the restaurant).

12 fresh black mission or Kadota **FIGS**, cut in half

2 tablespoons chopped fresh **ROSEMARY** leaves

2 tablespoons **BALSAMIC VINEGAR**

12 large sprigs Italian **PARSLEY**

8 ounces fresh **ARUGULA**, washed and spun dry to
    yield 2 cups

3 tablespoons extra-virgin **OLIVE OIL**

8 ounces **PROSCIUTTO** di Parma, sliced paper-thin

Preheat the grill or broiler.

Place12 fig halves cut side down on the grill or cut side up on the broiler pan and cook 3 minutes, until just lightly browned. Transfer to a mixing bowl and allow to cool.

Add the remaining figs, rosemary, balsamic vinegar, Italian parsley, arugula, and olive oil to the cooled grilled figs and gently mix with your hands so as not to break the figs up.

Divide the prosciutto among 4 plates. Arrange a portion of the fig salad on top of the prosciutto and serve immediately.

Prosciutto di Parma with
Baked Stuffed Figs

serves 4

Figs stuffed with Gorgonzola create an almost sweet and sour sensation in my mouth that *can* challenge the prosciutto. To achieve the perfect balance of flavors in each bite I generally cut the figs into quarters and wrap each quarter in a slice of prosciutto.

12 fresh black mission or Kadota **FIGS**

6 ounces **GORGONZOLA** cheese, softened to room temperature

2 tablespoons finely chopped **WALNUTS**

2 bunches Italian **PARSLEY**, finely chopped (½ cup)

8 ounces **PROSCIUTTO** di Parma, sliced paper-thin

Preheat the oven to 450° F.

Quarter the figs lengthwise, cutting down from the stem but leaving the segments attached at the base. Place on an ungreased baking sheet.

In a mixing bowl, stir together the Gorgonzola, walnuts, and parsley until well mixed. Using a tablespoon, stuff 1 tablespoon of the filling onto each opened fig. Bake the figs 8 to 10 minutes, until the cheese filling is bubbling.

Arrange 3 or 4 slices of prosciutto on each of 4 plates. Remove the figs from the oven, place 3 in center of each plate, and serve immediately.

FIGS

Figs are among the world's oldest cultivated fruits and today are found throughout California, the Mediterranean, and northern Africa. They are eaten raw, cooked, and preserved and are immensely versatile, beyond fig Newtonian applications. The fig trees in Borgo Capanne had double life, producing fruit early in the summer for most of the month of June then fruiting again near the end of August with the trees continuing to bear until the end of September.

One of my favorite uses for figs that have gotten too ripe is fig vinegar. Remove the stems from six overripe figs and blend in a food processor with two cups of balsamic vinegar for two minutes or until smooth and viscous. This intensely flavored nectar is outstanding on salads, makes a great addition to sandwiches, and keeps in the refrigerator, tightly covered for up to a month.

Prosciutto di San Daniele with Apple Salad

serves 4

San Daniele is a slightly sweeter prosciutto produced in the northeastern part of Friuli, and it is particularly harmonious with the apples of that region. I find that combining several kinds of apples in one dish allows the palate to appreciate even better the complexity of something so simple. My favorites include Macoun, Empire, and Jonagold.

8 ounces thinly sliced San Daniele or other imported **PROSCIUTTO**

1 **GRANNY SMITH** apple, peeled and cored

1 **MCINTOSH** apple, peeled and cored

1 **GOLDEN DELICIOUS** apple, peeled and cored

1 tablespoon **POPPY SEEDS**

3 tablespoons extra-virgin **OLIVE OIL**

1 tablespoon **RED WINE VINEGAR**

1 head **RADICCHIO** di Treviso, leaves separated

SALT and **PEPPER**

4 1-inch-thick slices Italian peasant **BREAD**,
     grilled or toasted

Arrange the prosciutto slices on a large platter.

Cut the apples into thin julienne strips and place in a mixing bowl. Add the poppy seeds, olive oil, vinegar, radicchio leaves, and salt and pepper to taste and toss to coat.

Mound the salad in the center of the platter and surround with the grilled bread. Serve immediately.

Paper-Thin Frittata Salad

Frittatine Verdi in Insalata

serves 4

This interesting *antipasto* is actually Sicilian inspired and can be made successfully with egg whites alone for those with cholesterol issues. The combination of mint leaves and fennel fronds closely approximates the flavor of Sicilian wild fennel and makes this particularly light and flavorful salad taste quite exotic.

½ cup fresh **MINT** leaves

½ cup fresh **BASIL** leaves

½ cup fresh **OREGANO** leaves

½ cup **FENNEL FRONDS**

6 **EGGS**

SALT and black **PEPPER**

2 tablespoons extra-virgin **OLIVE OIL**

1 head **ESCAROLE**, washed and spun dry

zest and peeled segments from 2 **ORANGES**

¼ cup extra-virgin **OLIVE OIL**

juice and zest of 1 **LEMON**

Chop together the mint, basil, oregano, and fennel until the herbs are as fine as bread crumbs and place in a large mixing bowl. Crack the eggs into the same bowl, mix well, and season with salt and black pepper.

Place an 8- to 10-inch nonstick sauté pan over medium heat, add 1 tablespoon of the olive oil, and heat until smoking. Add one-quarter of the egg-herb mixture to the pan and cook until golden brown. Flip the frittata and cook 1 minute on the second side; remove to a plate to cool. Make 3 more thin frittatas in the same fashion, adding more oil as needed and placing each on its own plate.

When the frittatas have cooled, stack them one on top of the other and cut into ¼-inch julienne strips. Place in a clean mixing bowl and toss with the escarole, orange zest and segments, extra-virgin olive oil, and lemon juice and zest. Season with salt and pepper, toss to coat well, and serve.

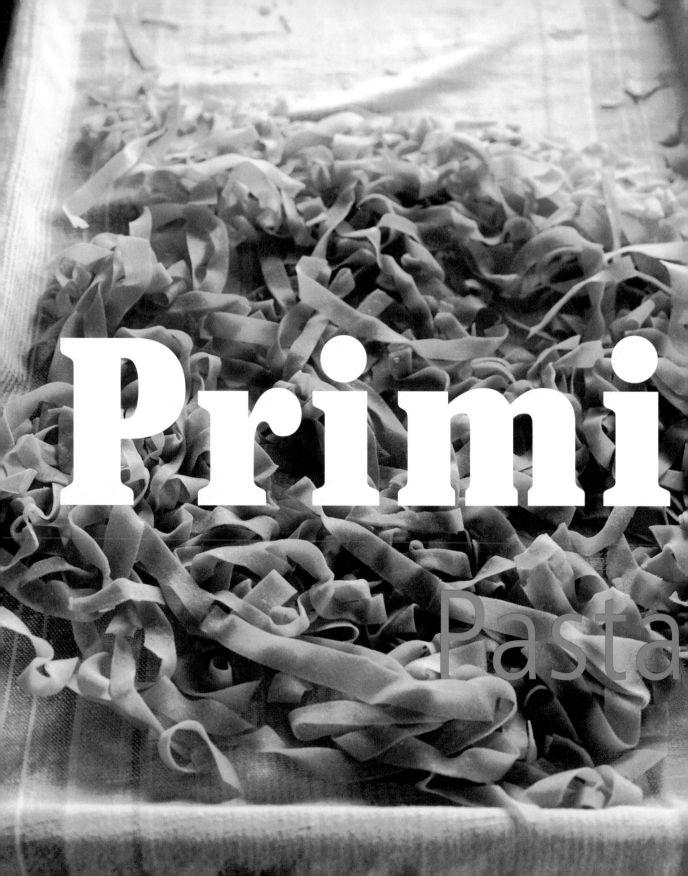

Primi

Pasta

and Risotto

PRIMI

To my mind the single most satisfying dish on the planetary menu is properly prepared pasta and it may be the most important category of food anywhere; noddles from Asia compete in complexity and nuance with many of Italy's great dishes, and there are few modern restaurants in America that do not have at least one or two pasta offerings on the menu. In Italy, there are more names for pasta shapes than there are names for the children.

With such a vast number of pasta permutations around there are obviously going to be at least as many flubs as there are hits. This is because pasta, as it is prepared in Italy, reflects very specific philosophies and techniques that are not always observed as assiduously in this country as they are there. Choosing the style and shape of the noodle, matching it with a complementary *condimento*, or sauce, cooking the noodle properly, and serving the dish as one harmonious player in the overall game plan of a great meal are aspects of pasta cookery that cannot be learned simply by reproducing a recipe from a book or a TV show. I rarely eat pasta in restaurants because I have found there are few, even in New York City, in which all of these details are covered. This is not meant to intimidate the home cook, but to suggest that as simple as pasta is, it must be prepared and served with care or the whole dish can be lost.

In Emilia-Romagna, pasta in all of its elaborate intricacies is elevated to the level of the church, and certainly many of the most labor intensive pasta dishes, such as tortelloni, tortellini, lasagne, cannelloni, and tagliatelle, can be traced back to Bologna. That said, there are as many delicious pasta dishes as there are days of the year in every region of Italy and very few require techniques or skills beyond an accomplished cook's abilities.

At La Volta, we began each day by making twenty-five "eggs" of pasta in the traditional well method, using 2½ kilos of flour. We'd cut the larger ball of dough into five pieces, knead them individually, then use a *matarello* (a dowel-like wooden rolling pin) to roll them by hand into paper-thin sheets. These pasta sheets were then cut into the different shapes and sizes of pasta for which we were famous. In America, it may not be possible to work as hard as we do and still enjoy fresh pasta every day, and if using a pasta machine makes the task of preparing fresh pasta less onerous to you, by all means use one. But even if you never try your hand at fresh pasta (which would be a shame), that should not preclude *all* pasta; cooking pasta at home, when everybody is ready to eat and hungry, is still one of my favorite things to do. Many of the dishes in this chapter are made with dry pasta and can be on the table in no more time than it takes me to demonstrate the dish on my television show—as little as ten minutes once the water boils. Stopping at the farmer's market on the way home from work for seasonal treasures can yield a meal such as spaghetti with artichokes and pecorino in a half hour, and it's twice as satisfying as take out on more levels than one.

A further note: Many of the recipes in this and later chapters call for my basic homemade tomato sauce. If making sauce from scratch seems too time-consuming, by all means feel free to use one of myriad prepared sauces available at your grocery store; just choose the one with the shortest ingredient list, and certainly avoid those with added meat or cheeses.

One of the big issues when comparing the Italian way with pasta to the American is portion size. Restaurants in Italy expect nearly every customer to order at least a pasta and a main course as part of every meal. In that spirit, the portions in this chapter are designated to serve four *as either a first course or an appetizer.* Cooking in Greenwich Village, I have found that many Americans like to have pasta as the main or even only course for their meal, *in which case these recipes will serve just two.* To serve four or more as a main course, simply double the quantities of everything, as they easily can be scaled up.

Basic Pasta Dough

makes 1 pound

This yields enough fresh pasta to serve four as a first course pasta dish or two as a main course. Divided into 4 portions and rolled to the thinnest setting on a pasta machine, it can be used to make ravioli and other stuffed pastas. Rolled slightly thicker the sheets can be cut into varying widths, as follows:

Tagliolini: ¼ inch
Fettuccine: ½ inch
Tagliatelle: ¾ inch
Pappardelle: 1½ inches

3½ to 4 cups unbleached all-purpose **FLOUR**

4 extra-large **EGGS**

½ teaspoon extra-virgin **OLIVE OIL**

Mound 3½ cups of the flour in the center of a large wooden cutting board. Make a well in the middle of the flour and add the eggs and olive oil. Using a fork, beat together the eggs and oil and begin to incorporate the flour starting with the inner rim of the well.

As you expand the well, keep pushing the flour up from the base of the mound to retain the well shape. Do not worry that this initial phase looks messy. The dough will come together when half of the flour is incorporated.

Start kneading the dough with both hands, using the palms of your hands. Once you have a cohesive mass, remove the dough from the board and scrape up and discard any leftover crusty bits. Lightly reflour the board and continue kneading for 6 more minutes. The dough should be elastic and a little sticky. Wrap the dough in plastic and allow to rest for 30 minutes at room temperature. Roll or shape as desired.

Note: Do not skip the kneading or resting portions for the dough. They are essential for a light pasta.

Green Pasta Dough

makes 1 pound

3½ to 4 cups unbleached all-purpose **FLOUR**

4 extra-large **EGGS**

½ teaspoon extra-virgin **OLIVE OIL**

6 ounces frozen chopped **SPINACH**, defrosted, squeezed very dry, and
finely chopped

Mound 3½ cups of the flour in the center of a large, well-floured wooden cutting board. Make a well in the middle of the mound and add the eggs, olive oil, and spinach. Using a fork, beat together the eggs, oil, and spinach and begin to incorporate the flour starting with the inner rim of the well. As you expand the well, keep pushing the flour up from the base of the mound to retain the well shape. Do not worry that this initial phase looks messy. The dough will come together when half of the flour is incorporated.

Start kneading the dough with both hands, using the palms of your hands. Once you have a cohesive mass, remove the dough from the board and scrape up and discard any leftover crusty bits. Lightly reflour the board and continue kneading for 6 more minutes. The dough should be elastic and a little sticky. Wrap the dough in plastic and allow to rest for 30 minutes at room temperature. Roll or shape as directed.

Note: Do not skip the kneading or resting periods for the dough. They are essential for a light pasta.

FLAVORED PASTAS

Pastas flavored with anything from black squid ink to roasted beets are served all over Italy in both traditional and creative kitchens. My favorite variations include pureed blanched chives, lemon thyme, golden or purple beets, roasted red peppers, and red wine. In this country, pasta producers have taken the concept to unfortunate extremes with such variations as licorice, strawberry, and chocolate.

To infuse Basic Pasta with herbs or cooked vegetables, first chop or puree them to the texture of fine flour. Incorporate the flavoring agent—two to three tablespoons per pound of pasta—by stirring or blending it into the eggs and carefully kneading it into the pasta as usual. The ball formed may be too wet, in which case extended kneading with a little extra flour may be necessary. From this point, proceed as you would with the basic pasta recipe, being gentle in the rolling machine as flavored pastas tear more easily.

Black Pepper Pasta

makes 1 pound

I use a coffee grinder to get the pepper really finely ground.

3½ to 4 cups all-purpose **FLOUR**

4 jumbo **EGGS**

1 tablespoon extra-virgin **OLIVE OIL**

2 tablespoons finely ground fresh black **PEPPER**

Make a mound of the flour in the center of a large wooden cutting board. Make a well in the middle of the flour and add the eggs, olive oil, and pepper. Using a fork, beat together the eggs, oil, and pepper and begin to incorporate the flour, starting with the inner rim of the well.

As you expand the well, keep pushing the flour up to retain the well shape. Do not worry that this initial phase looks messy. The dough will come together when half of the flour is incorporated.

When all the flour is incorporated, start kneading the dough using the palms of both hands. Once you have a cohesive mass, remove the dough from the board and scrape up and discard any crusty bits. Lightly flour the board and continue kneading for 6 more minutes. The dough should be elastic and a little sticky. Remember to dust your board when necessary. Wrap the dough in plastic and allow to rest for 30 minutes at room temperature.

Note: Do not skip the kneading or resting portions for this dough. They are essential for a light pasta.

Eggless Orecchiette

makes enough for 4 first course portions

2 cups **SEMOLINA** flour (see sidebar, below)

2 cups all-purpose **FLOUR**

1 to 1¼ cups tepid **WATER**

Place both types of flour in a large mixing bowl and stir to mix well. Make a well in the center of the flour and add the water a little at a time, stirring with your hands until a dough is formed. You may need more or less water, depending on the humidity in your kitchen.

Place the dough on a floured work surface and knead it like bread for 8 to 10 minutes, until smooth and elastic. Cover and let stand for 10 minutes at room temperature.

Roll the dough into long dowels about ¾ inch thick. Cut into flat disks about ¼ inch to ½ inch thick. Press the center of each disk with a thumb to form a saucer shape. Set aside under a dish towel until ready to cook.

FLOUR TYPES

Flours are distinguished by the types of wheat they are derived from. For Italian cooks, the main distinction is between hard and soft wheat. As its name implies, soft wheat flour makes a softer final product because it is high in starch, yet low in protein and gluten. So while soft flour produces soft and light cakes, it does not have the glutinous elasticity necessary to harness yeast's expanding power, so essential to bread making. Soft wheat flour does, however, produce the tender pasta at the heart of Emilia-Romagna's cuisine. Hard wheat flour, conversely, is lower in starch and higher in protein and gluten, producing firm and resilient pasta and superior bread. Durum wheat is high in gluten and is usually ground into semolina, a slightly coarser flour used in pasta production, particularly in the south of Italy.

When purchasing flour, look at the nutrition panel for the protein content, which is listed in grams per pound. For fresh pasta, choose flour with 8 to 11 grams of protein and for breads, look for 13 to 15 grams. In Italy, double zero (00) is the pasta maker's choice: the 00 refers to its sift fineness. Since it's hard to come by here, I like to blend 80 percent cake flour and 20 percent all-purpose flour, but if you want to buy only one type of flour for making fresh pasta which isn't such a tragedy, buy cake flour. Be sure to avoid "self-rising" cake flour.

Bigoli

makes enough for 4 first course servings

A meat grinder is essential for making this pasta; if you do not have one, substitute the thickest possible dried whole wheat spaghetti.

fine **CORNMEAL**, for dusting

3 to 3½ cups **WHOLE WHEAT FLOUR**

3 large **EGGS**, beaten

2 tablespoons **BUTTER** melted in ½ cup warm **MILK**, cooled

Dust 2 large sheet pans heavily with cornmeal. Set aside.

Mound 4 cups of the flour in the center of a large wooden cutting board. Make a well in the middle of the flour and add the eggs and milk mixture. Using a fork, beat together the eggs and milk mixture and begin to incorporate the flour, starting with the inner rim of the well. As you expand the well, keep pushing the flour up to retain the well shape. Do not worry that this initial phase looks messy. The dough will come together when half of the flour is incorporated.

Start kneading the dough, using the palms of both hands. Once you have a cohesive mass, remove the dough from the board and scrape up and discard any crusty bits. Lightly flour the board and continue kneading for 6 more minutes, remembering to dust your board when necessary. The dough should be elastic and firm. Wrap the dough in plastic and allow to rest for 30 minutes at room temperature. Do not skip the kneading or resting portions of this recipe. They are essential for a light pasta.

Cut the dough into 6 equal portions and roll each into a 1-inch thick log. Run each log through a meat grinder set to the smallest extrusion size using the plunger to push the dough. As the pasta exits, cut it into 12-inch pieces and let it fall onto the prepared sheet pan. Shake the pasta in the cornmeal, gently separating the strands while rolling them in the cornmeal. Repeat with the remaining dough.

Cavatelli with Garlic, Crab, Chile, and Trebbiano

serves 4

Chiles combine well with the austere richness of crab to bring out the clean sea flavor to its maximum. When buying crab meat at your fishmonger, avoid any that has been pasteurized, as it will have lost most of the great brininess so essential to the success of this dish.

¼ cup extra-virgin **OLIVE OIL**

6 **GARLIC** cloves, thinly sliced

1 tablespoon finely sliced serrano **CHILE**

2 cups Trebbiano or other dry **WHITE WINE**

4 tablespoons (½ stick) **BUTTER**

1 pound fresh lump **CRAB MEAT** (not pasteurized), picked over

1 pound fresh or dried **CAVATELLI**

SALT and **PEPPER**

Bring 6 quarts of water to a boil and add about 2 tablespoons salt.

In a 12- to 14-inch sauté pan, heat the olive oil. Add the garlic and sauté over medium heat until lightly browned, 2 to 3 minutes. Add the chile, wine, and butter and bring to a boil. Stir in the crab meat and immediately remove from the heat.

Cook the pasta until tender yet al dente, about 6 to 8 minutes. Drain well and add to the crab mixture. Return to the heat and cook briefly until most of the liquid is absorbed. Pour into a warm serving bowl and serve.

CRABS

Most of the crabs served in Italy come from the Adriatic Sea, and recipes for preparing the prized crustaceans are found up and down Italy's east coast. I grew up in Washington state, where the ready availability of freshly boiled and picked Dungeness crabs or huge claws of Alaskan king crabs made crab meat one of my favorite indulgences. Buy only fresh crab meat, not pasteurized, and try to find a purveyor who cooks it on the premises or can be trusted to buy from reputable suppliers in Maine or the Chesapeake Bay areas on the East Coast and from good harvest grounds on the West Coast. When making hot dishes, do not add the crab until the last minute, as it quickly becomes stringy and tough if overcooked.

Tagliatelle with Fresh Tuna Ragu

serves 4

At La Volta, we made this at least once a week with canned tuna, but at Pó I use the scraps and trimmings from the belly of a whole tuna. Either way, it's enticing.

Basic Tomato Sauce

¼ cup extra-virgin **OLIVE OIL**

1 Spanish **ONION**, chopped in ¼-inch dice

4 **GARLIC** cloves, peeled and thinly sliced

3 tablespoons chopped fresh **THYME** leaves, or 1 tablespoon dried

½ medium **CARROT**, finely shredded

2 28-ounce cans peeled whole **TOMATOES**, crushed by hand and juices reserved

SALT to taste

In a 3-quart saucepan, heat the olive oil over medium heat. Add the onion and garlic and cook until soft and light golden brown, about 8 to 10 minutes. Add the thyme and the carrot and cook 5 minutes more, until the carrot is quite soft. Add the tomatoes and juice and bring to a boil, stirring often. Lower the heat and simmer for 30 minutes until as thick as hot cereal. Season with salt and serve. This sauce holds one week in the refrigerator or up to six months in the freezer. Makes 4 cups.

1 medium **RED ONION**, thinly sliced

2 tablespoons extra-virgin **OLIVE OIL**

2 cups **BASIC TOMATO SAUCE**

8 ounces fresh **TUNA**, cut into ½-inch cubes

2 tablespoons finely chopped fresh **ROSEMARY** leaves

SALT and **PEPPER**

1 pound fresh **TAGLIATELLE** (page 78)

¼ cup finely chopped Italian **PARSLEY**

Bring about 6 quarts of water to a boil and add about 2 tablespoons salt.

In a large skillet, cook the onion in the olive oil over medium heat until wilted, 3 to 4 minutes. Add the tomato sauce and bring to a boil. Add the tuna and rosemary, return to a boil, and remove from the heat. Season with salt and pepper.

Drop the tagliatelle into the boiling water and cook until just al dente, about 1 minute. Drain the pasta and add to the pan with the tuna sauce. Return to medium-high heat, stirring carefully to coat the pasta. Add the parsley and cook for 1 minute. Pour into a warm serving bowl and serve immediately.

Tagliatelle with Texas Boar Ragu

serves 4

My amazing game purveyor, D'Artagnan, turned me on to the rich and flavorful boar being raised in Texas, but I've also made this with lamb and even venison. While the ragu requires a long cooking time, it is even better the second day, making it the perfect choice to make ahead for a quick and satisfying fall meal. It also freezes well for up to six months.

¼ cup extra-virgin **OLIVE OIL**

½ medium Spanish **ONION**, cut into ⅛-inch dice

½ small **CARROT**, cut into ⅛-inch dice

½ **CELERY** stalk, sliced ⅛ inch thick

1 teaspoon **ANCHOVY PASTE**

1 tablespoon hot red **PEPPER FLAKES**

1 teaspoon chopped fresh **ROSEMARY** leaves

1 cup dry **RED WINE**

1 cup **BASIC TOMATO SAUCE** (page 84)

8 ounces fresh **BOAR**, lamb, or venison shoulder, cut into 1-inch cubes

SALT and **PEPPER**

1 pound fresh **TAGLIATELLE** (page 78)

In a heavy 6- to 8-quart saucepan, heat the olive oil until smoking. Add the onion, carrot, and celery and cook until softened and light brown, 12 to 15 minutes. Add the anchovy paste, red pepper flakes, rosemary, wine, and tomato sauce and bring to a boil.

Season the meat cubes with salt and pepper and add to the tomato sauce. Return to a boil, then reduce the heat to a simmer and cook for 90 minutes. The meat should fall apart with the poke of a fork. Cool for 10 minutes.

Working in batches, transfer the ragu to a food processor, ½ cup at a time, and briefly pulse once or twice until the ragu resembles meat sauce. Check for seasoning and set aside or cover and refrigerate until ready to serve.

Bring about 6 quarts of water to a boil and add about 2 tablespoons salt.

Drop the pasta into boiling water and cook until tender yet still firm, about 1 minute. Drain the pasta and add to the ragu. Toss gently to coat, pour into a warm serving dish, and serve immediately.

Pappardelle with Crawfish, Tomatoes, and Lemon Basil

serves 4

Cleaned cooked crawfish meat is available in fancy fish stores throughout the summer, but it is definitely better if you boil and peel the crawfish yourself. For this dish I prefer lemon basil, which adds an almost Southeast Asian scent, but you could substitute Thai basil, opal basil, or regular basil. Cooked shrimp or lobster meat can also stand in for the crawfish meat.

5 pounds **CRAWFISH**, boiled, cooled, and tail meat
   removed (1½ cups)

¼ cup extra-virgin **OLIVE OIL**

2 **GARLIC** cloves, thinly sliced

4 **JALAPEÑO** peppers, cored, seeded, and julienned

1 pound very ripe plum **TOMATOES**

1 pound fresh **PAPPARDELLE** (page 78)

¼ cup fresh lemon **BASIL** leaves, lightly packed

zest of 1 **LEMON**

SALT and **PEPPER**

Pick through the crawfish meat and discard any shell bits.

Bring about 6 quarts of water to a boil and add about 2 tablespoons salt.

In a 12- to 14-inch sauté pan, heat the olive oil until almost smoking over medium heat. Add the garlic and jalapeños and cook until the garlic is light golden brown, about 2 minutes. Meanwhile, trim off the stem ends from the tomatoes and cut into ¾-inch cubes. Add the tomatoes to the pan with garlic and chiles and cook until soft and beginning to get saucy, 8 to 10 minutes. Lower the heat to a simmer while you cook the pasta.

Drop the pappardelle into the boiling water and cook until tender, about 2 minutes. Drain the pasta. Toss the crawfish meat into the tomato sauce, add the pappardelle, and toss to coat well over low heat. Add the lemon basil and lemon zest, season to taste with salt and pepper, toss again, and serve immediately.

Stinging Nettle Tagliatelle with Sausage, Kale, and Pecorino

serves 4

Stinging nettles have a slightly tangy, almost artichoke flavor that works really well with the richness of the sausage and the pecorino in this filling plate of pasta. To make stinging nettle pasta, use the green pasta recipe on page 79, substituting steamed nettles for the spinach, or add ½ cup dried nettles and another egg to the green pasta ingredients.

8 ounces fresh hot Italian **SAUSAGE** with fennel seeds, cut into ¼-inch pieces

8 ounces **KALE**, stems discarded and leaves finely chopped (about 4 cups)

½ cup **CHICKEN STOCK**

SALT and **PEPPER**

1 recipe **BASIC GREEN PASTA DOUGH** (page 79) flavored with stinging
    nettles (see above) or plain

½ cup freshly grated **PECORINO** cheese

Bring about 6 quarts of water to a boil and add about 2 tablespoons salt.

In a 10- to 12-inch sauté pan, cook the sausage over low heat until the fat begins to render, about 6 minutes. Turn the heat up to medium and cook until most of the fat from the sausage has rendered and the sausage is golden brown, 8 to 9 minutes. Add the kale and chicken stock and cook until very soft, 8 to 9 minutes. Season to taste with salt and pepper and remove from the heat.

Drop the pasta into the boiling water and cook until tender, about 1 minute. Drain the pasta and add to the sauté pan with the kale and sausage. Cook over high heat until coated, about 1 minute. Add the grated cheese and toss to mix. Pour into a heated serving bowl and serve.

STINGING NETTLES

Having fallen into stinging nettles many times as a child, I was very surprised to see them used for cooking in Borgo Capanne. Nettles (*ortica* in Italian) are very traditional and popular for vegetable dishes or flavoring pasta and are considered therapeutic for digestive, blood pressure, and reproductive problems. Once cooked, the prickly thistles are rendered harmless, and the stems and leaves can be treated like cooked spinach for soups, pasta-making, or simple side dishes.

Bigoli in Salsa

serves 4

When I first ate this Venetian specialty at a restaurant called Antica Bessetta behind the Rialto market, I was blown away by the firm texture of the noodle, which was emphasized by the scant quantity of sauce served with it. Although I often concede the use of oil-packed anchovies in other delicacies, the best-quality salt-packed anchovies are the only ones that work in this fragrant dish.

1 recipe **BIGOLI** (page 82)

6 tablespoons extra-virgin **OLIVE OIL**

8 **ANCHOVY** fillets, soaked in milk for 2 hours and drained

1 medium Spanish **ONION**, minced

½ cup finely chopped Italian **PARSLEY**

Bring about 6 quarts of water to a boil and add about 2 tablespoons salt.

In a 12- to 14-inch sauté pan, combine the olive oil, anchovies, and onion and cook over medium heat, stirring often to break up the anchovies, until a paste is formed, 8 to 10 minutes.

Drop the noodles into the boiling water, and cook until al dente, 8 to 9 minutes. Drain the pasta and toss into the pan with the anchovies. Add the parsley, toss through, and divide among 4 serving plates. Serve immediately.

DRESSING PASTA

The most disappointing aspect of pasta service in America seems to be a misunderstanding of the ratio of noodles to sauce. The dish should be treated like a salad—that is to say, the noodles should be coated but not swimming in the sauce, or the *condimento*, as the Italians call it. Pasta, both dried and fresh, should go into the water only when the *condimento* is ready. When the pasta is about half a minute short of being perfect, it should be quickly drained and tossed immediately into the pan (or the bowl in specific cases) with the *condimento*. It should be delicately tossed or stirred until the noodles and the sauce are evenly distributed and have become one with their lord. If the mixture seems a little sticky, add a tablespoon of the pasta water; if it seems a little soupy, continue cooking it a little more. When it is perfect, serve it immediately.

Bigoli with Duck Ragu

serves 4

Duck ragu is typical of the cooking in the Veneto. I poached this recipe from an Agriturism restaurant outside of Vicenza, where guests stay on a working farm and enjoy the bounty of the hunt or the garden.

4 **DUCK** legs and thighs, skin removed

SALT and **PEPPER**

¼ cup extra-virgin **OLIVE OIL**

1 medium Spanish **ONION**, cut into ¼-inch dice

1 medium **CARROT**, finely chopped

2 **GARLIC** cloves, thinly sliced

1 **CELERY** stalk, cut into ¼-inch dice

4 whole fresh **SAGE** leaves

2 cups dry **RED WINE**, preferably Valpolicella

1 pound canned peeled whole plum **TOMATOES**

1 cup **CHICKEN STOCK**

SALT and **PEPPER**

1 recipe **BIGOLI** (page 82)

Wash the duck pieces and remove all visible fat. Pat dry.

In a thick-bottomed casserole or Dutch oven, heat the olive oil until almost smoking over medium-high heat. Season the duck pieces with salt and pepper and cook until brown on all sides, 10 to 12 minutes.

Remove the duck pieces to a plate and add the onion, carrot, garlic, celery, and sage to the casserole and cook over low heat until softened, 7 to 9 minutes. Add the wine, tomatoes, and chicken stock and bring to a boil. Add the duck pieces, then lower the heat, cover, and simmer for 1 hour.

Remove the duck pieces, and when cool enough to handle pull all meat off the bones. Return the meat to the pot and simmer uncovered for 30 minutes, or until quite thick. Season with salt and pepper and set aside.

Fill a large pot with about 6 quarts of water and add about 2 tablespoons salt. Add the bigoli and cook until al dente, 8 to 9 minutes. Reheat the sauce if necessary, drain the pasta, and toss into the pan. Toss to coat over medium-high heat and serve immediately.

White Bean Ravioli with Balsamic Brown Butter

serves 6

I made this for my television show with beet-flavored pasta (see sidebar, page 79), but either way it is a Pó classic. The syrupy flavor of the balsamic brown butter makes it an easy sell to children and sweet tooths alike.

FILLING

2 cups cooked **WHITE BEANS** (see page 65)

½ cup extra-virgin **OLIVE OIL**

1 **EGG**

¼ cup **BALSAMIC VINEGAR**

½ cup freshly grated **PARMIGIANO-REGGIANO** cheese

2 tablespoons finely chopped Italian **PARSLEY**

SALT and **PEPPER**

1 recipe **BASIC PASTA DOUGH** (page 78)

¾ cup (1½ sticks) unsalted **BUTTER**

¼ cup **BALSAMIC VINEGAR**

¼ cup freshly grated **PARMIGIANO-REGGIANO** cheese

2 tablespoons finely chopped Italian **PARSLEY**

Make the filling. Set aside 1 cup of the cooked white beans. Combine the remaining filling ingredients in a food processor and blend until smooth, about 1 minute. Transfer the puree to a medium mixing bowl and stir in the reserved white beans. Season to taste.

Divide the pasta dough into 4 equal portions and roll each in a pasta machine on the thinnest setting. Lay out 1 sheet of pasta and cut into 8 pieces 3½ inches square. Place 1½ tablespoons of filling in the center of each square and fold in half diagonally to form a triangle. Press firmly around the edges to seal. Continue with the remaining pasta and filling; you should have 32 ravioli. These can be set aside on a baking tray, the layers separated by a dish towel, in the refrigerator for 6 hours.

Bring about 6 quarts of water to a boil and add about 2 tablespoons salt.

Drop the ravioli into the water and cook just below boiling for 3 minutes.

Place the butter in a 10- to 12-inch sauté pan and heat until the foam subsides and the butter begins to brown. Turn off the heat and add the balsamic vinegar (careful—it will spatter).

Remove the ravioli from the cooking liquid with a slotted spoon or strainer and add to the pan with the butter and vinegar. Toss over medium heat and sprinkle with the grated cheese and parsley. Serve immediately.

Crab Tortelloni with Scallions and Poppy Seeds

serves 4

Each Valentine's Day, Pó offers a special menu highlighting the food and wine of Venice, perhaps the most romantic city in the world. This pasta is a consistent winner and, from what I understand, quite an aphrodisiac.

1 pound fresh lump **CRAB MEAT** (not pasteurized)

8 **SCALLIONS**, thinly sliced

¼ cup **BASIC TOMATO SAUCE** (page 84)

1 recipe **BASIC PASTA DOUGH** (page 78), rolled out to thinnest setting on pasta machine

6 tablespoons (¾ stick) unsalted **BUTTER**

1 tablespoon **POPPY SEEDS**

Bring about 6 quarts of water to a boil and add about 2 tablespoons salt.

In a mixing bowl, stir together the crab, half of the scallions, and the tomato sauce until well blended.

Cut the pasta into 4-inch squares and place 1 tablespoon of filling in the center of each square. Fold into triangles, press out any air around the filling, and press to seal the edges. Bring the points of the long side together to form a ring (or a hat) and seal between your fingers.

Drop the tortelloni in the boiling water and cook for 8 to 10 minutes at a high simmer. Meanwhile, in a 10- to 12-inch sauté pan, melt the butter with the poppy seeds. Drain the cooked tortelloni carefully and gently place in the pan. Add the remaining scallions and toss to coat. Serve immediately.

Goat Cheese and Scallion Ravioli with Black Olive–Tomato Butter

serves 6

I first made this dish for a demonstration at a great supermarket in Short Hills, New Jersey, called Kings. Since then I've used it whenever I want to plug Coach Farm's amazing fresh goat cheese.

FILLING

3 cups soft **GOAT CHEESE**, preferably Coach Farm

¼ cup freshly grated **PECORINO ROMANO** cheese

¼ cup extra-virgin **OLIVE OIL**

1 extra-large **EGG**, lightly beaten

6 **SCALLIONS**, thinly sliced

pinch of grated **NUTMEG**

SALT and **PEPPER**

1 recipe **GREEN PASTA DOUGH** (page 79)

SAUCE

¾ cup (1½ sticks) unsalted **BUTTER**

2 tablespoons **BLACK OLIVE PASTE**

4 tablespoons slivered oil-packed **SUN-DRIED TOMATOES**

¼ cup freshly grated **PECORINO ROMANO** cheese

Make the filling. Combine all the ingredients in a large mixing bowl and mix until well incorporated. Set aside.

Divide the pasta dough into 4 portions and roll out to a 9 × 12-inch rectangle on the thinnest setting of a pasta machine. Place 1 sheet of the dough on a lightly floured cutting board. Cut the sheet into thirds lengthwise, then score each length in half and in half again, yielding four 3-inch squares per length of pasta. Cover with a towel.

Place 1½ teaspoons of filling onto each square. Fold opposing corners together to form a triangle, gently pressing out any air between the filling and the pasta dough. If the pasta is a little dry, moisten the edges with a little water to help them adhere. Be certain to seal the ravioli well on both flat sides or they will burst while cooking. Repeat with the remaining sheets of green pasta and filling. At the halfway point, check to be sure that you've used half the filling. If not, adjust the quantity of filling accordingly for the remaining ravioli.

Bring about 6 quarts of water to a boil and add about 2 tablespoons salt.

Make the sauce. Melt the butter with the black olive paste in a 10-inch skillet over medium heat. When it is just starting to bubble, add the tomatoes and remove from the heat.

Gently drop the ravioli into the boiling water and cook 3 to 4 minutes on a low boil, until the pasta is cooked through. Remove from the water with a slotted spoon and add to the skillet with the sauce. Simmer together for 1 minute over low heat; then sprinkle with the grated cheese and place on a warm serving platter.

FREEZING PASTA

One of the great secrets of restaurant pasta cookery consists of two elements: sealable plastic bags and a freezer. Maintaining a menu of five or six stuffed pastas, from tortellini to tortelloni or agnolotti and ravioli, would be quite difficult if we had to make each type each day. In reality what we do is make enough of one kind of stuffed pasta each day to last a week. We layer the freshly stuffed shapes on clean dish towels and place them on cookie sheets overnight in the freezer. The next day we freeze them in plastic bags until they're ordered in the restaurant. You can do this at home and stock up for improvised dinners or fancy dinner parties, eliminating valuable time from youir "day of party" prep list.

Agnolotti

serves 4

I cooked this pasta for a luncheon at VinItaly, the huge wine fair held each year in Verona, at the back of the Marchese Alberto di Gresy's stand. It is a Piemontese classic that goes so well with his brilliantly structured and powerful wines. Try it with a bottle of his fabulous Martinenga Barbaresco.

10 tablespoons (1¼ sticks) unsalted **BUTTER**

1 medium Spanish **ONION**, cut into ⅛-inch dice

¾ cup **RICOTTA** cheese

¾ cup grated **FONTINA** cheese

9 tablespoons fresh **GOAT CHEESE**

3 tablespoons fresh **MARJORAM** leaves

¾ cup finely chopped Italian **PARSLEY**

¾ teaspoon freshly grated **NUTMEG**

SALT and **PEPPER**

1 recipe **BASIC PASTA DOUGH** (page 78), rolled to thinnest setting
   on pasta machine.

4 ounces fresh porcini or cremini **MUSHROOMS**, sliced paper-thin

¼ cup freshly grated **PARMIGIANO-REGGIANO** cheese

Bring 6 quarts of water to a boil and add about 2 tablespoons salt.

In a 12- to 14-inch sauté pan, heat 4 tablespoons of the butter over medium heat until the foam subsides. Add the onion and cook until soft and golden brown, 7 to 8 minutes. Remove the pan from the heat and cool. Stir in the cheeses, marjoram, parsley, and nutmeg, and season with salt and pepper.

To form the agnolotti, drop heaping teaspoons of filling down one side of each pasta sheet at 3-inch intervals. Fold the pasta over the filling, pressing the dough flat between the lumps of filling. Using a pastry cutter, cut half-moons using the fold as the flat side of the moon.

Drop the agnolotti into the boiling water and simmer rapidly until tender.

Meanwhile, melt the remaining 6 tablespoons butter with the mushrooms in a 12- to 14-inch sauté pan. Drain agnolotti and add to the pan. Sprinkle with Parmigiano-Reggiano and toss over medium heat to coat. Serve immediately.

Cappellacci di Zucca

Pumpkin Hats

serves 4

We serve these "little hats" all autumn long at Pó, and in the tradition of Mantova, we add a particularly delicious sprinkling of crushed amaretti cookies over them to finish.

3-pound **PUMPKIN** or butternut squash

2 large **EGGS**

1¼ cups freshly grated **PARMIGIANO-REGGIANO** cheese

½ teaspoon freshly grated **NUTMEG**

SALT and **PEPPER**

1 recipe **BASIC PASTA DOUGH** (page 78), rolled out to thinnest setting on
   pasta machine

½ cup (½ stick) unsalted **BUTTER**

4 **SAGE** leaves

Preheat the oven to 350°F. Halve the squash and remove the seeds. Bake cut side down for 1 hour. Scoop out the flesh, discarding the shells.

Bring about 6 quarts of water to a boil and add about 2 tablespoons salt.

In a large mixing bowl, mix the squash, eggs, 1 cup of the cheese, and the nutmeg until smooth and homogeneous. Season with salt and pepper and set aside.

Cut the pasta sheets into 3-inch squares. Place 1 teaspoon squash filling in the center of each, fold to form triangles, pressing firmly around the edges. Bring the two ends together and press firmly to form "little hats." Drop the cappellacci in the boiling water and lower the heat to a high simmer. Cook until tender, 2 to 3 minutes.

Melt the butter in a 12- to 14-inch sauté pan and add the sage. Gently drain the pasta and add to the pan with the butter. Cook gently for 1 minute, and serve sprinkled with the remaining ¼ cup cheese and perhaps a bit of crushed amaretti cookie crumbs.

Tortelli of Potato and Chives with Brown Butter and Sage

serves 4

When I first made these tortelli at Pó, all of my New York friends jokingly called them pierogi because they resemble that Russian delicacy, in looks and flavor. However, they are much less chewy and are never served with sour cream. An improvisation on the wondrous food turned out by the poor kitchens of wartime Bologna, these satisfying pillows are my version of comfort food.

4 russet **POTATOES**, boiled 40 minutes until tender and peeled

¾ cup freshly grated **PARMIGIANO-REGGIANO** cheese

¾ cup chopped **CHIVES**

2 extra-large **EGGS**

½ teaspoon freshly grated **NUTMEG**

1 recipe **BASIC PASTA DOUGH** (page 78)

4 tablespoons (½ stick) **BUTTER**

8 **SAGE** leaves

juice of ½ **LEMON**

Bring about 6 quarts of water to a boil and add about 2 tablespoons salt.

In a large mixing bowl, crush the potatoes with a masher until smooth. Add ½ cup of the cheese, ½ cup of the chives, the eggs, and nutmeg and mix well.

Roll out the pasta to the thinnest setting and cut into 4-inch squares. Place 1 tablespoon potato mixture in the center of each square and fold to form triangles, pressing firmly to seal. Bring the opposite points of the triangle together and press firmly to join. Continue until all the pasta is stuffed and formed into tortelli. Drop the pasta into the boiling water and cook until tender, 6 to 7 minutes.

Meanwhile, melt the butter in a 12- to 14-inch sauté pan and, over medium-high heat, cook until a golden brown color (*noisette*) appears in the thinnest liquid. Add the sage leaves and remove from the heat, then stir in the lemon juice. Drain the tortelli well, gently pour into the sauté pan, and return to the heat. Add the remaining ¼ cup cheese and ¼ cup of chives, toss to coat, and serve immediately.

Baked Lasagne with Asparagus and Pesto (page 104)

Tagliatelle with Texas Boar Ragu (page 85)

Baked Goat Cheese Tortellini with Radicchio (page 105)

Green Gnocchi with Caduta di Formaggio (page 108)

NEXT PAGE: **Linguine with Manila Clams, Pancetta, and Chiles (page 115)**

Tortellini with Goat Cheese and Scallions

serves 4 to 6

These delicious little navel-shaped dumplings are my geographical response to the amazing tortellini of Bologna. There, each is filled with its local treasures of prosciutto, mortadella, and Parmigiano-Reggiano and served in a broth as a regal opener to a special family meal. Here, we use local goat cheese. I like to allow 15 to 20 tortellini and 1½ cups of broth per serving.

2 cups soft **GOAT CHEESE**, preferably Coach Farm

8 **SCALLIONS**, thinly sliced

2 extra-large **EGGS**, beaten

½ teaspoon freshly grated **NUTMEG**

½ cup freshly grated **PARMIGIANO-REGGIANO** cheese

¼ teaspoon **SALT**

¼ teaspoon **PEPPER**

6 to 9 cups **CHICKEN STOCK**

1½ recipes **BASIC PASTA DOUGH** (page 78)

SALT and **PEPPER**

Bring about 6 quarts of water to a boil and add about 2 tablespoons salt.

In a large mixing bowl, mash the goat cheese until soft. Add 6 of the sliced scallions, the eggs, nutmeg, ¼ cup cheese, and salt and pepper and stir well. Refrigerate until firm, 30 minutes or more.

Bring the chicken stock to a simmer in a 4-quart saucepan. Using a pasta machine, roll out the pasta to the thinnest setting and then cut the sheets into 2-inch squares. Place 1 teaspoon of goat cheese filling in the center of each 2-inch square. Fold the opposite corners together to form a triangle and press the edges together firmly to seal. Bring the long points of the triangle together and join with firm finger pressure. Continue filling and shaping tortellini until all the pasta and filling are used.

Drop the tortellini in the boiling water and cook until tender, 7 to 10 minutes. Drain the tortellini well and drop into the simmering chicken broth. Add the remaining 2 sliced scallions and ¼ cup cheese, check for seasoning, and serve immediately in warmed soup bowls.

Chicken Tortellini in a Sweet Onion Lambrusco Broth with Grana and Leeks

serves 6

Tortellini in brodo is the ultimate holiday indulgence in and around Bologna. Making the tortellini from scratch, as opposed to buying them, really separates the rookies from the pros in the home kitchen. This is not a dish to make after a long day at work, so avoid it if you do not have ample time to enjoy the meditative quality of this repetitive but satisfying task.

2 tablespoons unsalted **BUTTER**

7 ounces boneless, skinless **CHICKEN** breast

½ cup dry **WHITE WINE**

3-ounce piece **PROSCIUTTO**, chilled

5-ounce piece **MORTADELLA**, chilled

1 cup grated **GRANA** cheese

½ teaspoon freshly grated **NUTMEG**

¼ cup **MILK**

1 large **EGG**, beaten

SALT

2 medium **RED ONIONS**, cut into ¼-inch dice

2 cups **LAMBRUSCO** wine

3 tablespoons **SUGAR**

1½ recipes **BASIC PASTA DOUGH** (page 78)

6 cups good **CHICKEN STOCK**

1 **LEEK**, washed and cut into fine julienne (about 1 cup)

1 cup freshly grated **PARMIGIANO-REGGIANO** cheese

In a 12- to 14-inch sauté pan, melt the butter over medium heat until just starting to foam. Slice the raw chicken very thin across the grain and place in the pan with the butter. Cook over medium heat, stirring constantly, until very lightly browned. Add the wine, cover, and cook for 3 minutes. Uncover and continue to cook until liquid is gone, 5 more minutes. Set aside to cool.

Cut the prosciutto and mortadella into ¼-inch dice and place in a food processor. Add the cooled contents of the sauté pan and pulse just until coarsely ground—like meat, not mousse. Transfer to a large mixing bowl and add the Grana, nutmeg, milk, and egg. Fold together carefully, season with salt only, and refrigerate for 1 hour.

In a stainless steel saucepan, combine the onions, Lambrusco, and sugar. Cook over low heat until thick like marmalade, about 20 minutes; cool.

Roll the pasta dough out to the thinnest setting on the machine and cut into 2-inch squares. Place 1 teaspoon of filling in the center of each square. Bring the two opposite corners together to form a triangle, pressing the edges firmly together to seal. Bring the ends of the triangle together and join with firm finger pressure. It should now look like tortellini, but may resemble Venus's navel. Continue until all the pasta or filling is used up.

Bring the chicken stock to a boil in a large soup pot and add the onion mixture. Drop the tortellini and leek into the broth and simmer for 8 to 10 minutes, until tender. Spoon into 6 bowls with ample broth and serve with grated Parmigiano-Reggiano cheese.

FRESH VS. DRIED

Fresh pasta and dried pasta are as different as night and day. In Italy, the idea of using different shapes of pasta interchangeably with different sauces or condiments simply does not exist. The same holds true for fresh versus dried pasta.

Dried, hard pasta is made of 100 percent hard wheat (durum) flour; it is high in protein, low in starch, and retains its shape when cooked al dente. Pressed through metal dies in special machines, the pasta itself is relatively solid, smooth, and difficult to penetrate. For this reason, dried pasta is most often served with sauces in which olive oil, shellfish, or firm vegetables play a large role—the pasta maintains a clean, firm texture yet remains separate from the sauce, dancing in a close embrace with the oil without soaking up too much.

Fresh, soft pasta is made of the soft wheat flour that grows on the plains near Parma and whole eggs and is rolled between a wooden board and a wooden rolling pin to produce flat noodles of the most porous, sauce-clinging, and absorbent quality possible, or rolled on a pasta machine to produce slightly less thirsty results. Porous, hand-rolled pasta served with oil-rich tomato or vegetable sauces would soak up too much oil and render the noodles slick and greasy. Serving it with an austere amount of rich ragu, or using it to enclose a rich ricotta mixture and saucing it with silken melted butter and sage, renders it poetic and full of passion.

Both styles of pasta have their place in Italian households; I tend to prefer dried pasta and its spartan condiments in the warmer months and fresh pasta and its rich accompaniments in the cooler months.

Ramp Ravioli with One-Hour Calamari

serves 4

The briny flavor of this rich calamari dish is a perfect contrast to the fresh and smoky grilled ramps. You can make the ravioli in advance and freeze in sealable plastic bags separated by layers of paper towels for up to a month.

12 **RAMPS**, cleaned, or 2 cups chopped chives and scallions

1 tablespoon freshly ground black **PEPPER**

2 plum **TOMATOES**, finely chopped

SALT

1 recipe **BASIC PASTA DOUGH** (page 78) flavored with squid ink

  (see sidebar, page 79)

1 cup **ONE-HOUR CALAMARI** (page 142)

¼ cup extra-virgin **OLIVE OIL**

2 bunches **CHIVES**, cut into 2-inch pieces

Preheat the grill or broiler.

Grill or broil the ramps until tender and smoky, about 1 minute, turning occasionally. Cool briefly, then chop into ¼-inch pieces and place in small mixing bowl with the pepper and tomatoes. Season with salt and set aside.

Bring about 6 quarts of water to a boil and add about 2 tablespoons salt.

Roll the pasta to the thinnest setting on a pasta machine and cut into 3-inch squares. Place 1 tablespoon of the ramp mixture in the center of each square and fold into a triangle, pressing the sides to seal. Continue until all the pasta and filling are used.

Place the ravioli in boiling water and cook at a fast simmer until cooked, 4 to 5 minutes.

Meanwhile, bring the calamari and olive oil to a boil in a 12- to 14-inch sauté pan. Lower the heat to a simmer and add the chives. Drain the ravioli and add to the pan with the calamari. Toss to coat and mix gently. Pour onto a warm platter and serve immediately.

Fresh pasta and dried pasta are as different as night and day.

Crespelle with Radicchio and Goat Cheese

serves 4

Betta made these *crespelle* (the Italian word for crepes, the French word for pancakes) using young fresh goat cheese produced at the Cervaro della Sala winery, owned by the Antinori family in Umbria. Of course, you can't get this cheese in the United States, but you can certainly get Coach Farm goat cheese and it is a fine substitute. The rich, creamy goat cheese makes a perfect foil for the slightly bitter radicchio. Serve the hot *crespelle* with a radicchio salad.

CRESPELLE

¾ cup all-purpose flour

2 **EGGS**

1 cup **MILK**

1 pinch of **SALT**

5 tablespons extra-virgin **OLIVE OIL**

1 medium **RED ONION**, finely chopped

3 heads **RADICCHIO** di Treviso, chopped into ½-inch pieces

1 teaspoon chopped fresh **ROSEMARY**

8 ounces **GOAT CHEESE**, preferably Coach Farm

2 tablespoons **BALSAMIC VINEGAR**

1/4 cup finely chopped Italian **PARSLEY**

4 tablespoons (½ stick) unsalted **BUTTER**

Make the *crespelle* batter. Sift the flour into a bowl. Crack the eggs into the bowl and beat, adding the milk a little at a time until all is incorporated. Stir in the salt and allow to rest 30 minutes.

Preheat the oven to 350°F.

Heat 4 tablespoons of the olive oil in an 8-inch sauté pan until smoking. Add the onion and sauté over medium-high heat until soft, 5 to 6 minutes. Add the radicchio and sauté until soft, 5 to 6 minutes. Transfer the mixture to a bowl and stir in the goat cheese, vinegar, and parsley, then set aside.

Heat a 6-inch nonstick pan until hot and brush with some of the remaining tablespoon olive oil. Turn the heat down to medium and pour 1½ tablespoons of batter in the pan. Cook until pale golden, about 1 minute, and flip. Cook 15 seconds on second side and remove. Continue the process until all the batter has been used, yielding between 8 and 10 *crespelle.*

Set aside ¼ cup of the goat cheese mixture. Fill each *crespella* with 2 tablespoons of the remaining goat cheese mixture and fold in half.

Butter the bottom and sides of a 10 × 8-inch ceramic baking dish. Lay the filled *crespelle* overlapping in the baking dish. Smear the remaining goat cheese mixture over the top and place in the oven until piping hot and crispy on top, 12 to 15 minutes. Serve hot.

BAKED PASTA

Almost any combination of noodle and condiment combination can be prepared "al forno," and dishes such as cannelloni, lasagne, and vincigrassi are classic examples. Baked pastas are especially versatile for large gatherings, as they can be held warm up to 30 to 45 minutes until the guests arrive. The real trick to creating a great baked pasta is striking the proper balance between sauce and noodle; while more condiment is obviously necessary to keep a dish that will be baked for 40 minutes moist, often the addition of bechamel, or even milk or cream, to the noodles and condiment makes more sense than drowning the pasta in too much of the sauce itself. Most important, the noodles themselves must be cooked just al dente and no more, then refreshed and well drained prior to dressing and baking.

Baked Lasagne with Asparagus and Pesto

serves 4

Pesto Sauce

3 tablespoons **PINE NUTS**

2 cups **BASIL** leaves, preferably picolo fino

1 **GARLIC** clove

pinch of **SEA SALT**

½ cup grated **PARMIGIANO-REGGIANO** cheese

3 tablespoons grated **PECORINO** cheese

1¼ cups extra-virgin **OLIVE OIL**

In a food processor, place pine nuts, basil, garlic, and sea salt and process to a paste. Add the cheeses and drizzle in the olive oil. Store in a jar, topped with oil. Makes 2½ cups.

In Italy, the term *lasagna* refers to the width of the noodle, not a particular preparation, so baked is an important part of the recipe description. We serve these baked lasagne in the early spring, when the asparagus first becomes available. It is far better to have too much *balsamella* sauce than not enough—its what makes the dish so good.

1½ pounds medium **ASPARAGUS** spears

1 recipe **BASIC PASTA DOUGH** (page 78),
    rolled to thinnest setting on pasta machine

2 cups **BALSAMELLA** (page 229)

1 cup **PESTO SAUCE**

1 cup grated **PECORINO SARDO** cheese

½ cup **BREAD CRUMBS**

Preheat the oven to 400°F.

Bring about 6 quarts of water to a boil and add about 2 tablespoons salt. Prepare a bowl of ice water.

Trim the asparagus and boil 1 minute. Use tongs to remove the asparagus from the hot water, reserving the cooking water, and refresh in the ice bath. Use tongs to transfer the asparagus to a colander, drain well, and cut each spear in half crosswise. Set aside.

Cut the pasta into 20 5-inch squares and drop into the same boiling water as used for the asparagus. Cook 1 minute, until tender. Drain well and refresh in the ice bath. Drain on towels and set aside.

In a mixing bowl, stir the balsamella, pesto, and grated cheese together until mixed well. Butter four 6-inch oval gratin dishes and place 1 piece of pasta on the bottom of each. Top each piece of pasta with 3 pieces of asparagus and 2 tablespoons of pesto, followed by another piece of pasta. Continue with this layering until you have 4 pieces of pasta and 4 layers of asparagus and pesto mixture. Lay one more piece of pasta on top, followed by a spoonful of pesto mixture and sprinkle with bread crumbs. Place the dishes on a baking sheet and bake for 20 to 25 minutes, or until bubbling and golden brown on top. Serve immediately.

Baked Goat Cheese Tortellini with Radicchio

Tortellini al Forno with Radicchio and Goat Cheese

serves 4

I devised this fantastic baked dish to cope with an overabundance of tortellini I'd prepared for a large party of friends at Pó. The absolute best part is the crunchy, crusty bit around the edges of the dish.

3 tablespoons extra-virgin **OLIVE OIL**

1 medium **RED ONION**, sliced paper-thin

2 heads **RADICCHIO** di Treviso, cut into ½-inch pieces

1 recipe **TORTELLINI WITH GOAT CHEESE AND SCALLIONS**
   (page 97), scallions, stock, and grated cheese omitted

2 cups **BALSAMELLA** (page 229)

½ cup freshly grated **PARMIGIANO-REGGIANO** cheese

Preheat the oven to 425°F. Bring about 6 quarts of water to a boil and add about 2 tablespoons salt.

Heat the olive oil in a 12- to 14-inch sauté pan until almost smoking and add the onion. Cook until softened but not brown, 1 to 2 minutes. Add the radicchio and cook until softened and lightly gray in color, 5 to 6 minutes. Remove from the heat and allow to cool.

Meanwhile, drop the tortellini into the boiling water and cook until tender, about 6 to 7 minutes. Gently drain and place in a large mixing bowl. Add the cooled radicchio mixture, balsamella, and half the grated cheese. Gently stir to mix well. Divide among 4 buttered gratin dishes, sprinkle with the remaining cheese, and bake until bubbly and crusty on top, about 20 minutes. Serve immediately.

Basic Gnocchi

makes 12 servings

The recipe for this velvet-textured gnocchi has been in my family since my dad can remember. I was surprised when I arrived in Borgo Capanne to find they used the exact same one—of the hundreds of variations used in Italy.

3 pounds russet **POTATOES**

2 cups all-purpose **FLOUR**

1 extra-large **EGG**

1 teaspoon **SALT**

½ cup canola **OIL**

Place the whole potatoes in a saucepan with water to cover. Bring to a boil and cook at a low boil until they are soft, about 45 minutes. While still warm, peel the potatoes and pass them through a vegetable mill onto a clean pasta board.

Bring about 6 quarts of water to a boil. Set up an ice bath with 6 cups ice and 6 cups water near by.

Make a well in the center of the potatoes and sprinkle all over with the flour. Break the egg into the center of well, add the salt, and, using a fork, stir into the flour and potatoes as if you were making pasta. Once the egg is mixed in, bring the dough together, kneading gently until a ball is formed. Knead gently another 4 minutes, until ball is dry to the touch.

Divide the dough into 6 large balls. Roll each ball into ¾-inch-diameter ropes and cut the ropes into 1-inch-long pieces. Flick the pieces off of a fork or along the concave side of a cheese grater to score the sides. Drop the dough pieces into the boiling water and cook until they float to the surface, about 1 minute. Use a slotted spoon to transfer the gnocchi to the ice bath. Meanwhile, continue with the remaining dough, forming ropes, cutting 1-inch pieces, and flicking them off of a fork. Continue until all the gnocchi have been cooked and allow them to sit several minutes in the ice bath.

Drain the gnocchi and transfer to a mixing bowl. Toss with the canola oil and store covered in the refrigerator for up to 48 hours or until ready to serve.

Green Gnocchi

serves 8

1 pound russet **POTATOES**

2 pounds fresh **SPINACH**, rinsed and partially dried

1¼ cups all-purpose **FLOUR**

1 extra-large **EGG**, beaten

1 teaspoon **SALT**

2 tablespoons extra-virgin **OLIVE OIL**

Fill a medium bowl with cold water and ice cubes. Set aside.

Place the unpeeled potatoes in a saucepan with water to cover. Bring to a boil and cook until very tender, 20 to 25 minutes.

Peel the warm boiled potatoes and run them through a ricer or food mill on the finest setting onto a clean cutting board. In a pot with a lid, cook the spinach over medium heat, allowing it to steam in just the liquid remaining on the leaves, about 1 minute. Transfer the cooked spinach to the ice bath to cool rapidly. Use tongs to remove the spinach (reserving the ice bath). Drain well, then wrap in a clean dish towel and twist to extract as much liquid as possible. Chop the spinach fine (and I mean *fine*) with a knife. Add to the potatoes on the pastry board and sprinkle with the flour. Make a well in the center, add the egg and salt, and knead to form a dough.

Bring about 6 quarts of water to a boil.

Divide the dough into 4 balls. Roll each ball into 1-inch-thick ropes and cut each rope into 1-inch-long pieces. Flick the pieces off the fork tines to establish the classic shape and drop 10 to 15 at a time into the boiling water. When all the gnocchi float to the surface, use a slotted spoon or skimmer to transfer to the ice bath. Repeat until all the gnocchi are cooked. Remove from the ice bath and drain, then toss with the olive oil in a mixing bowl, cover, and refrigerate until ready to use.

Green Gnocchi with Caduta di Formaggio

serves 8

Caduta translates as "snowfall," and this rich winter pasta is perfect for a day with a blanket of winter wonder outside. The grappa, although not essential, really adds a grapey depth to the otherwise simple cheese *condimento*.

4 ounces **GORGONZOLA** cheese

4 tablespoons (½ stick) unsalted **BUTTER**, softened

2 tablespoons **GRAPPA**

1 recipe **GREEN GNOCCHI** (page 107)

½ cup freshly grated **ASIAGO** cheese

¼ cup chopped **CHIVES**

Bring about 6 quarts of water to a boil and add about 2 tablespoons salt.

In a 12- to 14-inch sauté pan, mash together the Gorgonzola and butter until smooth. Stir in the grappa and simmer over medium heat for 4 minutes.

Cook the gnocchi in the boiling water at a low boil until they float to the surface; drain well and toss into the pan with the Gorgonzola mixture. Toss over medium heat, add the Asiago and chives, pour into warmed bowls, and serve.

Gnocchi alla Romana

serves 4

These baked semolina shapes are great for dinner parties. You can make them in advance and even hold them in the oven for an extra ten minutes if you're having difficulty with guests hanging around the cocktails too long.

3 cups **MILK**

1 teaspoon **SALT**

½ cup (1 stick) unsalted **BUTTER**

1 cup **SEMOLINA** flour (see sidebar, page 81)

1 cup freshly grated **PARMIGIANO-REGGIANO** cheese

4 **EGG YOLKS**

Preheat the oven to 425° F. Butter a jelly roll pan that has ¾-inch sides.

In a 3- to 4-quart saucepan, heat the milk, salt, and 6 tablespoons of the butter nearly to the boiling point over medium heat. Whisking vigorously, add the semolina in a thin stream and cook for about a minute, switching to a wooden spoon as the batter thickens. Remove from the heat and stir in ½ cup of the grated cheese, then beat in the egg yolks. Working quickly pour the batter into the prepared pan and spread to a thickness of ½ inch. Allow to cool and cover with plastic until ready to cook.

Using a 3-inch diameter water glass, cut a row of rounds across the top of the sheet. Cut a second row 1 inch below the first, to create crescent moons. Repeat, moving the glass 1 inch each time. Arrange leaning up against one another in a buttered baking dish and sprinkle with the remaining ½ cup grated cheese. Place in oven and cook 15 to 20 minutes, or until top is light golden brown. Remove and serve immediately.

Roasted Pepper Gnocchi with Tomatoes, Olives, and Marjoram

serves 4 to 6

These gnocchi have the velvet texture of my grandma's recipe, but they get an extra touch of sweetness from the peppers. I prefer fresh marjoram to oregano in most recipes, for its exotic and sexy perfume.

ROASTED PEPPER GNOCCHI

1 pound russet **POTATOES**

2 medium red **BELL PEPPERS**, roasted, cored, seeded, and finely chopped

1 cup all-purpose **FLOUR**

1 extra-large **EGG**, beaten

1 teaspoon **SALT**

4 tablespoons extra-virgin **OLIVE OIL**

2 **GARLIC** cloves, thinly sliced

1 cup Gaeta **OLIVES**

2 pounds ripe plum **TOMATOES**, cut into ½-inch dice

1 tablespoon **MARJORAM**, leaves only

Make the gnocchi dough. In a large saucepan, boil the potatoes until they are soft, about 45 minutes. While still warm, peel and pass through a vegetable mill or ricer onto a clean pasta board. Place the chopped peppers in a towel and wring to extract as much liquid as possible.

Make a well in the center of the potatoes and sprinkle all over with the flour, using all the flour. Place the egg, salt, and chopped pepper in the center of the well and, using a fork, stir into the flour and potatoes, just like making pasta. Once the egg and roasted peppers are mixed in, bring the dough together, kneading gently until a ball is formed. Knead gently another 4 minutes until the ball is dry to the touch.

Bring 6 quarts of water to a boil and add about 2 tablespoons salt.

Heat the olive oil in a 12- to 14-inch sauté pan over medium heat until almost smoking. Add the garlic and cook until light brown, about 30 seconds. Add the olives and tomatoes and cook for 3 minutes. Keep warm.

Divide the dough into 4 balls. Flour the board and roll each ball into a 1-inch-thick rope. Cut the rope into 1-inch-long pieces and let the pieces dry slightly before shaping. Roll the pieces down the tines of a fork to establish the classic shape. Repeat with the remaining gnocchi dough. Drop the gnocchi, 10 to 15 at a time, into boiling water and cook until they float to the surface.

Gently remove with a slotted spoon and add to the pan with the olives and tomato. Add the marjoram. Toss until coated over medium heat, about 1 minute. Place in a warm bowl and serve.

POTATOES

Potatoes have been cultivated in South America for more than three thousand years and are actually the edible tuber, or swollen underground stem, from which sprouts a beautiful yet poisonous flower and leaf. Originally carried from the Americas to Europe in the early sixteenth century by the Spaniards, the potato was at first regarded with much suspicion, as were tomatoes and eggplant. However, potatoes were simple to cultivate and store, and many varieties of potatoes, from purple Peruvians to the American russet, eventually found their way into the European diet. In the early eighteen hundreds, potatoes served to sustain large groups of people through frequent food shortages in new urban areas, contributing to the infamous potato famine that caused huge numbers of people to leave Ireland when their potato harvest was decimated by a parasite.

Today, potato varieties differ immensely in starch content, flavor, sugar content, and appearance, so it is important to choose the right potato for each dish. In general, look for firm specimens with no green areas or distinct sprouting eyes, and with some sign of soil on the skin. Prewashed potatoes are more likely to spoil quickly. Avoid them always; you'll wash them before you eat them, anyway. Store potatoes for up to eight months in temperatures below 40° F. in a dark, well-ventilated place, as light and heat promote sprouting.

Spinach and Goat Cheese Gnocchi with Sun-dried Tomatoes, Pine Nuts, and Lemon

serves 4

Another creative use of Coach Farm's wonderful goat cheese, these gnocchi were inspired by the ricotta gnocchi that are served all over southern Lombardy with butter and Parmigiano-Reggiano.

RICOTTA GNOCCHI

1 pound fresh **SPINACH**, well washed, stems removed

1 pound **RICOTTA** cheese or substitute Coach Farm

    fresh goat cheese

2¼ cups all-purpose **FLOUR**

2 extra-large **EGGS**

1 teaspoon **SALT**

½ teaspoon freshly grated **NUTMEG**

¼ cup freshly grated **PECORINO** cheese

½ cup (1 stick) unsalted **BUTTER**

½ cup sliced **SUN-DRIED TOMATOES**

3 tablespoons **PINE NUTS**

juice and zest of 1 **LEMON**

freshly grated **PECORINO** cheese, for sprinkling

Bring about 6 quarts of water to a boil and add about 2 tablespoons salt.

Make the gnocchi. In a medium saucepan, steam the spinach over medium-high heat in just the water that clings to the leaves. When just wilted, drain well. Chop very fine, then wrap in a dish towel and press to remove as much moisture as possible.

In a large bowl, stir the ricotta cheese until softened. Add the spinach, then the flour, eggs, salt, nutmeg, and pecorino and stir to form a firm ball. Divide into 4 balls and knead on a cutting board until firm and slightly dry. Roll each ball into a 1-inch-thick rope. Cut into 1-inch pieces and roll down a fork to create traditional gnocchi shape. Continue until all the dough has been shaped.

Place all the gnocchi into the boiling water and stir once. Cook until all float to the top, 6 to 7 minutes.

While the gnocchi cook, combine the butter, sun-dried tomatoes, and pine nuts in a 12- to 14-inch sauté pan. Cook over medium heat until the butter is lightly browned, then add the lemon juice and zest and remove from the heat.

Drain the gnocchi gently, add to the pan with the lemon mixture, and return to medium heat. Toss to coat and serve immediately. Sprinkle with additional cheese at the table.

Bucatini with Olive Pesto, Sun-dried Tomatoes, and Basil

serves 4

As owner of La Volta, Gianni cooked less than rarely, so the two or three times a year when he decided to make a family meal it was always comical. This dish was created in a flurry of theatrical motions that obscured its easy technique. Olive paste is widely available at gourmet stores.

1 cup **BLACK OLIVE PASTE**

¼ cup oil-packed **SUN-DRIED TOMATOES**, cut into ⅛-inch julienne strips

2 bunches **BASIL** leaves, washed, spun dry, and chopped

(1 cup loosely packed)

1 pound **BUCATINI**

¼ cup roughly chopped Italian **PARSLEY**

Bring 6 quarts of water to a boil and add about 2 tablespoons salt.

In a large sauté pan, stir together the olive paste, sun-dried tomatoes, and basil. Set aside.

Drop the pasta into the boiling water and cook according to package directions, until tender yet still al dente. Drain the pasta and add to the sauté pan with the olive sauce. Cook together over medium heat, stirring gently to coat the pasta, just until warm through, about 1 minute. Add the parsley, toss to mix, pour into a warm serving bowl, and serve immediately.

Spaghetti with Artichokes, Mint, and Chiles

serves 4

When a dish contains as few ingredients as this one, it is essential that everything be perfect. I like the tiny violetta artichokes from Castroville best for this simple Tuscan classic. If you can't find them, substitute the hearts of fresh globe artichokes, with all of the leaves removed and sliced ¼ inch thick.

16 **BABY ARTICHOKES**

4 **GARLIC** cloves, thinly sliced

1 large **RED ONION**, cut into ¼-inch julienne

4 **JALAPEÑO** peppers, seeded and sliced

½ cup extra-virgin **OLIVE OIL**

10 ounces **SPAGHETTI**

1 bunch **MINT**, leaves only (about ½ cup)

¼ cup freshly grated **PECORINO** cheese

freshly ground black **PEPPER**

Bring about 6 quarts of water to a boil and add about 2 tablespoons salt.

Peel the stems and remove the outer leaves of the baby artichokes. Place them in a bowl of cool, acidulated water while you cut each artichoke top to bottom into four or five ¼-inch-thick slices.

In large sauté pan, combine the artichokes with the garlic, onion, jalapeños, and olive oil and sauté over medium-high heat until the artichokes are tender but not too brown, 8 to10 minutes. Set aside

Drop the spaghetti into the boiling water and cook according to package directions, until tender yet al dente. Drain the pasta, reserving ½ cup of the cooking water.

Add the hot pasta to the pan with the artichokes. Reduce the heat to medium and cook for 1 minute, gently tossing to coat the pasta with the sauce. If it seems too dry, add a little of the reserved pasta water and toss again. Add the mint leaves and grated cheese and toss to mix. Pour into a heated serving bowl, top with black pepper, and serve.

Linguine with Manila Clams, Pancetta, and Chiles

serves 4

Traditionalists scoff at the combination of pork and shellfish in this Pó classic, but I find that just a small amount of smoked bacon rounds out the flavor in a big way. Traditional Portuguese cooks were, of course, light-years ahead of me with their cataplana of chorizo and clams.

6 tablespoons extra-virgin **OLIVE OIL**

½ medium **RED ONION**, minced

4 ounces **PANCETTA**, cut into ⅛-inch dice

4 **GARLIC** cloves, thinly sliced

1 teaspoon hot red **PEPPER FLAKES**

1 pound Manila **CLAMS**, scrubbed and rinsed

2 cups dry **WHITE WINE**

4 tablespoons (½ stick) unsalted **BUTTER**

10 ounces dried **LINGUINE**

¼ cup finely chopped Italian **PARSLEY**

Bring 6 quarts of water to a boil and add about 2 tablespoons salt.

In a large sauté pan, heat the olive oil and sauté the onion, pancetta, and garlic over medium heat until the onion is very soft and the pancetta is translucent, about 10 minutes.

Add the red pepper flakes, clams, wine, and butter and bring to a boil. Cook just until all the clams have opened, 5 to 7 minutes, and then set aside. Discard any clams that did not open.

Boil the linguine according to package directions, until tender yet still al dente. Drain the pasta and toss into the pan with the clams. Stir gently to mix; this should still be a little brothlike. Add the parsley, pour into a warm serving bowl, and serve.

Fettuccine with Lobster alla Pantelleria

serves 4

Sicilian flavors are an interesting amalgamation of North Africa and southern Europe, and the cooking of the tiny island of Pantelleria is even more exotic. The world's best capers are grown on Pantelleria, so most dishes evoking its name will contain them. Ask your fishmonger for female lobsters; the bright red coral, or roe, adds great color to the dish.

2 1½-pound **LOBSTERS**, steamed and cooled, or ¾ pound
   cooked lobster meat

½ cup fresh **MINT** leaves

½ cup fresh **BASIL** leaves

1 cup **PARSLEY** leaves

2 **GARLIC** cloves

¼ cup **CAPERS**, rinsed well and drained

4 medium plum **TOMATOES**, roughly chopped

1 tablespoon hot red **PEPPER FLAKES**

1 tablespoon freshly ground black **PEPPER**

½ cup extra-virgin **OLIVE OIL**, or more as needed

10 ounces dried **FETTUCCINE**

Bring about 6 quarts of water to a boil and add about 2 tablespoons salt.

Crack the lobster shells and remove the meat and coral, if any. Cut the tail into ½-inch pieces and the claws into thirds. Set aside the tomalley.

In a blender, puree the mint, basil, parsley, garlic, capers, tomatoes, red pepper flakes, black pepper, and olive oil to form smooth paste. If needed, add a little more oil. Combine this with the lobster meat, coral, and tomalley in a large serving bowl.

Cook the fettuccine according to package instructions, until tender but still al dente, and drain well. Add the hot pasta to the bowl with the lobster and toss like a salad until well mixed. Serve immediately.

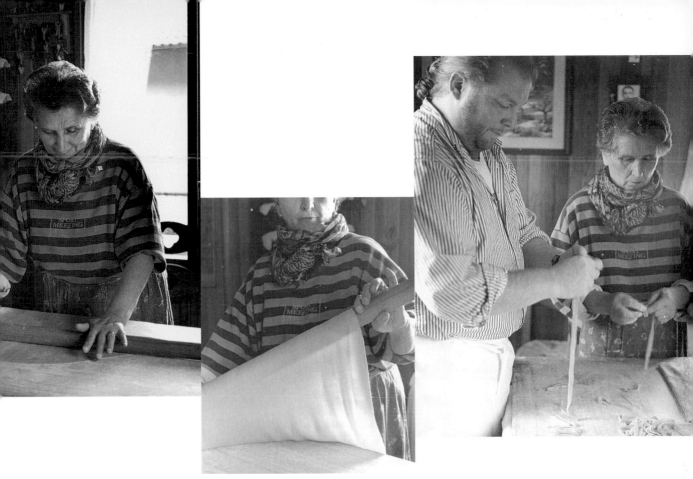

LOBSTER

Made famous in the B-52s' hit song of the same name, rock lobster (or spiny lobster) unfortunately enjoys the status of second-class citizen among crustacean lovers, loser to the North American lobster so much more popular on our tables. Spiny lobster is in fact a member of a different genus, the *Palinuridae*, and has no enlarged claws, so all of the meat is enclosed in the spine-covered tail. I've tasted spiny lobsters in Sicily, Puglia, California, and the Caribbean and found them all to have a more tender texture and sweeter flavor than the Maine variety, contrary to most books I've read on the subject. Both, of course, are delicious and they can be used interchangeably in the recipes in this book.

To kill a lobster humanely prior to cooking, insert the tip of a large knife (point aimed lengthwise) into the point where the head and body meet. The lobster will die immediately, although a nervous system reaction may cause it to continue to move. All lobster should be purchased live to ensure optimum freshness and should be quite lively and energetic. Japanese imitation shellfish such as surimi and kamaboko should be avoided at all costs; they have no place on our dining tables.

Spaghettini with Rock Shrimp, Anaheim Chiles, and Arugula

serves 4

Rock shrimp maintain their delicate, firm texture even if slightly overcooked, so this dish is great for the home cook. If you cannot find rock shrimp, substitute fresh bay shrimp or small gulf shrimp.

4 **GARLIC** cloves, thinly sliced

6 tablespoons extra-virgin **OLIVE OIL**

2 fresh Anaheim **CHILES**, cut into ¼-inch rounds

2 cups dry **WHITE WINE**

2 tablespoons unsalted **BUTTER**

1 pound fresh **ROCK SHRIMP**, peeled and deveined

SALT

10 ounces **SPAGHETTINI**

1 bunch **ARUGULA**, washed, spun dry, and chopped into ribbons (2 cups)

Bring 6 quarts of water to a boil and add about 2 tablespoons salt.

In a 12- to 14-inch sauté pan, sauté the garlic in the olive oil over moderate heat until lightly brown, about 1 minute. Add the chiles and continue cooking about 30 seconds longer. Add the wine and butter and boil over high heat for 3 minutes. Add the shrimp and cook, stirring, until just cooked, about 4 minutes. Season to taste with salt and remove from the heat.

Boil the spaghettini according to package instructions, until tender but still al dente. Drain the pasta, add to the skillet with the shrimp, and put pan back over medium heat. Stir gently until the spaghettini is coated with sauce, then toss in the arugula. Stir quickly to mix and just wilt, about 30 seconds. Check for seasoning, pour into a large serving bowl, and serve immediately.

Spaghetti with Fresh Anchovies, Caramelized Onions, and Thyme

serves 4

Sweet onions and anchovies sound like practically nothing on the page, but when cooked together in the correct quantities they form the backbone of many traditional seaside dishes. Pared down to their purest form, they are nothing short of transcendent.

1 pound fresh **ANCHOVIES**

½ cup extra-virgin **OLIVE OIL**

4 **GARLIC** cloves, peeled, left whole

1 large Spanish **ONION**, cut into ½-inch slices

1 tablespoon fresh **THYME** leaves

1 cup dry **WHITE WINE**

10 ounces **SPAGHETTI**

¼ cup freshly toasted **BREAD CRUMBS**

SALT and **PEPPER**

Bring about 6 quarts of water to a boil and add about 2 tablespoons salt.

Remove the fillets from the anchovies by holding the head between the thumb and forefinger of the left hand and scraping down the spine with the thumb and forefinger of the right hand.

In a large skillet, heat ¼ cup of the olive oil over medium heat. Add the garlic and onion and cook until golden brown, about 10 minutes. Discard the garlic. Add the thyme, anchovy fillets, and wine and bring to a boil. Add the remaining ¼ cup olive oil and remove from the heat.

Cook the spaghetti according to package instructions, until tender but still al dente, and drain. Toss the pasta into the anchovy mixture, place the pan over medium heat, and stir until well coated, 30 seconds. Pour into a heated serving bowl, sprinkle with the bread crumbs, salt and pepper to taste, and serve immediately.

Penne with Spicy Goat Cheese and Hazelnut Pesto

serves 4

I am always looking for new ways to use the authentic goat cheeses made by Susi's family and this dish includes her favorite hazelnuts as well. As with most pesto dishes, you do not want to heat the pasta with the sauce too long because the basil turns dark and bitter if it really cooks. Just toss them together quickly to coat and remove from the heat immediately.

Hazelnut Pesto

2 cups fresh **BASIL** leaves, lightly packed, washed and spun dry

2 **GARLIC** cloves

1 teaspoon hot red **PEPPER FLAKES**

¼ cup **HAZELNUTS**

½ cup extra-virgin **OLIVE OIL**

SALT

Place the basil, garlic, red pepper flakes, and hazelnuts in a food processor and pulse 3 times to start the chopping process. Turn the machine on and drizzle in the olive oil in a thin stream. Season with salt. Makes 1 cup.

8 ounces **PENNE**

1 recipe **HAZELNUT PESTO**

4 ounces fresh soft **GOAT CHEESE**, preferably Coach Farm, at room temperature

Bring about 6 quarts of water to a boil and add about 2 tablespoons of salt.

Cook the penne according to package instructions until tender but still al dente, and drain well. Transfer the pesto to a 12- to 14-inch sauté pan. Whisk in the cheese until smooth. Toss the penne into the pesto mixture and stir together over very low heat for 1 minute, until thoroughly coated. Pour into a warm serving dish and serve.

Fusilli Bucati with Soft-Shell Crabs, Hot Peppers, and Escarole

serves 4

The arrival of the year's first soft-shell crabs is always a certain sign that spring has come to Emeriltown, my staff's affectionate nickname for the southern seaports my Food Network colleague Emeril Lagasse calls home.

8 soft-shell **CRABS**, small to medium

6 tablespoons extra-virgin **OLIVE OIL**

1 medium **RED ONION**, thinly sliced

6 fresh **ANAHEIM** peppers, cored, seeded, and julienned

4 fresh red or green **JALAPEÑO** peppers, cored, seeded, and julienned

1 cup dry **WHITE WINE**

1 cup **BASIC TOMATO SAUCE** (page 84)

2 cups finely chopped **ESCAROLE**

SALT and **PEPPER**

1 pound **FUSILLI BUCATI**

Bring about 6 quarts of water to a boil and add about 2 tablespoons salt.

Clean the crabs by snipping off their faces with a pair of scissors and removing the skirts. Cut in half and set aside.

In a 12- to 14-inch sauté pan, heat the olive oil until almost smoking. Add the onion and peppers and cook over low heat until softened, 10 to 12 minutes. Increase the heat to medium, add the crab pieces, and continue cooking until the crabs are deep red and firm. Be careful not to break up the crabs with aggressive stirring. Add the wine and tomato sauce and cook until reduced by half, 6 to 7 minutes. Add the escarole and cook another minute until it has wilted. Remove pan from the heat and season with salt and pepper.

Drop the fusilli into boiling water and cook according to package instructions, until tender but still al dente, 7 to 9 minutes. Drain the pasta well and add to the pan with the crabs. Place over medium heat and toss the pasta and sauce until well coated, about 1 minute. Pour onto a heated serving platter and serve immediately.

Mostaccioli with Fennel, Mint, and Bread Crumbs

serves 4

Here's another example of the clean, easy cooking emblematic of southern Italy. Buy the rounder, plumper female fennel bulbs, as opposed to the thinner male specimens; the difference in sweetness is astounding.

²/₃ cup extra-virgin **OLIVE OIL**

2 **GARLIC** cloves

2 **FENNEL** bulbs, tops reserved, cut into ¼-inch strips

1½ cups toasted **BREAD CRUMBS**

1 tablespoon hot red **PEPPER FLAKES**

8 ounces **MOSTACCIOLI** or rigatoni

1 cup loosely packed fresh **MINT** leaves

Bring about 6 quarts of water to a boil and add about 2 tablespoons salt.

In a 12- to 14-inch sauté pan, heat 6 tablespoons of the olive oil until almost smoking. Add the garlic and fennel and cook, stirring frequently, until light golden brown and quite soft, about 10 minutes. Add 1 cup of the bread crumbs and the red pepper flakes and continue cooking for 4 to 5 minutes.

Chop the reserved fennel fronds roughly and set aside.

Cook the pasta according to package instructions, until tender but still al dente, and drain well. Add the hot pasta to the sauté pan, add the mint, and toss to mix well. Pour into a warm serving dish, sprinkle with the remaining ½ cup of bread crumbs and the fennel tops. Drizzle with the remaining olive oil and serve.

Rigatoni with Sheep's Milk Cheese, Black Pepper, and Arugula

serves 4

This dish was served to me in a working-class trattoria behind the Pantheon in Rome and impressed me with its big flavor and ingredients. Cacio is a semi-soft sheep's milk cheese from the hills outside of Rome, with a particular tangy flavor that really gives this dish its push. Its texture requires hand grating, so you'll never see it pregrated at the store.

1 pound **RIGATONI**

½ cup extra-virgin **OLIVE OIL**

2 cups grated **CACIO DI ROMA** or other semi-soft sheep's milk
   cheese, such as Tuscan pecorino or Spanish manchego

4 tablespoons freshly ground black **PEPPER**

2 bunches **ARUGULA**, washed, spun dry, and chopped

Bring about 6 quarts of water to a boil and add about 2 tablespoons salt.

Drop the rigatoni into the water and cook according to package instructions, until tender but still al dente. Drain well and toss into a warm serving bowl. Add the olive oil and toss like a salad. Add the cheese, pepper, and arugula, toss again, and serve immediately.

AL DENTE VERSUS AL DANTE

There is a certain urgency in my kitchen when pasta goes into the boiling water. Once pasta has started its travels, it will stop only to be digested. Fresh pasta will never be the same "al dente" as dried pasta, but each has its own distinct firmness. Six times out of ten, non-Italian-speaking customers at Pó ask to have their pasta served al Dante. Dante, of course, is the fourteenth-century Tuscan poet who has been dead for six hundred years; to serve pasta "al Dante" would be to offer it either ravaged by centuries under the earth (way! cooked) or with a sweet and vinegary sauce with nuts, as the poet might have eaten fresh pasta in his time. Noodles cooked al dente, or "to the tooth," are still quite firm but not crunchy. Each cook has his or her own way of serving pasta, and I have always found that Italians prefer their pasta and risotto much less cooked, or more firm, than Americans will tolerate. Cook it the way you like it, but leave poor Dante to rest.

Spaghetti alla Carbonara

serves 4

This common dish is a classic "breakfast" pasta often eaten after a night out on the town. The raw egg yolk is actually cooked by the heat of the noodles as you stir it through just before serving.

½ medium **ONION**, finely chopped

4 ounces **GUANCIALE** or pancetta (see Glossary), cut into ¼-inch cubes

½ cup heavy **CREAM**

4 **EGGS**

1 pound very thick **SPAGHETTI**

½ cup freshly grated **PECORINO** cheese

4 tablespoons freshly ground black **PEPPER**

Bring about 6 quarts of water to a boil and add about 2 tablespoons salt.

In a 12- to 14-inch sauté pan, cook the onion and guanciale over medium heat until both onion and guanciale are translucent, 8 to 10 minutes. Add the cream and cook for 1 minute.

Separate the eggs, being careful to keep the yolks whole.

Cook the spaghetti according to package instructions, until tender but still al dente, and drain well. Add the hot pasta to the sauté pan and toss over medium heat until coated. Add ¼ cup of the cheese and stir through. Remove from the heat and vigorously stir in the egg whites.

Divide the pasta among 4 plates and top each serving with 1 yolk. Sprinkle with the remaining ¼ cup grated cheese and the black pepper and serve.

Ziti al Telefono

serves 4

The "telephone" in this recipe title refers to the strings of melted mozzarella, which look like a telephone switchboard, that form over the plate as you eat.

2 cups **BASIC TOMATO SAUCE** (page 84)

2 medium **TOMATOES**, cut into ¼-inch cubes

1 bunch **BASIL**, stems removed (¼ cup)

1 pound **ZITI**

8 ounces fresh **MOZZARELLA** cheese, cut into ¼-inch cubes

Bring about 6 quarts of water to a boil and add about 2 tablespoons salt.

In a 12- to 14-inch sauté pan, combine the tomato sauce and tomatoes and bring to a boil. Lower the heat to a simmer and add the basil leaves without stirring.

Cook the pasta according to package instructions, until tender and just shy of al dente. Drain well, then add to the pan with the tomatoes and basil. Add the mozzarella pieces and toss over medium heat until the cheese is just melting. Pour into warm bowls and serve immediately.

SALT

Salt is an essential ingredient in much of Italian cooking. To season pasta and vegetable water, I always use sea salt for its intense and briny flavor. For seasoning meat, fish, and poultry, as well as cooked vegetables and salads, I always use kosher salt. I find kosher salt to be slightly less saline and a lot less likely to stick to my fingers when I reach for it while cooking.

Because salt causes meat and vegetables to exude their natural liquids, it is important not to season a dish before you want that to happen. For example, I salt salads with tomatoes immediately before I serve them. When I'm making a quick tomato sauce of meaty fresh plum tomatoes, I may add the salt right when I cut the tomatoes, if they're very firm, or not until I add the pasta, if they're soft and drippy. For slow-cooked dishes, I find it essential to season with salt conservatively all through the process. For soups, I tend to add salt only at the end. But to season with care; I've ruined many dishes' delicacy through aggressive seasoning.

Shellfish Couscous
"Sicilian Lifeguard" Style

serves 4

I've found that giving dishes funny names often leads to a comfortable banter between guests and my staff that demystifies Italian cooking and reduces the intimidation factor for rookies. To my knowledge this dish has never been made by a Sicilian lifeguard—I made it all up. But it's a good way to have fun with the customers.

1 medium **LEEK**, halved lengthwise, cleaned, and sliced into ¼-inch half-moons

4 **GARLIC** cloves, thinly sliced

6 tablespoons extra-virgin **OLIVE OIL**

1 tablespoon hot red **PEPPER FLAKES**

1 cup Sicilian **GREEN OLIVES**

1 cup chopped fresh **TOMATOES**

8 large cherrystone **CLAMS**

8 **MUSSELS**

8 jumbo **SHRIMP**, peeled and deveined

½ cup quick-cooking **COUSCOUS**

2 cups **FISH STOCK** or bottled clam juice

2 cups dry **WHITE WINE**

1¼ pounds cleaned **CALAMARI**, cut into ¼-inch rings

SALT and **PEPPER**

½ cup finely chopped Italian **PARSLEY**

In a large flameproof casserole suitable for serving, sauté the leek and garlic in the olive oil over medium heat until very soft, about 8 minutes.

Add the red pepper flakes, olives, tomatoes, clams, mussels, shrimp, and couscous and stir to mix. Add the fish stock and wine, and bring to a boil. Cover and cook for 3 minutes over high heat, then remove the cover and stir to mix.

Add the calamari and continue to cook uncovered, stirring often, until the calamari is cooked but still tender, about 3 minutes. Season to taste with salt and pepper, then stir in the parsley. Discard any clams or mussels that did not open. Pour into a warmed serving dish and serve.

RISOTTO

Among pasta courses, risottos are less familiar to non-Italians, but I expect them to become quite popular as consumers become more knowledgeable about regional Italian cooking. A proper risotto requires a roundish short grain rice with a plump, starch-filled center that allows each granule to absorb lots of liquid while still retaining a firm "al dente" texture. For risotto-making, Italians favor the vialone nano, carnaroli, and arborio varieties of short-grain rice. Technically, the process involves three important steps, as follows: *Rossolare*, the act of cooking the rice with the soffrito (before adding any liquid) until the rice turns opaque. This allows each grain to begin to absorb the flavor and helps develop a resiliant outer shell. Second, *coucere;* adding the liquid component, either broth or water, gradually so that the rice can absorb the broth fully before more is added. This causes each grain to release its starch, producing a dish with a creamy texture. Finally, *mantecare*, literally pounding the rice with butter, oil, or cheese, to enrich the finished dish.

Risotto Milanese

serves 4

If serving this with Osso Buco (page 202), spoon it onto a deep platter, top with the veal shanks, and sprinkle with gremolata.

¼ cup extra-virgin **OLIVE OIL**

1 medium **ONION**, cut into ¼-inch dice

1 teaspoon **SAFFRON** threads

2 cups **ARBORIO RICE**

4 cups **CHICKEN STOCK**, hot

4 tablespoons (½ stick) unsalted **BUTTER**

½ cup freshly grated **PARMIGIANO-REGGIANO** cheese

In a 12- to 14-inch skillet, heat the olive oil over medium heat. Add the onion and cook until softened and translucent but not browned, 8 to 10 minutes. Add the saffron and cook, stirring, for 1 minute. Add the rice and stir with a wooden spoon until toasted and opaque, 3 to 4 minutes.

Add a 4- to 6-ounce ladle of the stock and cook, stirring, until it is absorbed. Continue adding stock a ladle at a time, waiting until the liquid is absorbed before adding more. Cook until the rice is tender and creamy and yet still a little al dente, about 15 minutes. Stir in the butter and cheese until well mixed.

Risotto with Porcini, Shiitake, and Vin Santo

serves 4

Risotto is a tricky dish that must be served at the exact moment it is ready. Venetians like their risotto quite wet, or *sul'onda* ("on the wave"), and al dente, like spaghetti. In Emilia, it's served a bit drier. I prefer the former. If you cannot find Vin Santo, an Italian dessert wine, substitute a fino or amontillado sherry.

4 cups **CHICKEN STOCK**

4 tablespoons extra-virgin **OLIVE OIL**

$\frac{1}{2}$ medium **RED ONION**, finely chopped

8 ounces fresh **PORCINI** mushrooms, stems and caps sliced $\frac{1}{4}$ inch thick

8 ounces fresh **SHIITAKE** mushrooms, hard stems removed and sliced
$\frac{1}{4}$ inch thick

1$\frac{1}{2}$ cups **ARBORIO RICE**

4 tablespoons ($\frac{1}{2}$ stick) unsalted **BUTTER**

1 cup **VIN SANTO**

$\frac{1}{2}$ cup freshly grated **PARMIGIANO-REGGIANO** cheese

SALT and **PEPPER**

In a medium saucepan, heat the chicken stock to a simmer and place on a back burner over low heat.

Heat the olive oil in a heavy-bottomed 12- to 14-inch sauté pan over medium heat. Add the onion and sauté until translucent but not browned, about 5 minutes.

Add the mushrooms and sauté until lightly browned but not fully cooked, 6 to 7 minutes. Add the rice and stir 1 minute to coat thoroughly. Ladle $\frac{1}{2}$ cup of warm stock over the rice and cook, stirring constantly, until the liquid is absorbed. Add another ladle of broth and continue to cook, keeping the risotto at a slow boil and adding more stock. Repeat until rice is quite al dente (12 to 14 minutes). Add the butter, wine, and cheese and bring to a boil again, continuing to stir until the rice is done—firm and tender all the way through.

Season with salt and pepper and serve immediately.

Red Wine Risotto with Radicchio and Asiago

serves 4

This pleasingly straightforward dish was inspired by Mauro Cuppone's mother, a perfect *casalinga* ("homestyle") cook from Vicenza. This dish stands on its own as a pasta course but also serves as an excellent side dish for roasted meats.

3 cups **CHICKEN STOCK**

¼ cup extra-virgin **OLIVE OIL**

1 medium Spanish **ONION**, cut into ¼-inch dice

2 cups **ARBORIO RICE**

2 cups dry **RED WINE**

1 head **RADICCHIO**, cored and thinly sliced (2 cups)

½ cup freshly grated **ASIAGO** cheese

4 tablespoons (½ stick) unsalted **BUTTER**

SALT and **PEPPER**

In a medium saucepan, heat the chicken stock to a simmer and place on a back burner over low heat.

In a 12- to 14-inch skillet, heat the olive oil over medium heat. Add the onion and cook until soft, 8 to 10 minutes. Add the rice and stir with a wooden spoon until the rice is toasted and opaque, 3 to 4 minutes. Add the wine and continue cooking over medium heat until the liquid is absorbed.

Add the warm chicken stock 1 ladle at a time, waiting until stock is absorbed between additions, until the rice is cooked and has a creamy texture, about 15 minutes. Stir in the radicchio, cheese, and butter and stir until well mixed. Season to taste with salt and pepper and serve immediately.

Risotto with Asparagus and Fennel

serves 4

I got the idea for this vegetarian risotto from Faith Willinger, the outstanding teacher and cookbook author, whose views on cooking have been influenced by her Italian husband, Massimo. He would insist on eliminating the butter from this recipe, believing it to be a crutch for poor cooks. I like the roundness it adds to the final flavor.

4 quarts **WATER**

2 medium **FENNEL** bulbs, stalks trimmed and reserved

8 ounces **ASPARAGUS**, tough ends removed

¼ cup extra-virgin **OLIVE OIL**

1 medium Spanish **ONION**, chopped into ⅛-inch dice

1½ cups **ARBORIO RICE**

4 tablespoons (½ stick) unsalted **BUTTER**

¾ cup freshly grated **PARMIGIANO-REGGIANO** cheese

¼ cup finely chopped Italian **PARSLEY**

Bring the water to a boil in a large pot. Add the fennel stalks and 2 table-spoons salt. Set up an ice bath next to the pot. Blanch the asparagus for 1 minute, then remove with tongs to the ice bath, reserving the cooking water. (Discard the fennel stalks.) Cut the cooled asparagus into 1-inch pieces and set aside.

Chop the fennel bulbs into ½-inch matchsticks. In a 12- to 14-inch sauté pan with 3-inch sides sauté the fennel with the olive oil and onion. Cook over medium heat until softened but not browned, 6 to 8 minutes. Add the rice and cook, stirring constantly, until the rice turns opaque, about 2 minutes. Add enough of the asparagus cooking water to cover the rice, about ½ cup. Turn the heat up to high, and continue to cook, stirring constantly, until the liquid has been absorbed. Add another ladle of liquid and continue stirring and cooking for 15 minutes, adding the warm asparagus cooking liquid 1 ladle at a time to keep the rice just covered with liquid. Add the blanched asparagus pieces and cook until the rice is soft but still al dente. Remove from the heat, add the butter, cheese, and parsley, and stir through. Serve immediately.

Green Apple Risotto

serves 4

When I first encountered this dish in the home of my friends the Cuppones, in Vicenza, I smugly thought how tragic it was to find nouvelle cuisine intruding on a family Sunday lunch. Much to my surprise, I learned it is, in fact, a traditional first course in the fall, when apples are at their apex in the Veneto.

4 to 5 cups **CHICKEN STOCK**

4 tablespoons (½ stick) unsalted **BUTTER**

2 tablespoons extra-virgin **OLIVE OIL**

1 large **RED ONION**, finely chopped

2 **GRANNY SMITH** apples, peeled, cored, and cut into
⅛-inch slices

2 cups **ARBORIO RICE**

1 cup dry **WHITE WINE**, such as Albana di Romagna

½ cup freshly grated **PARMIGIANO-REGGIANO** cheese, plus more for
serving

¼ cup finely chopped Italian **PARSLEY**

SALT and **PEPPER**

In a medium saucepan, heat the chicken stock to a simmer and place on a back burner over low heat.

In a 12- to 14-inch sauté pan, heat 2 tablespoons of the butter and the olive oil until melted together. Add the onion and cook over medium heat until soft but not browned, about 5 minutes. Add the apples and rice and cook 3 to 4 minutes, until the rice has a pearly opaque appearance. Add the wine and simmer until it has evaporated.

Add enough warm chicken stock to cover the rice and cook until the level of the liquid goes below the top of the rice. Continue cooking, adding stock and stirring constantly, until most of stock is gone, 15 to 18 minutes. The rice should be tender but still retain an al dente bite.

Stir in the remaining 2 tablespoons of butter, the grated cheese, and parsley and season to taste with salt and pepper. Serve immediately with additional grated cheese on the side.

Risotto Nero

serves 4

Venetians go wild for this strangely colored rice dish and justly so; the delicate flavor of squid ink or cuttlefish combines with the just-cooked freshness of calamari to create an out-of-body experience worth writing back to the planet about.

½ medium **ONION**

½ medium **CARROT**

1 **BAY LEAF**

1 pound cleaned **CALAMARI** or cuttlefish

¼ cup extra-virgin **OLIVE OIL**

1 medium Spanish **ONION**, cut into ¼-inch dice

2 packets **SQUID INK**, available at good fish markets

1½ cups **ARBORIO RICE**

1 cup dry **WHITE WINE**

SALT and **PEPPER**

2 tablespoons (¼ stick) unsalted **BUTTER**

¼ cup finely chopped Italian **PARSLEY**

Bring about 3 quarts of water to a boil with the onion, carrot, and bay leaf. Prepare an ice bath with cold water and ice cubes. Plunge the calamari into the boiling water and cook for 30 seconds. Use a slotted spoon to remove the calamari and submerge in the ice bath for 1 minute. Drain and set aside. Keep the cooking water warm on the stove.

In a 12- to 14-inch frying pan with 3-inch sides, heat the olive oil, onion, and squid ink over medium heat until the onion is softened but not brown, 8 to 10 minutes. Add the rice and, stirring constantly, cook until opaque, about 2 minutes.

Add the wine, then add the water in which the calamari cooked, ladle by ladle, until the rice is covered. Turn the heat to high and, stirring constantly, continue to cook, maintaining the level of liquid just about the level of rice, for 15 minutes. Chop the calamari into 1-inch pieces and add to the risotto. Continue cooking until the rice is soft but still al dente. Season to taste with salt and pepper, remove from the heat, and stir in the butter and parsley. Serve immediately.

Spiny Lobster Risotto

serves 4

I prefer the flavor and texture of spiny lobster to its Maine counterpart, but both work well in this deceptively easy classic. Crab meat is also a good option that gives very different results on the plate—and the palate.

½ medium **ONION**

½ medium **CARROT**

1 **BAY LEAF**

2 1½-pound spiny **LOBSTERS** (see sidebar, page 117)

4 tablespoons extra-virgin **OLIVE OIL**

1 medium Spanish **ONION**, chopped into ¼-inch dice

2 tablespoons **TOMATO PASTE**

1½ cups **ARBORIO RICE**

1 cup dry **WHITE WINE**

SALT and **PEPPER**

2 tablespoons (¼ stick) **BUTTER**

½ cup finely chopped Italian **PARSLEY**

Bring 3 quarts of water to a boil with the onion, carrot, and bay leaf. Prepare an ice bath. One at a time, plunge the lobsters into the boiling water and cook for 2 minutes. Remove and submerge in the ice bath 1 minute. Drain and set aside. Repeat with the second lobster. Keep the cooking liquid warm on the stove.

In a 12- to 14-inch sauté pan with 3-inch sides, heat the olive oil, onion, and tomato paste over medium heat until softened but not brown, 8 to 10 minutes. Add the rice and, stirring constantly, cook until opaque, about 2 minutes. Add the wine, then the lobster cooking liquid, ladle by ladle, until the rice is covered. Turn the heat to high and, stirring constantly, continue to cook, maintaining the level of liquid at just about the level of rice, for 15 minutes.

Remove the lobster from its shell, chop the meat into 1-inch pieces, and add to the rice. Continue cooking until the rice is soft but still al dente. Season with salt and pepper, remove from the heat, and stir in the butter and parsley. Serve immediately.

Pesc

e Fish

PESCE

Absolute freshness without compromise is what Italians demand from their seafood. The flesh must be firm, the eyes must be clear, the skin shiny with all of its scales, the gills blood red and rigid. Best of all is finding a fish still in rigor and almost impossible to bend. With perfect fish the cook's job is made simple. At Pó, we always acknowledge the sea's contribution to a great seafood dish, which is far more important than that of the cook.

In Bologna, as in most of Italy, fish is traditionally cooked as simply and as whole as possible, and then served unadorned with just a little lemon. At La Volta, fish was rarely served before my arrival in the kitchen, as it was essentially a mountain **trattoria,** and both Betta and Mara were born and raised far from the sea. Gianni and Roberto, however, were intrigued by the idea of serving fish as another way to distinguish La Volta from the other local *trattorie.* Over the course of several field trips we sampled the fish of the Adriatic and the Mediterranean, discussing the food and its preparation, and this led to experimentation at La Volta. While none of the recipes I offer here is traditional to a mountain *trattoria*, they are all reflective of the Emilian and Tuscan coastlines nearby.

In America, an incredible bounty of fresh fish is available across the country. Maine lobster and cod, full-flavored mid-Atlantic striped bass, sweet shrimp and grouper from the Gulf of Mexico, California halibut and Pacific Northwest salmon, plus the incredible variety of freshwater lake and stream fish available in every corner of every state give Americans ready access to the most elusive and essential ingredient in any fish and seafood recipe—freshness. Finding a good source for fish is the single most important step in cooking the following dishes. Beyond that, the greatest difficulty in trying to translate the Italian spirit in fish cookery into a specific recipe, given that we have different species in our waters, is the overriding importance of simplicity.

Steamed Mussels with Cinzano, Scallions, and Tomatoes

serves 4

I love the flavor of sweet vermouth with shellfish, and in this dish it makes a great sauce or dipping broth for tender mussels. You may be able to find both wild and cultivated mussels at the store; for this dish I recommend the fuller-flavored wild mussels, which will stand up better to the powerful and intense broth.

1 medium **RED ONION**, finely chopped

4 **GARLIC** cloves, thinly sliced

4 tablespoons extra-virgin **OLIVE OIL**

2 pounds **MUSSELS**, scrubbed and debearded

1 cup Cinzano Rosso or other sweet red **VERMOUTH**

¾ cup **WATER**

2 cups chopped ripe **TOMATOES**

4 **SCALLIONS**, thinly sliced

SALT and **PEPPER**

In a 12- to 14-inch sauté pan, sauté the onion and garlic in the olive oil until softened but not browned, 6 to 7 minutes. Add the mussels, Cinzano, water, and tomatoes and bring to a boil. Cover and steam until all the mussels are opened, 1½ to 2 minutes. Discard any mussels that do not open.

Uncover the pan, add the scallions, and stir until well mixed. Season the broth to taste with salt and pepper, pour into a warm serving bowl, and serve.

Clam Stew with Shiitakes, Cinzano, Chorizo, and Guido's Garlic Bread

serves 4

This is my adaptation of a great dish served at one of my favorite restaurants in New York, the world-renowned Blue Ribbon. Eric and Bruce Bromberg serve their version in a beautiful white clay pot with garlic bread on the side. In my somewhat murkier version, the clam's delicate brine flavor is a perfect match for the rich broth of the mushrooms, chorizo, and vermouth.

Guido's Garlic Bread

1 **BAGUETTE**

¼ cup dry **RED WINE**

¼ cup extra-virgin **OLIVE OIL**

6 **GARLIC** cloves, thinly sliced

2 tablespoons fresh **THYME** leaves, finely chopped

Preheat the oven to 400° F.

Slice the baguette as if to make a submarine sandwich. Brush both halves with the wine, then the olive oil, and sprinkle with garlic and thyme. Put the halves back together and place in the oven, unwrapped, for 5 minutes. Remove and cut into 4-inch lengths. Serve warm.

4 tablespoons extra-virgin **OLIVE OIL**

1 medium **RED ONION**, cut into ½-inch dice

8 ounces **SHIITAKE** mushrooms, hard part of stems removed

8 ounces cooked **CHORIZO** sausage, thinly sliced

½ cup Cinzano Rosso or other sweet **RED VERMOUTH**

1½ cups **BASIC TOMATO SAUCE** (page 84)

1 cup dry **WHITE WINE**

24 littleneck **CLAMS**, scrubbed and rinsed

1 recipe **GUIDO'S GARLIC BREAD**

In a heavy-bottomed 6-quart saucepan, heat the olive oil until smoking. Add the onion, shiitakes, and chorizo and cook over medium heat until the onion is softened, about 8 minutes. Add the Cinzano and bring to a boil. Add the tomato sauce, wine, and clams. Cover and cook until the clams open, about 10 minutes. Remove from heat.

Uncover clams and discard any that did not open. Serve immediately in shallow bowls with the warm garlic bread.

Sautéed Scallops with Wild Mushrooms and Frisée

serves 4

This fabulous earth and sea combo was served to me in a strangely down-scale restaurant in Mestre, Italy, with one Michelin star, called dell'Amelia. The pristine scallops arrived with the pinkish roe still attached and the mushrooms were just barely acidic from the vinegar. The dish was pure goosebumps in its harmony of flavors. Choose hand-harvested, or "diver," scallops if you have the opportunity; they are superior. The real trick to this dish is using a nonstick pan and not moving the scallops as they cook. This way they get a beautiful golden crust—if you shake the pan around, the scallops exude their liquid, thus causing them to steam or poach instead.

12 large **SEA SCALLOPS** (about 1 pound)

freshly ground black **PEPPER**

½ cup extra-virgin **OLIVE OIL**

4 **SHALLOTS**, thinly sliced

8 ounces mixed **WILD MUSHROOMS**, such as oyster, chanterelle,
   or cremini, sliced ¼ inch thick

4 tablespoons **BALSAMIC VINEGAR**

3 heads **FRISÉE** or mixed baby lettuce washed and spun dry (6 cups)

SALT and **PEPPER**

Season the scallops with pepper and set aside.

In a 10- to 12-inch nonstick pan, heat 2 tablespoons of the olive oil until smoking. Add 6 scallops to the pan and cook without moving them until crisp and golden brown, 5 to 6 minutes; do *not* turn. Remove to a plate and repeat with the remaining 6 scallops. Set aside.

In a 12- to 14-inch sauté pan, heat 2 tablespoons of the olive oil until smoking over high heat. Add the shallots and sauté until softened, 3 to 4 minutes. Add the mushrooms and toss 3 to 4 minutes, until softened. Stir in the vinegar and then add the frisée. Toss quickly, season with salt and pepper, and divide among 4 plates. Arrange 3 scallops on each salad, browned side up, drizzle with the remaining ¼ cup of olive oil, and serve.

Steamed Taylor Bay Scallops in a Spicy Caper Zuppetta

serves 4

These spectacular scallops arrive at the fishmonger washed and ready to eat, still in their pink and white shells. They are available from September to February, and though they are expensive, their exquisite flavor and dramatic presentation make them well worth it.

1 medium **RED ONION**, thinly sliced

2 **GARLIC** cloves, thinly sliced

¼ cup extra-virgin **OLIVE OIL**

2 tablespoons **CAPERS**, rinsed and drained

1 teaspoon hot red **PEPPER FLAKES**

28 Taylor Bay **SCALLOPS** in the shell

1½ cups dry **WHITE WINE**

juice and zest of 2 **LEMONS**

4 tablespoons (½ stick) unsalted **BUTTER**

¼ cup finely chopped Italian **PARSLEY**

In a 12- to 14-inch sauté pan, sauté the onion and garlic in the olive oil over moderate heat until softened but not brown, about 5 minutes.

Add the capers, red pepper flakes, scallops, wine, lemon juice and zest, and butter and bring to boil. Cover and steam until the scallops are all open, about 3 minutes. Discard any scallops that do not open.

Stir in the parsley, pour into a warm serving bowl, and serve.

SCALLOPS

Scallops are slow-growing bivalve mollusks native to both Mediterranean and American waters. Since they are extremely perishable, they are often sold shucked from their rounded shell pairs and packed in plastic buckets. Scallops in the shell can vary from two and a half to ten inches across, with the former known as bay scallops and the latter as sea scallops. Edible both raw and cooked, scallops can be prepared ceviche-style, steamed, grilled, sautéed, or baked in their shells. Most scallops in Italy arrive in the shell, while most in America do not. Several varieties of scallops are cultivated with great success in U.S. waters, however, the best are diver scallops and their quality merits the extra search to find them.

To open a live scallop (a dead one should be discarded), first rinse in cool water, then carefully slide a flat knife blade through the rounded edge beyond the skirt and beard to where the muscle is attached to the shell. Sever carefully, remove the beard and skirt and discard, then release the muscle from the other shell in the same fashion. Remove the prize and treat very gently; cooking more than two or three minutes will render a scallop dry, stringy, and nothing to be proud of.

One-Hour Calamari in Umido with Ramp Bruschetta

serves 4

To be tender, calamari should be cooked for just two minutes—or for one hour. This recipe utilizes the latter technique. We serve this dish at Pó in the late spring, when the ramps are free and delicious. If you cannot find ramps, substitute green garlic or young scallions.

3 pounds cleaned **CALAMARI**

½ cup extra-virgin **OLIVE OIL**

10 **GARLIC** cloves, peeled and left whole

1 tablespoon hot red **PEPPER FLAKES**

1 cup dry **WHITE WINE**

2 cups **BASIC TOMATO SAUCE** (page 84)

2 bunches (about 16) **RAMPS**, cleaned

1 bunch **MARJORAM**, leaves only

SALT and **PEPPER**

4 thick slices Italian peasant **BREAD**

Check the calamari for any cartilage and cut into 1-inch pieces. Place the calamari in a 6-quart saucepan, add ¼ cup of the olive oil, the garlic, red pepper flakes, wine, and tomato sauce, and bring to a boil. Lower the heat to a rapid simmer and cook 1 hour.

Preheat the grill or broiler.

Grill the ramps until wilted, about 1 minute. Set aside to cool, then chop the cooled ramps into ½-inch pieces. Place in a mixing bowl with remaining ¼ cup olive oil and the marjoram leaves and stir to blend. Keep grill hot.

When the calamari is tender, season with salt and pepper. Toast the bread on the grill. Spoon the ramp mixture over the bread, divide the calamari among 4 bowls, top each with a bruschetta, and serve.

Sautéed Spot Prawns with Acorn Squash, Campari, and Scallions

serves 4

Spot prawns are a seasonal delicacy that I first tasted when working at the Four Seasons Biltmore in Santa Barbara. Delivered live by local divers, their incredible sweet flesh has a firm texture and pleasantly briny aftertaste that works well with the sweetness of acorn squash and the bitterness of Campari. They are in season from mid-fall to the end of February, but are often difficult to find and can be successfully replaced by large Gulf shrimp.

1 acorn **SQUASH**, peeled, seeded, and cut into ½-inch cubes (about 1½ cups)

½ cup extra-virgin **OLIVE OIL**

12 whole **SCALLIONS**, trimmed at both ends

20 large **SPOT PRAWNS** or shrimp, peeled

1 cup **CAMPARI**

1 cup dry **WHITE WINE**

1 cup chopped fresh **TOMATOES**

SALT and **PEPPER**

1 tablespoon chopped fresh **ROSEMARY** leaves

Bring about 6 quarts of water to a boil. Prepare a bowl of ice water.

Drop the squash cubes into the boiling water and cook until al dente, 7 to 8 minutes. Remove the squash and refresh in ice water until cool. Drain and set aside.

In a large nonstick sauté pan, heat ¼ cup of the olive oil until almost smoking over medium heat. Sauté the scallions until limp but still green, and remove to a warm plate.

In a large saucepan, sauté the spot prawns in the remaining ¼ cup olive oil until golden on one side, about 3 minutes. Turn the prawns over, add the Campari, wine, squash cubes, and tomatoes, and bring to a boil. Reduce by half over high heat, about 2 minutes. Season to taste with salt and pepper and add rosemary leaves; stir to mix.

Arrange 3 sautéed scallions on each of 4 plates. Place a mound of the tomato and squash mixture in the center of each plate and prop the prawns around the squash mixture like a tepee. Serve immediately.

Scampi with Garlic, Chiles, and Herbs

serves 4

Nepitella is a kind of mint that grows wild only in Italy. It has a flavor that is slightly reminiscent of both fennel and marjoram, and to re-create it I add both to fresh mint with very interesting herby results. Crawfish work quite well as a substitute for the scampi in this dish, as would Gulf shrimp.

2 pounds **SCAMPI** or jumbo shrimp (12 pieces)

½ cup extra-virgin **OLIVE OIL**

4 **GARLIC** cloves, thinly sliced

4 red **JALAPEÑO** peppers, seeded and thinly sliced

½ cup dry **WHITE WINE**

¼ cup fresh **MINT** leaves

¼ cup chopped fresh **FENNEL FRONDS**

3 tablespoons fresh **MARJORAM** leaves

Split the scampi in half lengthwise.

In a 12- to 14-inch sauté pan, heat ¼ cup of the olive oil until smoking. Add the scampi, garlic, and jalapeños and cook until scampi have turned red on one side but the garlic is still light brown, 4 to 5 minutes. Add the wine and the remaining olive oil and turn the scampi over to cook 2 to 3 minutes more, until bright red all over and still flexible. Add the mint, fennel, and marjoram and toss through. Pour into a warm serving bowl and serve.

Shrimp Spiedini with Pesto, New Potatoes, and Chickpea Aïoli

serves 4

This dish is perfect for a party, as you can prepare it a day in advance and hold it wrapped in the refrigerator until your guests arrive. The chickpea sauce is relatively stable, but may break or separate on occasion; if this happens, just pop it back into the blender with another squeeze of lemon and blend until smooth again. I love the fat flavor of shrimp from the Gulf of Mexico, but Asian or Indian Ocean shrimp are good, too.

20 tiny new **POTATOES**, boiled with skins on until tender, drained, and cooled

1 recipe **PESTO SAUCE** (page 104)

28 jumbo **SHRIMP**, preferably with heads on

SALT and **PEPPER**

½ cup **CHICKPEA AÏOLI**

Prepare a charcoal fire or preheat the grill or broiler. Soak 4 bamboo skewers in water for at least 30 minutes.

Cut the potatoes into quarters and place in a mixing bowl. Dress with half the pesto and mound in the center of 4 individual serving plates.

Peel the shrimp, leaving the tail piece and head on. Thread 7 each on bamboo skewers. Season with salt and pepper. Grill the skewered shrimp for 3 minutes per side and place 1 skewer on each plate. Spoon the remaining pesto over the shrimp and drizzle with the aïoli.

Chickpea Aïoli

½ cup cooked **CHICKPEAS**
   (see page 65)

½ cup fresh **MINT** leaves

juice of 1 **LEMON**

1 **EGG**

1 **GARLIC** clove

1 cup extra-virgin **OLIVE OIL**

In a food processor, combine the chickpeas, mint, lemon juice, egg, garlic, and ½ cup of olive oil and blend until smooth, 1 minute. Slowly drizzle in the remaining oil to create a creamy sauce. Makes 1½ cups.

Sautéed Langostinos in Almond Flour Crust with Sweet and Hot Chiles

serves 4

Langostinos can be prohibitively expensive for an everyday meal, but for a special occasion the splurge will be obvious to your guests. The almond crust does not color, nor does it add that much textural crunch, but it contributes a subtle sweetness that contrasts exquisitely with the heat of the peppers.

½ cup extra-virgin **OLIVE OIL**

3 large **BELL PEPPERS** (red, green, and yellow), cored, seeded, and cut into
    ¼-inch-thick strips

3 **JALAPEÑO** peppers, seeded and thinly sliced lengthwise

1 tablespoon chopped fresh **THYME** leaves

20 fresh **LANGOSTINOS** or jumbo shrimp, in the shell

½ cup **ALMOND FLOUR** (available at specialty food stores)

juice of 1 **LEMON**

1 cup opal or regular **BASIL** leaves, loosely packed

SALT and **PEPPER**

Heat ¼ cup of the olive oil in a large sauté pan, and over medium heat, sauté the bell peppers and jalapeños until softened and starting to lightly brown, 8 to 9 minutes. Add the thyme and set aside to cool.

In another large sauté pan, heat the remaining ¼ cup oil until smoking. Cut the langostinos in half lengthwise and dredge the cut sides in the almond flour.

Cook the langostinos cut sides down until golden brown, about 1 minute. Turn and cook another minute on the other side, or until golden brown. Add the lemon juice and remove from the heat.

Add the basil leaves to the sautéed peppers and season to taste with salt and pepper. Divide the pepper mixture among 4 plates, stack 5 warm langostinos on each plate of peppers, and serve.

SCAMPI, LANGOSTINOS, PRAWNS, AND JUMBO SHRIMP

These crustaceans are found throughout the world in both fresh and salt waters. All but jumbo shrimp refer to shellfish with the appearance of miniature lobsters, while jumbo shrimp are simply large shrimp, 11 to 15 pieces per pound. All are found in various colors from gray-green to reddish brown to bright blue when raw in both sweet and salt waters. Scampi and the langostinos are definitely more expensive, due to their rarity even where they grow, probably because they more often end up on the fisherman's table than at the market, but all four are eminently substitutable one for the other.

Grilled Soft-Shell Crabs with Braised Scallions, Broccoli Rabe, and Dried Tomato Pesto

serves 4

Choose medium-size softies for this dish and always check to be sure that they are not leathery before you buy them. Some weeks are better than others for these farm-raised delicacies, so always buy from a fishmonger with whom you have developed a relationship—it really makes a difference.

Dried Tomato Pesto

¼ cup **SUN-DRIED TOMATOES**,
   soaked in ½ cup boiling water for
   10 minutes

2 tablespoons **BALSAMIC VINEGAR**

1 tablespoon **CAPERS**, rinsed and drained

½ cup extra-virgin **OLIVE OIL**

In a blender, puree the tomatoes, their liquid, and the remaining pesto ingredients until smooth, about 1 minute. Remove from the blender and set aside. Makes 1 cup.

8 ounces **BROCCOLI RABE**, trimmed

3 tablespoons extra-virgin **OLIVE OIL**

24 **SCALLIONS** or spring onions, root ends trimmed

½ cup sweet **VERMOUTH**

SALT and **PEPPER**

12 prime, medium **SOFT-SHELL CRABS**

½ cup **DRIED TOMATO PESTO**

Bring about 3 quarts of water to a boil in a large saucepan, and prepare an ice bath.

Drop the broccoli rabe in the boiling water and cook for 3 minutes; drain, then plunge into the ice bath to refresh. Remove the florets from the broccoli rabe and cut the stems and leaves into 1-inch pieces.

In a 10- to 12-inch sauté pan, heat the olive oil until just smoking. Add the scallions and cook 2 minutes, stirring often, until just wilted. Add the broccoli rabe and vermouth and continue cooking 2 to 3 minutes, until the scallions are quite soft. Season with salt and pepper. Set aside and cool to room temperature.

Preheat the grill or broiler.

Clean the soft-shell crabs by snipping off their faces with a pair of scissors and removing the skirt. Grill the crabs until crisp and bright red, about 5 minutes on each side.

Divide the rabe mixture among 4 plates. Place 3 crabs on each plate, drizzle 2 tablespoons of the pesto around each serving, and serve immediately.

SOFT-SHELL CRABS

Blue crabs caught between May and September that have shed their hard shells in the annual effort to further their growth process are known as soft-shell crabs. Avoid leathery, tough-skinned crabs and certainly the dead or seemingly asleep, selecting lively, energetic crustaceans with soft pliable skin that is flexible even along the outer edges and with all ten legs intact. To clean them use sharp scissors to snip off the eyes, mouth, and facial features, and pull away the cartiliginous tail piece shaped like the underside of a turtle, beneath the abdomen in the back. Many remove the gills but I find them delicious and leave them in. Always clean soft-shell crabs immediately prior to cooking and cook until well done, as some crustacean harbor bacteria that can cause gastrointestinal problems—even death—if not fully cooked.

COOKING IN OLIVE OIL

Many U.S. cooks stock three or four different qualities of olive oil, assigning each a special and specific use and reserving the extra-virgin for dressing salads and vegetables. Even in Italy, many cooks use one oil for cooking and another for serving raw. This is not the case in Tuscany, however. Owing to the spectacular quality and quantity of great oil available in every corner of the region, many Tuscans use only extra-virgin olive oil for everything in the kitchen.

Because of the high content of olive solids in cold-pressed extra-virgin olive oil, many cooking "experts" scoff at cooking in the emerald liquid, claiming that a lower smoking point (the point at which the fatty solids suspended in the oil actually start to burn) causes burnt or bitter flavors in the food. Since cooking

temperatures in Italian home kitchens rarely ascend beyond 360°F. (in part because of lower BTU, nonprofessional stoves and in part because of a slower paced, Italian grandma approach to cooking), I have not encountered burnt tastes in the foods I have tried. What cooking in extra-virgin olive oil *does* impart is a subtle yet substantial improvement in the flavor and spirit of the final dish.

Grilled Lobster with Herb Salad

serves 4

This is as simple and as elegant as seaside cooking gets, yet few chefs have the confidence to serve a dish so simple in our competitive industry. The fresher the better with the herbs, so use my list as a guide only, creating the salad from your garden or the best your greengrocer has to offer.

2 **LOBSTERS**, 1½ pounds each

2 tablespoons extra-virgin **OLIVE OIL**

HERB SALAD

½ cup chopped **FENNEL FRONDS**

½ cup **BASIL** leaves, washed and spun dry

½ cup **MINT** leaves, washed and spun dry

½ cup **CHERVIL** leaves

½ cup Italian **PARSLEY** leaves, washed and spun dry

½ cup julienned **SCALLIONS**

½ cup **CHIVES**, cut into 4-inch pieces

4 tablespoons extra-virgin **OLIVE OIL**

juice and zest of 1 **LEMON**

SALT and **PEPPER**

Preheat the grill or broiler.

Split the live lobsters lengthwise, brush the flesh of each half with ½ tablespoon olive oil, and place cut side down on the grill. Cook 7 to 10 minutes, turning once, until fully cooked and the shell is bright red all over.

Combine the herbs in a large mixing bowl. Add the oil and lemon juice and zest; season with salt and pepper, and toss to dress.

Mound the salad on a platter next to the lobsters. Serve immediately.

Variation: Grilled Snapper with Herb Salad

Substitute a whole 3-pound fish such as snapper, bream, sea bass, or porgy for the lobster and grill as above until cooked through, 15 to 20 minutes.

Scungilli alla Sorrentina

serves 4

Scungilli is a large whelk of Mediterranean waters and, though available here, can be difficult to find fresh in the United States. There is, however, a good supply of fresh conch from the warm waters of the Caribbean, and it is delicious. In New York's Chinatown, conch is available raw or precooked in bags and can be a pretty good deal; when cooking it on your own, watch carefully that you do not undercook the conch as it is much tougher undercooked than overcooked. And don't forget to add a cork to the cooking water. As with octopus (page 65), it magically keeps the conch tender.

2 pounds fresh cooked **SCUNGILLI** or conch

2 tablespoons **RED WINE VINEGAR**

½ cup extra-virgin **OLIVE OIL**

1 medium **RED ONION**, chopped into ¼-inch dice

1 bunch fresh **THYME**, leaves only (about 2 tablespoons)

1 yellow **BELL PEPPER**, cored, seeded, and cut into ¼-inch dice

1 cup dry **WHITE WINE**

3 plum **TOMATOES**, chopped into ¼-inch dice (¾ cup)

SALT and **PEPPER**

2 **LEMONS**, cut into wedges

Place the scungilli in a pot with water to cover. Add a wine cork and the vinegar and bring to a boil; boil 1 hour until tender. Drain and cool. Slice into ¼-inch-thick rounds and set aside.

In a deep 4-quart saucepan, heat ¼ cup of the olive oil over medium heat. Add the onion, thyme leaves, and bell pepper and cook until softened, 8 to 10 minutes. Add the wine, tomato pieces, and scungilli and bring to a boil. Lower the heat to a simmer and cook 15 minutes.

Season with salt and pepper and serve in shallow bowls with lemon wedges and the remaining olive oil.

Marinated Mackerel with Crispy Red Lentils and Oregano Aïoli

serves 4

This cooking technique is based on Mexican *escabeche* and results in a very creamy, soft fish. The lentil technique I learned from my friend Tom Colicchio of New York's Gramercy Tavern, where he serves them with wild striped bass, cooked quickly on the grill. Mackerel is quite oily, so it must be exceptionally fresh for this dish to succeed.

1 medium **RED ONION**, finely chopped

1 cup **RED WINE VINEGAR**

1 teaspoon dried **OREGANO** leaves

1¼ cups extra-virgin **OLIVE OIL**

2 **MACKEREL** fillets, 8 ounces each, bones removed, skin intact

SALT and **PEPPER**

1 cup **RED LENTILS**, soaked overnight in 4 cups cold water and drained

1 recipe **OREGANO AÏOLI**

In a medium saucepan, combine the onion, vinegar, oregano, and 1 cup olive oil. Bring to a boil over medium heat, lower the heat, and simmer 10 minutes.

Cut each mackerel fillet in half diagonally to form a pointed wedge. Season with salt and pepper on the flesh side, and place in a nonreactive casserole just large enough to hold the fish. Pour the vinegar mixture over the fish, moving the fillets around so they are surrounded by liquid. Let stand until cool, 10 to 15 minutes.

Meanwhile, sauté the lentils in ¼ cup olive oil over high heat until crispy, 7 to 8 minutes. Pour into a strainer to drain off the oil, then mound in the center of a serving platter. Place the mackerel pieces on top of the lentils, drizzle with the aïoli, and serve.

Oregano Aïoli

1 large **EGG** yolk

juice of 1 **LEMON**

½ cup extra-virgin **OLIVE OIL**

¼ cup finely chopped fresh **OREGANO** leaves

2 **GARLIC** cloves, finely minced

SALT and **PEPPER**

In a bowl, whisk the yolk and lemon juice until smooth. Whisk in the olive oil in a thin stream until a thick emulsion is formed. Stir in the oregano and garlic and season with salt and pepper. Makes ½ cup.

Snapper Livornese

serves 4

My customers go nuts for this classic dish from Livorno, on the southern Tuscan coast. The sauce keeps the fish moist and delicious, which enables you to hold the finished dish quite well for up to half an hour if you have difficulties timing the meal.

2 cups **BASIC TOMATO SAUCE** (page 84)

1 cup Gaeta **OLIVES**

¼ cup **CAPER BERRIES**, drained (about 12)

1 tablespoon hot red **PEPPER FLAKES**

1 cup dry **WHITE WINE**

1 1½-pound red **SNAPPER** fillets

SALT and **PEPPER**

Preheat the oven to 450°F.

In a 12-inch ovenproof skillet, combine the tomato sauce, olives, caper berries, red pepper flakes, and wine and bring to a boil over medium heat.

Rinse the fish and pat dry, then cut into 4 equal portions. Season with salt and pepper and place skin side up in the skillet with the sauce. Bake 7 to 10 minutes, until just cooked through.

Place a portion of fish on each of 4 plates, spoon some of the sauce over each, and serve.

MACKEREL

Mackerel is an oily fish related to tuna. In the summer and early fall, it is often found in waters off the United States and Canada, but it is most common to the warmer waters of the Mediterranean. Spanish mackerel usually weighs in between one and two pounds, while common mackerel, a bluer species with dark tigerlike stripes, can grow to up to five pounds. Italians prize the mackerel's strongly flavored oily flesh when it is served with a mixed grill, but it is also often marinated in vinegar with herbs and served at room temperature as an *antipasto*.

As with all oily fish (bluefish, tuna, herring, and sardines), freshness is fleeting; fish out of the water more than three days will be obviously deteriorated, so eat these fish the same day you buy them.

Bluefish with Oranges and Oregano Flowers al Cartoccio

serves 4

In New Jersey, where I went to college, bluefish is so plentiful in the summer that it is practically free. Sicilians love its oily flesh and often serve it steamed in a paper package, or *al cartoccio*. Because the fish is so rich in omega-3 fatty acids, which become quite smelly quickly, it must be served the day it is caught.

¼ cup extra-virgin **OLIVE OIL**

4 pieces **BLUEFISH** fillet (1½ pounds total)

SALT and **PEPPER**

6 **ORANGES**, zested, peeled, and cut into segments

1 cup **OREGANO FLOWERS** or other late-summer herb flowers

1 medium **RED ONION**, sliced paper-thin

½ cup finely chopped Italian **PARSLEY**

Preheat the oven to 400°F.

Cut four 16-inch square pieces of parchment paper and grease each piece with 1 tablespoon olive oil. Season each bluefish fillet with salt and pepper and place just to the right of center on a piece of parchment. Arrange the orange segments, oregano flowers, and onion slices on top of the bluefish fillets and sprinkle each with parsley. Fold the left half of the parchment over the fish and crimp the edges to seal securely. Place the packages on a cookie sheet and bake for 10 minutes.

Transfer the sealed packages to serving plates and, as you place them before each guest, use a pair of scissors or a knife to cut the *cartoccio* open. The fish should be eaten immediately.

Ciuppin

serves 4

Originally from Liguria, this great fish stew's alleged San Franciscan prove-nance is a fallacy. The fish is served completely cooked through, almost falling apart, the little bits contributing to the eventual thickness of the broth. The fish varieties are only suggestions, as the true dish is best when dictated by the market itself. My friend John Farber lives for this stew, so I invite him over every time I make it.

6 tablespoons extra-virgin **OLIVE OIL**

1 medium **ONION**, chopped into ¼-inch dice

1 **CELERY** stalk, sliced into ¼-inch pieces

1 **CARROT**, scraped and chopped into ¼-inch-thick half-moons

4 **GARLIC** cloves, thinly sliced

1 cup dry **WHITE WINE**

1 cup **BASIC TOMATO SAUCE** (page 84)

8 ounces **GROUPER** fillet, cut into 1-inch cubes

8 ounces **SNAPPER** fillet, cut into 1-inch cubes

8 ounces **HALIBUT** fillet, cut into 1-inch cubes

8 ounces **COD** fillet, cut into 1-inch cubes

SALT and **PEPPER**

1 cup **WATER**

¼ cup finely chopped Italian **PARSLEY**

4 slices Italian peasant **BREAD**, grilled or toasted

In a heavy-bottomed Dutch oven, heat the olive oil until smoking over medium heat. Add the onion, celery, carrot, and garlic and cook until softened and light brown, 7 to 8 minutes. Add the wine and tomato sauce and bring to a boil.

Add the fish cubes, cover, and bring to a boil, then lower the heat and simmer for 25 minutes. Check for seasoning with salt and pepper and add some of the water if too thick. Stir in the parsley.

Place a bread slice in the bottom of each of 4 bowls. Ladle the soup over the bread and serve.

Sweet and Sour Tuna Involtini

serves 4

Sweet and sour preparations are quite popular in Sicily, where years of North African trade have left an indelible mark on the palates and culinary styles of the great island cooks. These fish rolls can be prepared up to four hours in advance and reheated, or even served at room temperature. When you buy the fish from your fishmonger, ask for ¼-inch-thick slices.

1½ pounds fresh **TUNA**, cut into 8 thin steaks

8 **ANCHOVY** fillets, soaked in water for 1 hour

2 tablespoons chopped fresh **THYME** leaves, plus more for garnish

½ cup chopped **FENNEL FRONDS**

¼ cup extra-virgin **OLIVE OIL**

SALT and **PEPPER**

1 medium **RED ONION**, chopped into ¼-inch dice

2 medium **CARROTS**, chopped into ¼-inch dice

2 **CELERY** stalks, chopped into ¼-inch dice

3 **BAY LEAVES**

2 cups **BASIC TOMATO SAUCE** (page 84)

½ cup **RED WINE VINEGAR**

½ cup dry **RED WINE**

¼ cup chopped Italian **PARSLEY**

Lay the tuna pieces on a cutting board. Place 1 anchovy fillet, a pinch of fresh thyme, and a fennel frond on each and roll up to form an *involtino.* Secure each with 2 toothpicks.

Heat the olive oil in a 12- to 14-inch nonstick pan over medium-high heat until smoking. Season the rolls with salt and pepper and cook 2 to 3 at a time until lightly browned; remove to a plate. Add the onion, carrots, celery, and bay leaves to the pan and cook over medium heat until softened, 8 to 10 minutes. Add the tomato sauce, vinegar, and wine and bring to a boil. Lower the heat and simmer 30 minutes, stirring often, until thick as porridge. Season with salt and pepper.

Add the rolls to the sauce, cover, and simmer for a few minutes, just to warm through. Remove the toothpicks from the *involtini,* remove the bay leaves, sprinkle with the parsley and fresh thyme, and serve.

Monkfish Scaloppine with Shiitakes, Chianti, and Sage

serves 4

Shiitakes and red wine combine well with the firm texture of monkfish in this great winter dish. Although not even slightly traditional, this fish and mushroom combination derives its spirit from the cooking of the Adriatic in Romagna, where the bounty of wild mushrooms such as porcini pervades every course when they are in season.

¼ cup all-purpose **FLOUR**

SALT and **PEPPER**

1-pound piece **MONKFISH** fillet, cut into 8 ½-inch-thick slices

4 tablespoons extra-virgin **OLIVE OIL**

8 ounces **SHIITAKE** mushrooms, stemmed and halved

8 **SAGE** leaves

1 cup dry **RED WINE**, preferably Chianti

1 cup **BASIC TOMATO SAUCE** (page 84)

2 tablespoons cold unsalted **BUTTER**

2 tablespoons finely chopped **PARSLEY**

Place the flour on a plate and season with salt and pepper.

Pound each monkfish slice with a meat mallet to flatten and thin it to a ¼-inch thickness. Heat the olive oil in a 12- to 14-inch nonstick pan over medium heat. Dredge the fish in the seasoned flour and sauté in the hot oil until golden brown on both sides, 5 to 6 minutes total. Remove the fish and keep warm.

Add the mushrooms and sage to the pan and sauté 3 minutes, until softened and starting to brown. Add the wine, turn the heat to medium-high, and cook until the wine is reduced by half, 6 to 7 minutes. Add the tomato sauce and bring to a boil.

Return the fish to the pan, add the cold butter, and simmer for 10 minutes. The sauce should thicken slightly to coat the fish. Add the parsley, swirl to mix, and serve on a warmed serving platter.

WHOLE FISH

Cooking and serving fish whole is very dramatic, very Euro, and, sadly, perceived as very difficult by many home cooks. Cooking the fish in its natural state actually preserves the internal juices better and allows the outer flesh to char to a beautiful crispy shell. The trick is to buy fish no larger than 3 to 4 pounds and have your fishmonger scale and gut the catch. To roast or grill a whole fish requires the confidence that only experience can bring, but bear in mind that it is better to overcook a whole fish by one minute than to undercook it by a second, so follow the time guidelines provided in each recipe and allow an extra thirty seconds on each side if you're uncertain. When the fish is finished, place it on a platter for three or four minutes before portioning it. Fish is easier to cut when it has rested, just like meat. To carve it place the sharp edge of a long knife just below the gills and press gently until you feel resistance at the spine. Using the firm spine bone as your guide, slide the knife horizontally, using a deliberate yet gentle sawing motion from the head forward toward the tail, all the way through. Carefully remove the top fillet. Using your fingers, pull the skeleton and head away from the bottom fillet. Check both fillets carefully for small bones, and serve.

Mina's Baked Snapper

serves 4

I learned this dish from a woman from Lecce who is probably the most natural and intuitive cook I've ever met. The dish is deceptively simple and yet so delicious that it was the dish I chose to cook for Mark Franz, the original chef at Stars in San Francisco. Mark is the angel on my right shoulder, my inspirational mentor. The look on his face when he tasted it told me I had truly mastered the Italian way with fish. An excellent *contorno* for this dish would be tiny potatoes, roasted with garlic and rosemary.

1 3-pound **WHOLE FISH**, such as snapper, bream, porgy, or sea
   bass, scaled and gutted

½ cup dry **WHITE WINE**

1 cup Gaeta **OLIVES**

2 **JALAPEÑO** peppers, seeded and chopped

1½ cups **BASIC TOMATO SAUCE** (page 84)

1 **FENNEL** bulb, fronds chopped and reserved,
   bulb sliced paper-thin

1 bunch fresh **OREGANO**, leaves only (about ¼ cup)

4 tablespoons extra-virgin **OLIVE OIL**

Preheat the oven to 450° F.

Rinse the fish and use kitchen shears to remove the top and bottom fins and gills. Stand the fish up in a shallow casserole just large enough to hold the fish. Pour the wine over the fish and add the olives, jalapeños, tomato sauce, sliced fennel, and oregano leaves.

Drizzle the fish with the olive oil, place in oven, and cook until just cooked through, 25 to 35 minutes, or when the flesh is opaque at the skeleton near the gills. Sprinkle the fish with the reserved fennel fronds and serve immediately.

Whole Fish Baked in a Salt Crust

serves 4

When a fish is cooked whole, encased in a thick salt crust, the juices are all retained within and the briny essence of the fish is released only when the crust is cracked at tableside. It is a little risky as dinner party fare, though, since you really won't know if the fish is properly cooked until the moment of truth. Practice this dish on family members before breaking it out for the president's wife. A tomato and arugula salad would make an excellent accompaniment.

1 3-pound **WHOLE FISH**, such as snapper, bream, sea bass, or porgy,
  scaled and gutted

1 bunch fresh **THYME**

4 **EGG WHITES**

2 cups **KOSHER SALT**

4 tablespoons extra-virgin **OLIVE OIL**

1 **LEMON**, cut into wedges

Preheat the oven to 450°F.

Using kitchen shears, remove the fish's top and bottom fins and gills. Place the thyme in the body cavity and set aside.

Beat the egg whites until soft peaks form and fold in the salt. Place ¼ cup of egg white mixture on a large platter suitable for oven-to-table use. Place the fish on top of the mixture and spoon the remaining mixture over the fish, covering it completely. Place the fish and platter in the oven and bake for 30 to 35 minutes.

Bring the baking platter to the table and strike the crust to crack. Carefully remove the salt crust from the top of the fish and divide the flesh among 4 plates. Serve with the olive oil and lemon wedges.

Sautéed Langostinos in Almond Flour Crust with Sweet
and Hot Chiles (page 146)

Polenta-Crusted Pompano Salad with Sautéed Spicy Peppers, Chicory,
and Tomato Oil (page 169)

PREVIOUS PAGE: Fettuccine with Lobster alla Pantelleria (page 116)

**Clam Stew with Shiitakes, Cinzano, Chorizo, and Guido's
Garlic Bread (page 138)**

**Barbecued Red Mullet with Warm Fennel Salad and
Tangerines (page 168)**

Bluefish with Oranges and Oregano Flowers in Cartoccio (page 154)

Snapper Livornese (page 153)

NEXT PAGE: **Steamed Taylor Bay Scallops in a Spicy Caper
Zuppetta (page 140)**

Roasted Porgy with Peas, Garlic, Scallions, and Mint

serves 4

Porgy, also known as sea bream, is highly prized in France and Italy, but costs very little here in the States. Roasting a fish whole on the bone keeps the delicate flesh deliciously moist and delicate flesh is totally worth the effort. The peas should still have a bit of crunch for the textural contrast to make any sense. Grilled yellow squash makes an excellent *contorno*.

1 3-pound **PORGY** or sea bass, scaled and gutted

SALT and **PEPPER**

2 pounds fresh **PEAS** in the pod

¼ cup extra-virgin **OLIVE OIL**

6 **GARLIC** cloves, thinly sliced

½ cup dry **WHITE WINE**

4 **SCALLIONS**, thinly sliced

¼ cup fresh **MINT** leaves

Preheat the oven to 450° F.

Rinse the fish and season inside and out. Shell the peas and set aside.

In an ovenproof sauté pan large enough to hold the fish, heat the olive oil over medium heat until smoking. Place the fish in the pan and shake vigorously. Sauté 2 or 3 minutes, shaking frequently until fish is starting to crisp on the first side; turn the fish to the other side, add the garlic, and place the sauté pan in the oven for 12 to 15 minutes, or until fish is just cooked through.

Transfer the fish to a service platter and return the pan to the stove. Add the peas, wine, and scallions, and sauté 1 minute over medium heat. Stir in the mint leaves and immediately pour over the fish. Serve at once.

With perfect fish, the cook's job is made simple.

Grilled Whole Black Bass with Onions, Olives, and Red Chard

serves 4

Here is a good example of the Two Villages concept. While Italians like their fish served plain and unaccompanied by *contorni*, or side dishes, Americans prefer vegetable accompaniments with their entrées and they like sauces. This recipe addresses those preferences, but since the pesto is passed separately, it preserves the spirit of the Italian preparation while satisfying those customers who insist on ordering their meals "with sauce on the side," a practice I hate but have learned to tolerate.

2 **BLACK BASS**, approximately 2 pounds each, scaled, gutted, and rinsed

SALT and **PEPPER**

6 tablespoons extra-virgin **OLIVE OIL**

1 large **RED ONION**, thinly sliced

1 cup cured black **OLIVES**, preferably Ligurian

4 cups chopped red **SWISS CHARD** (about 2 pounds), cut into 1-inch-wide
   strips

juice and zest of 1 **LEMON**

½ cup **GREEN OLIVE PESTO** (page 29)

2 **LEMONS**, cut into 12 wedges

Preheat the grill or broiler.

Pat the fish dry, season inside and out with salt and pepper, and brush with 2 tablespoons olive oil. Place on the grill and cook 12 to 15 minutes, turning every 3 to 4 minutes, until the skin is nearly charred and crispy and yet the flesh is still moist near the bone. (You can check with a meat thermometer; internal temperature at the bone should get to 135 to 140° F.)

Heat a 12-inch skillet over medium heat and add 4 tablespoons olive oil. Add the onion and cook 1 minute, until wilted. Add the black olives, chard, and lemon juice and zest and toss until wilted, 2 to 3 minutes. Season with salt and pepper.

Place the fish on a large serving platter, arrange the chard around the edges, and serve immediately. Pass the green olive pesto and lemon wedges separately, so diners can serve themselves.

Grilled Tuna with Borlotti, Onion Pickles, Arugula, and Red Pepper Mustard

serves 4

Combining beans with canned tuna is practiced in *osterie* and *trattorie* throughout Tuscany and Emilia, but given the incredible quality of the fresh tuna available to me on the East Coast, I choose to substitute it for the canned. Pickled onion replaces the raw onions, and the red pepper mustard sauce creates both a visual and a flavor contrast to the rich grilled fish.

Red Pepper Mustard

¼ cup Dijon **MUSTARD**

1 teaspoon **CAYENNE** pepper

¼ cup **RED WINE VINEGAR**

½ cup extra-virgin **OLIVE OIL**

In a blender, mix the mustard, cayenne, vinegar, and olive oil until smooth. Transfer to a bowl. Makes 1 cup.

ONION PICKLES

1 large **RED ONION**, sliced into ¼-inch-thick rounds

½ cup **RED WINE VINEGAR**

½ cup **WATER**

¼ cup **SUGAR**

2 tablespoons **KOSHER SALT**

1 cup cooked borlotti (cranberry) **BEANS** (see page 65)

2 tablespoons finely chopped fresh **THYME** leaves

1 **GARLIC** clove, thinly sliced

3 tablespoons extra-virgin **OLIVE OIL**

1 tablespoon **BALSAMIC VINEGAR**

4 **TUNA** steaks, 6 ounces each, rubbed with salt and pepper

2 bunches **ARUGULA**, washed, stemmed, and spun dry

½ cup **RED PEPPER MUSTARD**

Preheat a grill or broiler.

In a mixing bowl, combine the pickle ingredients and mix well. Allow to stand 1 hour, then drain and set aside.

In a bowl, combine the beans, thyme, garlic, olive oil, and vinegar. Set aside.

Grill or broil the tuna steaks until medium rare, 3 to 4 minutes per side. While the tuna cooks, toss the arugula with the bean mixture and divide among 4 plates. Arrange some of the pickles around the border of the plate, and place the hot tuna in the center. Drizzle with the red pepper mustard and serve.

MUSTARD

Senape is the Italian word for that sprightly hot-dog enhancement served at ballparks across America, mustard. (The often-confused *mostarda* is a sweet fruit condiment served with tongue, brisket, zampone, or the king of Bolognese meat cookery, the bollito misto, a mixed boil of all of the above with capon, veal sausage, and turkey.) Although not a very traditional Italian condiment, mustard is invaluable for creating light sauces and vinaigrettes with explosive flavor. At Pó, mustard can be found in the house vinaigrette and in many of the sauces based on cooked vegetables or fruits. Used carefully, prepared mustard facilitates light emulsification to thicken sauces based on vinegar and oil.

Barbecued Swordfish with Black Olive–Cucumber Salad and Red Wine–Chive Vinaigrette

serves 4

Italians would pooh-pooh this dish for the salad and the sauce, but it is the number one seller at Pó whenever it's on the list of specials. Fresh swordfish is easy to find in the summer, but mako shark works quite well at less than half the price.

Red Wine–Chive Vinaigrette

½ cup extra-virgin **OLIVE OIL**

6 tablespoons **RED WINE VINEGAR**

3 tablespoons Dijon **MUSTARD**

¼ cup chopped **CHIVES**

SALT and **PEPPER**

In a blender, combine the olive oil, vinegar, and mustard and blend until smooth. Stir in the chives, and season with salt and pepper. Makes 1 cup.

4 6-ounce **SWORDFISH** steaks, about 1 inch thick

BARBECUE SAUCE

½ cup **BASIC TOMATO SAUCE** (page 84)

2 tablespoons **SUGAR**

2 tablespoons **BALSAMIC VINEGAR**

1 tablespoon hot red **PEPPER FLAKES**

BLACK OLIVE–CUCUMBER SALAD

1 large English **CUCUMBER**, peeled, halved, seeded, and cut into ¼-inch half-moons

1 cup black **OLIVES**, such as Gaeta

2 plum **TOMATOES**, cut into ⅛-inch cubes

2 tablespoons fresh **OREGANO** leaves

SALT and **PEPPER**

1 recipe **RED WINE–CHIVE VINAIGRETTE**

Prepare a hot fire in the charcoal grill or preheat the broiler.

Rinse the swordfish and pat dry.

Make the barbecue sauce. In a small mixing bowl, mix the tomato sauce, sugar, vinegar, and red pepper flakes and set aside.

Make the salad. In a medium mixing bowl, combine the cucumber and olives. Add the tomatoes and oregano, and mix well.

Brush the swordfish steaks with barbecue sauce and season with salt and pepper. Cook 3 minutes, then turn and spoon 2 tablespoons of barbecue sauce over each steak. Cook without turning about 4 minutes longer or until done.

Meanwhile, divide the cucumber salad among 4 plates. Lean 1 swordfish steak up against the salad on each plate. Drizzle with the vinaigrette and serve.

FLAVORED VINAIGRETTES

Here is the recipe for a basic flavored vinaigrette and several variations on the theme.

Blood Orange Vinaigrette
    2 tablespoons blood orange juice and pulp
    1 tablespoon Dijon mustard
    2 tablespoons red wine vinegar
    3/4 cup extra-virgin olive oil

Place all the ingredients in a blender and process until smooth.

To create variations on this theme you can substitute any of the following for the blood orange: 1/4 cup chopped roasted peppers; 1/4 cup chopped raw green apple with peel; 1/4 cup chopped roasted beets; 1/4 cup pureed cooked pumpkin.

Barbecued Red Mullet with
Warm Fennel Salad and Tangerines

serves 4

Small red mullet show up at fancier fish stores in the United States and every-where in the Mediterranean, and have a distinctive and rich flavor. If mullet is unavailable, use small snapper or even ocean perch for this delicate dish.

1 **FENNEL** bulb

6 tablespoons extra-virgin **OLIVE OIL**

4 **RED MULLET** (about 1 pound), scaled, gutted, and gills removed

SALT and **PEPPER**

4 **TANGERINES**

½ cup tiny green **OLIVES**, such as Anbequinas or Nyons

Preheat the grill or broiler.

Place a 12-inch skillet over medium-high heat. Cut off the fennel stalks, reserving the fronds. Cut the fennel bulb in half and then into ¼-inch match-sticks. Add 3 tablespoons of the virgin olive oil to the hot pan and toss in the fennel. Sauté until lightly browned and wilted, about 4 minutes. Set aside.

Brush the fish with 1 tablespoon olive oil. Season with salt and pepper and place on the grill. Cook 3 to 5 minutes per side or to your preferred degree of doneness. Keep warm.

With a very sharp knife or zester, remove the zest from the tangerines and reserve. Cut off any remaining peel and the pith, then cut between the mem-branes to free the individual segments, working over a bowl to catch the juice. Place the juice and segments in a large mixing bowl and toss in the warm cooked fennel, remaining olive oil, olives, and reserved fennel fronds. Season with salt and pepper and divide among 4 plates. Place a grilled fish on each plate and serve immediately.

Polenta-Crusted Pompano Salad with Sautéed Spicy Peppers, Chicory, and Tomato Oil

serves 4

Pompano from Florida is available in the winter months. It can be relatively tricky to fillet, so have your fishmonger do it if you're not up to the task—a slip-up could destroy the thin and fragile flesh. The hot and sweet peppers really make this a colorful plate.

8 ounces **CHICORY**, washed and spun dry

6 tablespoons extra-virgin **OLIVE OIL**

juice of ½ **LEMON**

SALT and **PEPPER**

4 fillets of **POMPANO**, sole, or trout

½ cup quick-cooking **POLENTA** or yellow cornmeal, for dredging

4 tablespoons freshly ground black **PEPPER**

1 recipe **SAUTÉED SPICY PEPPERS WITH MARJORAM VINAIGRETTE** (page 240)

½ cup **TOMATO OIL**

Tomato Oil

1 medium **TOMATO**

1 tablespoon **BALSAMIC VINEGAR**

1 tablespoon **CAPERS**, rinsed and drained

½ cup extra-virgin **OLIVE OIL**

Roughly chop the tomato and place in the blender with the vinegar, capers, and olive oil. Blend until smooth. Makes ¾ cup.

In a large mixing bowl, toss the chicory with 2 tablespoons olive oil, lemon juice, and salt and pepper to taste. Divide among 4 plates, placing a mound of salad in the center of each.

In a 10- to 12-inch sauté pan, heat the remaining olive oil until smoking over medium heat. Dredge the fish fillets in the polenta and sprinkle with pepper. Carefully place the fillets in the sauté pan and cook until golden brown, about 3 minutes per side.

Place a pompano fillet on each plate atop the chicory. Arrange the peppers around the plates, drizzle with the tomato oil, and serve immediately.

Eel Livornese

serves 4

I hesitated to include this classic Christmas Eve dish, but have opted to offer it because it represents everything delicious about the traditional meal of six fishes served at this special family meal. Eel can be purchased up and down the East Coast in midwinter, and is readily available around the holidays when there is a strong demand. If the eels are alive, have the fishmonger kill and skin them for you; it's rather daunting to nail them in the head at home.

2 pounds **EEL**, from sea or river, skinned and gutted

2 cups **BASIC TOMATO SAUCE** (page 84)

1 cup dry **RED WINE**

12 **CAPER BERRIES**

12 Gaeta **OLIVES**

1 tablespoon hot red **PEPPER FLAKES**

SALT and **PEPPER**

2 tablespoons chopped **FENNEL** fronds

Rinse the eel, pat dry, and cut into 4-inch-long pieces.

Preheat the oven to 450°F.

In a flameproof earthenware casserole, combine the tomato sauce, wine, caper berries, olives, and red pepper flakes and bring to a boil over medium heat. Season the eel pieces with salt and pepper and add to the boiling sauce. Place the casserole in the oven and bake until the eel is cooked through, about 20 minutes. Sprinkle with the chopped fennel and serve immediately.

Frogs' Legs with Garlic, Nosiola, and Radicchio

serves 4

Gianni and I ate this dish near Lago di Garda on our way to a casino in Ticino, a Swiss-Italian duty-free zone on the Swiss border. The food there is quite delicate and the local oil is surprisingly perfumed, resulting in a very pleasant combination of flavors at the base of the Alps somehow reminiscent of the seaside. Be careful not to overcook the radicchio at the end, as it will quickly discolor and become bitter.

4 pairs of **FROGS' LEGS**

SALT and **PEPPER**

½ cup extra-virgin **OLIVE OIL**, preferably
    from Lago di Garda

4 **GARLIC** cloves, thinly sliced

juice and zest of 1 **LEMON**

1 green **APPLE**, peeled, cored, and cut into
    ⅛-inch dice

½ cup dry, fruity **WHITE WINE**, such as
    Nosiola, Moscato Giallo, or Müller-Thurgau

2 tablespoons unsalted **BUTTER**

1 small head **RADICCHIO**, finely shredded

¼ cup fresh **BREAD CRUMBS**

¼ cup finely chopped Italian **PARSLEY**

Rinse, clean, and separate the frogs' legs. Pat dry. Season with salt and pepper.

In a large 12- to 14-inch sauté pan, heat the olive oil until smoking over medium heat. Add the frogs' legs and sauté until light golden brown on one side. Turn the legs over and add the garlic. Cook until the garlic is light golden brown, then add the lemon juice, apple pieces, and wine. Cook until the liquid is reduced by half, about 2 minutes. Add the butter, shaking the pan until incorporated. Add the radicchio and bread crumbs, toss to coat the frogs' legs, and pour into a bowl. Sprinkle with the lemon zest and parsley and serve.

Carne

Meat

CARNE

Some of the most glorious and elaborate meat and game dishes in all of Italy come from Bologna and its environs. At La Volta, we served them on holidays and weekends, most often at lunch, to affluent families on country excursions, as well as to locals giving mom or grandma a special day off. One of Italy's greatest dishes of all, the Homeric bollito misto, is a specialty of Bologna, served with green sauce, red sauce, and *mostarda*, pickled sweet fruits with mustard seeds and pepper. We also served zampone and cotecchino sausage, both elaborate paeans to Bologna's rich tradition of hog butchering and her flavorful, fat, and educated history. Being so near the Tuscan border, we also served the straightforward grilled meats favored by the slender, sober steak eaters to the south. Dishes like the classic steak Fiorentina were served with nothing more than simple sautéed spinach and a drizzle of exquisitely perfumed oil.

Notwithstanding the great beef to the east in Romagna, the Emiliani mostly used the pig, and at La Volta we used pork even for our scaloppini and our cotoletta Milanese. These pork dishes are traditionally made only in the Emilia part of Emilia-Romagna, not in the rest of northern Italy, where Italy's only plain stretches from the mountain's feet in Piemonte to the hills of Friuli and affords the inhabitants a wealth of beef and rich cow's milk cheeses. Elsewhere, where the land is too austere to support cattle, lamb and sheep are the meats of choice. Rome's lamb chops *scottaditi* are a national treasure, and the braised lamb shanks served in Foggia epitomize the splendor of this dish. Every region in Italy has recipes for poultry, especially rabbit (which has yet to catch on here in Bugs Bunny town), but also chicken, turkey, and both farmed and wild game birds.

To Europeans, the meat in America is the stuff of dreams. Unfortunately, artisanal butchery here has fallen by the wayside, giving way to bins of plastic-wrapped steaks at massive supermarkets. It is rare to find organ meats or hand-made sausages in such outlets, and even rarer to see such labors of love as cotecchino sausages hanging in the butcher shops. As with all food products, I recommend finding a good purveyor and developing a relationship with him or her, but with meat it becomes a reason to live. Cured and smoked meats are best purchased from the artist-butcher who made them.

Chicken Thighs with Saffron, Green Olives, and Mint

serves 6

The thighs are without a doubt the favorite part of the chicken for many of my chef and foodie friends. Nearly impossible to overcook, their juicy flesh can be reheated several times and never dries out. Unfortunately, the average restaurant customer tends to think just about the opposite, so whenever a dish like this is on the menu, it's pretty easy to guess what the staff meal will be. Serve this on a bed of couscous.

12 **CHICKEN THIGHS** (2½ to 3 pounds)

SALT and **PEPPER**

all-purpose **FLOUR**, for dredging

¼ cup extra-virgin **OLIVE OIL**

2 large **RED ONIONS**, thinly sliced

½ teaspoon **SAFFRON** threads

1 cup small green **OLIVES**

1 medium **CARROT**, finely chopped

3 cups **CHICKEN STOCK**

½ cup fresh **MINT** leaves

Season the chicken thighs liberally with salt and pepper and dredge in flour. In a heavy-bottomed casserole, heat the olive oil until smoking. Add 6 thighs at a time and brown well on all sides over medium-high heat. Transfer to a plate and repeat with the remaining thighs. When well browned, remove the thighs and add the sliced onions and saffron to the casserole. Cook over low heat until the onions have softened, 8 to 10 minutes. Add the olives, carrot, and stock and bring to a boil.

Return the chicken pieces to the casserole, submerging them in the stock, and bring to a boil. Lower the heat to a simmer, cover the pot tightly and simmer 1 hour. Remove the lid and cook 10 minutes uncovered.

Remove the chicken thighs from the casserole and arrange on a platter. Season the sauce with salt and pepper and stir in the mint leaves. Pour the sauce over the chicken thighs and serve.

Balsamic Glazed Chicken with Grilled Radicchio

serves 4

Around my house this simple roasted chicken is one of our favorite things to have on my day off. There are few things more satisfying to eat—or as easy to prepare and clean up—than a whole roasted bird. It's also a great way to use up the flavorful but inedible rinds from prosciutto and Parmigiano-Reggiano cheese. I love bitter radicchio di Treviso, and it is particularly delicious with the pan juices from the roasted onions and chicken splashed over it.

1 3½- to 4-pound **CHICKEN**

2 **GARLIC** cloves, finely minced

4 tablespoons chopped **ROSEMARY** leaves

2 tablespoons freshly ground black **PEPPER**

1 teaspoon **SEA SALT**

5 tablespoons extra-virgin **OLIVE OIL**

2-ounce piece **PROSCIUTTO RIND** or bacon

2-ounce piece **PARMIGIANO-REGGIANO RIND**

2 medium **RED ONIONS**, sliced into 1-inch disks

¾ cup **LAMBRUSCO** or other dry red wine

½ cup **BALSAMIC VINEGAR**

6 large heads **RADICCHIO** di Treviso

Rinse the chicken and pat dry. Remove the giblets and set aside.

Combine the garlic, rosemary, black pepper, and sea salt and mix with 3 tablespoons olive oil. Rub the outside of the chicken all over with the rosemary mixture. Place the prosciutto and cheese rinds inside the cavity, cover, and refrigerate for 3 hours or overnight.

Preheat the oven to 475° F.

Place the onion slices and reserved giblets in the bottom of a small, heavy-bottomed roasting pan. Place the chicken on top of the onions, breast side up. Pour the wine over the chicken and rub all over with ¼ cup of the vinegar. Roast in the oven for 1 hour and 10 minutes, or until a skewer pushed into the thickest part of the thigh shows clear—not bloody—juices. Remove the pan from the oven and let the chicken rest for 5 minutes.

Preheat the grill or broiler.

Halve the radicchio lengthwise and grill for 3 to 4 minutes per side. Brush with the remaining olive oil and set aside.

Transfer the chicken to a carving platter and degrease the pan juices. Combine the onions and giblets with the pan juices. Carve the chicken, drizzle with the remaining ¼ cup vinegar, and serve immediately over the radicchio. Pass the giblet gravy separately.

CHICKEN

Chickens have been domesticated for their meat in the Mediterranean since 400 B.C. and since 1000 B.C. in Southeast Asia. Hens have been traditionally killed at the end of their productive days, generally about two years, an age by which muscle tissue has toughened and become sinewy and difficult to eat simply roasted (hence the phrase "from old hens, you make good broth"). Capon is a castrated male bird, fattened to two to three times the size of its sexually able brothers, with a more delicate flavor, even in its leg meat. Prized in Italy, particularly around Christmas, capons sell for exorbitant prices compared to equally delicious yet less chic turkeys.

Guinea hens are black pullets that originated in Africa. They have a darker, richer flesh than their Kentucky fried cousins. Quite popular in Italy, they are usually a hunter's catch as opposed to domesticated and should be consumed young, weighing in at less than a kilo.

When buying chickens, look for whole birds with shiny, flexible skin devoid of discoloration or worn areas. Birds with heads should have flexible, rubbery beaks and those with feet should have flexible toes with no hard scales or cracking. To store, always wipe birds with a moist towel, remove the gizzards and liver, and wrap in waxed paper. I always prefer higher to lower heat for cooking poultry, and this is one food that should never be served medium-rare. Always cook until the juices that run from a hole stuck in the thickest part of the thigh run clear, not pink.

Cool Chicken Braciole Messinese

serves 4

Braciole generally refers to the braised, rolled beef concoction sold from food stands at street fairs, but I have taken poetic license with the technique and substituted boneless chicken legs. This dish is perfect for a party because it can be made a day in advance. The Messinese style refers to the Strait of Messina, between Sicily and the mainland of Italy, and generally implies the presence of pine nuts, tomatoes, and often capers.

1¼ cups **PINE NUTS**

½ cup freshly grated **PECORINO ROMANO** cheese

1 teaspoon grated **NUTMEG**

4 **CHICKEN LEG** quarters, butterflied open and thigh and drumstick bones

removed (this can be done by your butcher)

SALT and **PEPPER**

2 cups chopped fresh **TOMATOES**

¼ cup small black **OLIVES**, such as Niçoise

2 tablespoons **CAPERS**, rinsed and drained

3 tablespoons extra-virgin **OLIVE OIL**

2 tablespoons **BALSAMIC VINEGAR**

1 teaspoon hot red **PEPPER FLAKES** or more to taste

2 tablespoons dried **CURRANTS**

Preheat the oven to 450° F.

In a mixing bowl combine 1 cup of the pine nuts, the pecorino, and nutmeg.

Place the chicken legs skin side down on a cutting board and season with salt and pepper. Divide the pine nut mixture among the chicken legs, filling them as full as possible. Fold the meat up and around the mixture and tie tightly with butcher's twine. Place the legs in a small roasting pan, flap side down. Roast for 25 to 30 minutes, or until browned and crispy and cooked through. Remove from oven and allow to cool.

In a medium bowl mix the chopped tomatoes, olives, capers, olive oil, vinegar, red pepper flakes, and currants. Place 1 piece of chicken on each plate and remove the butcher's twine. Season the sauce with salt and pepper and spoon some over each piece of chicken and serve.

Grilled Chicken in Tapenade with Broccoli Rabe

serves 4

At the restaurant I make this with baby chickens, but made with more readily available small chickens it's an easy, earthy dish for a backyard barbecue.

2 bunches **BROCCOLI RABE**

¾ cup **TAPENADE** (page 38)

1 cup extra-virgin **OLIVE OIL**

2 teaspoons fresh chopped **THYME LEAVES** or 1 teaspoon dry

2 teaspoons freshly ground black **PEPPER**

1 teaspoons hot red **PEPPER FLAKES**

2 small (2 to 2½ pound) **CHICKENS**, split down the backbone and flattened

2 **GARLIC** cloves, peeled and thinly sliced

SALT and **PEPPER**

Preheat the grill or broiler.

Bring a large pot of salted water to a boil and prepare an ice bath. Trim the bottom 2 inches from the broccoli rabe and boil for 2 minutes. Drain and refresh in the ice bath. Drain again and set aside.

In a large mixing bowl, mix ½ cup of the tapenade, ¾ cup of the oil, the thyme, pepper, and red pepper flakes until will blended. Add chickens and toss to coat.

Place the chickens skin side up on the grill, 8 to 10 inches from coals. (If using broiler, start skin side toward the heat 5 to 6 inches from heat source). In either case, cook slowly about 15 to 20 minutes per side until skin is crisp and brown and juices run clear when bird is pricked with a sharp knife at thickest part of thigh. Set aside and keep warm.

Heat the remaining olive oil and sliced garlic over medium heat until the garlic is lightly browned. Add the broccoli rabe and toss until well heated but not browned. Season with salt and pepper and arrange on 4 plates. With a sharp knife, cut the birds down the breast bone. Place one half over the broccoli rabe on each plate. Spoon 1 tablespoon tapenade over each half and serve immediately.

Stuffed Turkey Breast with Pears, Chestnuts, and Rosemary

serves 4 to 6

I usually serve a whole turkey prepared in this manner at Thanksgiving, with the legs boned and filled with the same stuffing. It makes carving a breeze and also significantly reduces the cooking time, leaving me more time to enjoy my company. Cooked and chilled, this makes a great base for a light salad, served in thin slices with some lightly dressed greens sprinkled on top. Serve this with Red Wine Risotto (page 129).

¼ cup dried **CHESTNUTS** (available at Italian specialty stores)

½ large **TURKEY BREAST** with skin (approximately 2½ pounds), boned

2 Bosc **PEARS**, peeled, cored, and cut into ¼-inch cubes

3 tablespoons chopped fresh **ROSEMARY** leaves

1 cup fresh **BREAD CRUMBS**

2 **EGGS**, beaten

SALT and **PEPPER**

In a small saucepan, combine the chestnuts with water to cover. Bring to a boil and boil for 20 minutes. Drain well.

Preheat the oven to 425°F.

Have your butcher butterfly the raw turkey breast to a consistent ½-inch thickness. In a mixing bowl, stir together the chestnuts, pear cubes, rosemary leaves, bread crumbs, and eggs and mix well. Season the surface of the turkey breast with salt and pepper and lay the stuffing mix on top. Roll the breast and stuffing up like a jelly roll and tie with butcher's twine. Place in a roasting pan and roast for 60 to 75 minutes, until an instant-read thermometer reads 155°F. at the center. Remove from the oven and allow to rest 10 minutes before carving.

Braised Duck Legs with Dried Orange and Almonds

serves 4

Dried orange peel is available at many specialty shops and it contributes a great deal of orange flavor to slow-cooked dishes without adding too much sweetness. If you can't find it, substitute the zest of 4 oranges. The almonds add an almost Moroccan hint to the dish.

4 large **DUCK LEGS** (2 to 3 pounds)

SALT and **PEPPER**

6 tablespoons extra-virgin **OLIVE OIL**

FLOUR, for dredging

2 medium Spanish **ONIONS**, cut into $\frac{1}{4}$-inch slices

1 medium **LEEK**, cleaned and cut into $\frac{1}{2}$-inch slices

1 medium **CARROT**, cut into $\frac{1}{4}$-inch slices

$\frac{1}{2}$ cup **GRAND MARNIER** or other orange liqueur

1 cup dry **WHITE WINE**

2 cups **CHICKEN STOCK**

6 tablespoons **DRIED ORANGE PEEL** or orange zest

$\frac{3}{4}$ cup blanched sliced **ALMONDS**

Preheat the oven to 375° F.

Trim the duck legs of excess fat and season well with salt and pepper.

In a 6- to 8-quart heavy-bottomed casserole, heat the olive oil until smoking. Dredge the duck legs in flour and place carefully in the hot oil. Brown well on both sides for 8 to 10 minutes and remove. Add the onion, leek, and carrot and cook until brown and just softened, 8 to 10 minutes. Add the Grand Marnier, wine, stock, $\frac{1}{4}$ cup of the orange peel, and $\frac{1}{2}$ cup of the almonds and bring to a boil. Return the duck to the casserole and submerge in liquid. Cover tightly, place in the oven, and cook until duck is tender, $1\frac{1}{2}$ to 2 hours.

Transfer the duck legs to a platter. Season the cooking liquid with salt and pepper and spoon over the duck. Sprinkle with the remaining orange peel and almonds.

Duck Stew Foggia Style
with Olives and Fennel Seeds

serves 4

I read about this duck dish while researching a series of shows on Puglia and was fascinated by its technical similarity to French cooking. The flavors, however, betray its southern Italian roots. The sweet Aleatico wine in the sauce creates a sublime contrast to the intensity of the duck flesh when slowly cooked. If you can't find Aleatico, I recommend a sweet red vermouth —not nearly the same, but equally interesting with its herby backbone.

1 4-pound Muscovy **DUCK** or 2 wild ducks

6 tablespoons extra-virgin **OLIVE OIL**

8 ounces **PANCETTA**, cut into ¼-inch dice

1 large Spanish **ONION**, chopped into ¼-inch dice

2 **CELERY** stalks, cut into ¼-inch pieces

2 **CARROTS**, cut into ¼-inch rounds

1 tablespoon **FENNEL SEEDS**

2 cups green **OLIVES**, preferably from Ascoli

2 cups sweet Aleatico di Puglia **WINE** or sweet red vermouth

2 cups **BASIC TOMATO SAUCE** (page 84)

2 dried hot **CHILES**

SALT and **PEPPER**

Cut the duck into 12 pieces by splitting the breast and cutting each half into 3 pieces, then separating the thighs, drumsticks, and wings. Reserve the liver and set aside.

In an 8- to 10-quart heavy-bottomed braising pan or Dutch oven, heat the olive oil over medium heat until smoking. Add the duck skin side down and cook until the pieces are golden brown and most of fat has been rendered, 10 to 15 minutes. You may need to work in batches, cooking 4 to 6 pieces at a time.

Drain all but 2 tablespoons of fat from the pan and add the pancetta. Cook over medium heat until lightly browned, then add the onion, celery, carrots, and fennel seeds and cook until the vegetables are softened, about 10 minutes. Add the olives, wine, tomato sauce, and chiles and bring to a boil. Add the duck pieces and liver, submerging them in the liquid, and bring to a boil. Lower the heat and simmer 1½ hours, or until the duck is falling off the bone. Remove the duck pieces to a platter.

Using a wooden spoon, mash the liver to a fine paste and stir back into the sauce. Season the sauce with salt and pepper, pour over the duck, and serve.

WILD GAME

In Emilia-Romagna, the phrase "wild game" is a redundancy. Apart from domesticated rabbits and pigeons (called courtyard animals, or *del cortile*), all game is wild.

Game birds predominate and include quail, pheasant, mallard and teal ducks, woodcock, and ortolan. The latter are considered rare, but are consumed regularly. Game birds are hunted from the end of the summer through the first snowfall or hard freeze, usually in late December.

In Italy, as in France, game is often smoked, salted, or cooked and packed in fat to preserve the season's catch for the off season. It's during the fall that game cooking and eating are at their peak, and game is often served matched with other autumnal favorites such as truffles, porcini mushrooms, cardoons, and wine grapes. Wild boar and venison are hunted a little earlier until a little later in the year, although the presence of snow on the ground leads many hunters to refrain for reasons of sportsmanship; the clear trails of footprints in the snow make running the beasts to the ground too easy.

In recipes calling for wild boar, domestic pork is an acceptable substitute, though it is often too lean for many Italian uses. Texas boar is becoming increasingly available in the American market, and venison from New Zealand, although not truly wild, is also an excellent product.

Barbecued Goose Breast with Apricot Vinaigrette

serves 4

Goose breast (I get mine from Quattro Farms in upstate New York) is very similar to red meat, with much less fat but great flavor that is accentuated here first by the marinade and then later by the apricot sauce. The marinade is quite like a paste and later helps to develop a nice crusty outer skin. If you do not feel comfortable eating poultry cooked medium, avoid this dish altogether; cooked any more than that, the flesh becomes tough and dry. If you substitute duck breasts, reduce the cooking time by 3 to 4 minutes.

Apricot Vinaigrette

½ cup dried **APRICOTS**

2 cups boiling **WATER**

6 tablespoons **RED WINE VINEGAR**

2 tablespoons Dijon **MUSTARD**

½ cup extra-virgin **OLIVE OIL**

Combine the apricots and water in a saucepan and boil for 2 minutes. Drain the apricots and place in a blender with the vinegar and mustard. Blend until smooth, then drizzle in the olive oil until emulsified. Makes ¾ cup.

2 large single or 1 large double **GOOSE BREAST**, 2 to 3 pounds, or 4 duck breasts

¼ cup extra-virgin **OLIVE OIL**

3 tablespoons **SUGAR**

1 tablespoon **SALT**

1 tablespoon ground **CINNAMON**

1 tablespoon **CAYENNE** pepper

1 recipe **BALSAMIC GLAZED ONIONS** (page 232)

1 recipe **APRICOT VINAIGRETTE**

Remove the skin and any fat from the goose breast. In a mixing bowl, stir the together olive oil, sugar, salt, cinnamon, and cayenne. Rub the goose breast with the spice mixture, cover, and marinate overnight in refrigerator or 2 hours at room temperature.

Prepare a charcoal fire or preheat the grill.

Place the goose breast or breast halves over the hottest part of the fire and grill 8 to 10 minutes on the first side and 4 to 5 minutes after turning. The meat should register 125°F. on an instant-read thermometer.

Transfer the goose breast to a cutting board and let rest for 10 minutes. Carve into ¼-inch-thick slices and arrange around the glazed onions. Drizzle the meat with apricot vinaigrette and serve.

Grilled Squab with Pomegranate Molasses and Kale

serves 4

Faith Willinger spit-roasts squab for guests in the hearth of her Florentine kitchen, inspiring this variation that I serve at Pó. The tangy sour-sweet molasses, which is my addition, is a beautiful complement to barbecued birds. Game hens would be fine replacements for the squab.

MARINADE

½ cup extra-virgin **OLIVE OIL**

2 tablespoons **HONEY**

2 tablespoons **RED WINE VINEGAR**

2 tablespoons **PAPRIKA**

4 **SQUAB**, backbones removed and flattened by butcher

SALT and **PEPPER**

1 medium **RED ONION**, thinly sliced

3 tablespoons extra-virgin **OLIVE OIL**

juice and zest of 1 **LEMON**

4 cups shredded **KALE**, cut in ¼-inch ribbons

¾ cup **POMEGRANATE MOLASSES**

In a shallow dish, combine the marinade ingredients. Add the squab and turn to coat. Cover and marinate overnight in the refrigerator or for 3 hours at room temperature.

Preheat the grill or broiler.

Place the squab skin side down on the hottest part of the grill. Sprinkle with salt and pepper. Cook until the breast meat nearest the bone is medium to medium rare, 8 to 10 minutes on the first side and 4 to 5 minutes when turned over.

In a 12- to 14-inch skillet, sauté the onion in the olive oil until softened, 8 to 10 minutes. Add the lemon juice and zest and the kale and toss until wilted, 3 to 4 minutes. Season with salt and pepper and pile in the center of a serving platter. Arrange the squab over the greens, pour 3 tablespoons of pomegranate molasses over each bird, and serve immediately.

Grilled Guinea Fowl with Lentils and Green Apple Vinaigrette

serves 4

Guinea hen has especially rich and flavorful flesh that is even more intense in the legs. Although it takes a little time to remove the bones from the legs, you'll find that the final result really justifies the effort. The green apple vinaigrette will keep well for several weeks in the refrigerator, and can be served successfully with any grilled meat, particularly pork.

MARINADE

¼ cup extra-virgin **OLIVE OIL**

¼ cup **BALSAMIC VINEGAR**

1 tablespoon **HONEY**

1 tablespoon dried **THYME** leaves

Green Apple Vinaigrette

1 medium **GREEN APPLE**, such as Granny Smith, cored, seeded, and peeled

3 tablespoons Dijon **MUSTARD**

3 tablespoons **RED WINE VINEGAR**

½ cup extra-virgin **OLIVE OIL**

Chop the apple into ½-inch pieces and place in a blender. Add the mustard and vinegar and blend until smooth. With the motor still running, drizzle in the olive oil and blend until smooth. Makes 1 cup.

4 **GUINEA FOWL** or chicken leg and thigh quarters, butterflied open and leg and thigh bones removed

1 cup **LENTILS**

3 tablespoons extra-virgin **OLIVE OIL**

3 tablespoons **RED WINE VINEGAR**

1 tablespoon chopped fresh **ROSEMARY** leaves

1 **CELERY** stalk, finely chopped

½ medium **CARROT**, finely chopped

SALT and **PEPPER**

1 recipe **GREEN APPLE VINAIGRETTE**

In a mixing bowl, stir together the marinade ingredients. Add the boned leg quarters, cover, and marinate overnight in the refrigerator or for 2 hours at room temperature.

Boil the lentils in about 3 cups of water until tender but still al dente. Drain and transfer to a sauté pan with the olive oil, vinegar, rosemary, celery, and carrot. Bring to a boil, then remove from the heat and season with salt and pepper. Cool to room temperature.

Preheat the grill or broiler.

Remove the poultry from the marinade and pat dry. Place skin side down over the hottest part of the grill and cook until dark brown and crisp on the skin side, 6 to 7 minutes, 8 if you're using chicken. Season with salt and pepper, turn, and cook on the flesh side until just cooked through, 4 to 5 minutes, or 6 to 7 for chicken.

Arrange the lentils in the center of a serving platter and place the cooked leg quarters on the top. Drizzle with the vinaigrette and serve.

GRILLING AND THE BARBECUE

Grilling over hot coals has a rich tradition in all of Italian regional cooking. From the best grilled Fiorentina in the Chianti region to the barbecued whole fish served along the Amalfi coast, the simplicity, elegance, and—most important—clarity of flavor seem to ring truest in grilled foods. In Italy, a hardwood fire is usually started in the same oven used for baking bread, making pizza, or roasting meats. The fire eventually burns out, leaving the hot coals as the true heat source. For roasting or pizza making, the coals are left in the back of the oven and occasionally fed a small log to generate the oxygen-consuming flame so essential for a crisp crust. For grilling, the coals are dragged forward to the hearth and an iron grill is place over them.

In this country, charcoal reigns, but unfortunately it offers only a 30- to 40-minute cooking window. This works fine, provided the cook is prepared, the food requires a brief cooking time, and the guests all arrive at the appointed time. For better flavor and an extended cooking period, I advocate owning both a gas or charcoal grill and building a small pit or wood-burning oven in the backyard that can be fueled with wood. Allow the fire to burn down and occasionally stoke the coals with more wood while you wait for your hopelessly hip friends to finally arrive. Then place a grill over the coals, arrange some foil-wrapped vegetables along the perimeter, and grill to your Fiorentina's desire. In a pinch, however, or if you're grilling just a few shrimp, the broiler is a fine alternative.

Pheasant Breasts with Cider Vinegar, Apples, and Pomegranate

serves 4

In the tiny little town of Quistello, nestled on the plains between Mantova and Ferrara, my good friend Romano Tamani and his family run an unbelievably good restaurant called Ambasciata. It consistently provides one of my most memorable dining experiences in Italy, because the kitchen manages to juggle brilliantly the flavors and techniques of the region with the evolving needs of a modern kitchen at an international level. I most recently enjoyed this fabulous pheasant dish, very reminiscent of nouvelle cuisine yet totally at home in Romano's comfortably elegant dining room.

4 single **PHEASANT BREASTS**, boned

SALT and **PEPPER**

3 tablespoons **BUTTER**

4 **SHALLOTS**, finely chopped

½ cup cider **VINEGAR**

2 medium tart **APPLES**, such as Granny Smith, peeled and thinly sliced

1 cup **CHICKEN STOCK**

¼ cup heavy **CREAM**

seeds from ½ **POMEGRANATE**

Preheat the oven to 350°F.

Pound the breasts lightly with a meat mallet between sheets of oiled waxed paper to a consistent thickness. Season well with salt and pepper.

In a 10- to 12-inch ovenproof sauté pan, heat the butter over medium heat until the foam subsides. Add the pheasant breasts skin side down and cook until golden brown, 8 to 10 minutes. Place the pan in the oven and roast for 8 to 10 minutes. Transfer the breasts to a warm platter.

Add the shallots to the pan and stir. Cook over medium heat until softened, 4 to 5 minutes. Add the vinegar and apples, and cook until the vinegar is reduced by half. Stir in the stock and cream and boil until the sauce is again reduced by half. Return the pheasant to the pan and heat through. Season with salt and pepper and remove the breasts to a serving platter. Spoon the sauce over, sprinkle with pomegranate seeds, and serve immediately.

Braised Rabbit with Leeks, Rutabagas, and Vin Santo

serves 6

This is a variation on a dish I sampled at the great Monte Vertine winery just outside of Radda, in Chianti. Sergio Manetti and his son Martino are both major forces in the development of great Super Tuscan wine in the Chianti region, in addition to being renaissance men and generally cool guys. To accompany this course, they selected an unbelievable 1982 Monte Vertine Riserva, some of the last bottles on the estate at that time.

2 whole **RABBITS**, each cut into 8 serving pieces (2 front haunches,
  2 rear haunches, and 4 saddle pieces)

SALT and **PEPPER**

FLOUR, for dusting

6 tablespoons extra-virgin **OLIVE OIL**

4 medium **LEEKS**, cut into ½-inch-thick rounds and cleaned

1 large **RUTABAGA**, peeled and cut into ½-inch-thick cubes

1 cup **VIN SANTO**

1 cup **BASIC TOMATO SAUCE** (page 84)

3 cups **CHICKEN STOCK**

Preheat the oven to 375° F.

Season the rabbit pieces liberally with salt and pepper and dredge with flour. In a heavy-bottomed 6- to 8-quart casserole, heat the olive oil until smoking. Add 4 pieces of rabbit and cook until golden brown, turning often, 8 to 10 minutes. Remove to a plate and brown the remaining 4 pieces. Set aside.

To the same pan add the leeks and rutabaga and, stirring constantly, cook until lightly browned, 5 to 7 minutes. Add the wine, tomato sauce, and chicken stock and bring to a boil. Return the rabbit pieces to the pot, submerging them in the liquid, and bring to a boil. Cover the casserole with a tight-fitting lid or aluminum foil and cook in the oven for 1 hour and 15 minutes, or until the meat is falling off the bone.

Remove the pan from the oven and carefully remove the rabbit pieces. Taste the sauce and season with salt and pepper. Place the rabbit pieces in the center of a serving dish, pour the sauce over, and serve.

Grilled Rabbit Loins with Sweet Potatoes and Green Sauce

serves 4

The combination of sweet and sour potatoes with juicy grilled rabbit and a tangy green sauce might strike Italians as perplexing. To me, it makes perfect sense and is quite easy to prepare. Don't skip the brining step; it adds immeasurably to the rabbit's rich flavor and firm texture.

Green Sauce

2 slices day-old **BREAD**

¼ cup **WHITE WINE VINEGAR**

1 cup **PARSLEY** sprigs, tightly packed

2 tablespoons **CAPERS**, rinsed and drained

1 **GARLIC** clove, thinly sliced

½ cup cooked and chopped **SPINACH**

1 tablespoon chopped **THYME** leaves

1 tablespoon chopped **FENNEL FRONDS**

1 cup extra-virgin **OLIVE OIL**

SALT and **PEPPER**

Soak the bread in the vinegar for about 10 minutes. Squeeze the vinegar out of the bread with your hands and place in a food processor with the parsley, capers, garlic, spinach, thyme, fennel fronds, and half of the olive oil. Process until finely chopped. With the motor running, drizzle in the remaining ½ cup oil until a smooth creamy sauce is formed. Season with salt and pepper. Makes 1½ cups.

4 boneless **RABBIT LOINS**, with flap intact

1 cup cold **WATER**

½ cup **RED WINE VINEGAR**

4 tablespoons **SALT**

10 **PEPPERCORNS**

2 large **SWEET POTATOES**

3 tablespooons extra-virgin **OLIVE OIL**

3 tablespoons **BALSAMIC VINEGAR**

SALT and freshly ground black **PEPPER**

1 recipe **GREEN SAUCE**

In a mixing bowl, combine the rabbit with the water, vinegar, salt, and peppercorns and soak for 1 hour. Drain the rabbit, rinse, and pat dry.

Prepare a charcoal fire or preheat the grill.

Peel the sweet potatoes and cut into ½-inch cubes. Cook in boiling water until al dente, about 10 minutes. Drain thoroughly and while still warm, place in a mixing bowl with the olive oil, balsamic vinegar, salt, and lots of freshly ground black pepper. Toss gently and set aside.

Season the rabbit pieces with salt and pepper. Grill with the flap on on the hottest part of the barbecue until cooked through, 7 to 8 minutes on the first side and 3 to 4 minutes on the second.

Divide the sweet potatoes among 4 plates. Place 1 piece of grilled rabbit on each plate, drizzle with green sauce, and serve immediately.

The rich, haunting smell of meat on the grill or in the pan brings sweet memories of family feasts to all Italians.

Rabbit alla Cacciatora Barese

serves 4

Many Italian-Americans trace their roots to Puglia, and most seem to come from the province of Bari. I was there in spring of 1997 and was totally impressed by the depth of the traditional cooking in this southern province. One of the best meals we had was in a restaurant called Il Fornello da Ricci. After five different *antipasti* and two pasta courses, they brought out this exquisite rabbit preparation. I'll never forget it.

½ cup all-purpose **FLOUR**

SALT and **PEPPER**

1 **RABBIT**, cut into 8 serving pieces (2 front haunches, 2 rear haunches, and 4 saddle pieces), liver, heart, and kidneys reserved

4 tablespoons extra-virgin **OLIVE OIL**

1 medium Spanish **ONION**, chopped into ½-inch dice

2 whole dried **CHILES**, preferably cayenne

8 ounces **CREMINI** mushrooms, halved

¼ cup **SUN-DRIED TOMATOES**, cut into ⅛-inch strips

2 tablespoons **SUGAR**

juice and zest of 1 **ORANGE**

2 cups dry **WHITE WINE**

1 cup **BASIC TOMATO SAUCE** (page 84)

2 tablespoons chopped fresh **ROSEMARY** leaves

Season the flour with about 1 teaspoon salt and 1 teaspoon freshly ground black pepper. Rinse the rabbit pieces and pat dry, including the liver, heart, and kidneys. Dredge all pieces in the flour and shake off excess.

In a heavy-bottomed Dutch oven or casserole, heat the olive oil over medium heat until smoking. Cook the rabbit, 3 to 4 pieces at a time, until dark golden brown, about 20 minutes, and remove to a plate. Add the onion, chiles, mushrooms, tomatoes, and sugar and cook until the onion has softened, 8 to 10 minutes. Add the orange juice and wine and boil for 5 minutes. Add the tomato sauce and rabbit pieces and simmer uncovered for 45 to 50 minutes, or until the meat is tender and the sauce has reduced by two-thirds. Stir in the rosemary and check for seasoning. Place on a serving platter, sprinkle with the orange zest, and serve.

Pork Loin alla Porchetta (page 196)

Cool Chicken Braciole Messinese (page 178)

NEXT PAGE: Osso Buco with Toasted Pine Nut Gremolata (page 202)

Braised Stuffed Rabbit Legs with Walnuts, Prosecco, Dried Cherries, and Apricots

serves 4

Just as with chicken, my favorite part of the rabbit is invariably the legs, because even when cooked through they remain moist and flavorful. This dish from Pó was inspired by a braised rabbit dish Quintiglio prepared after his late-spring expeditions for greens and early porcini. You could simply braise the legs and omit the labor-intensive stuffing, if you prefer; the cooking time remains approximately the same.

4 **RABBIT** leg and thigh quarters

½ cup **WALNUTS**

2 **GARLIC** cloves

½ cup extra-virgin **OLIVE OIL**

1 teaspoon chopped fresh **ROSEMARY** leaves

1 tablespoon freshly ground black **PEPPER**

1 medium **RED ONION**, cut into 1-inch dice

¼ cup dried **CHERRIES**

¼ cup dried **APRICOTS**, cut into ⅛-inch strips

1 bottle **PROSECCO** or other sparkling wine

Butterfly and bone the rabbit legs or have it done by your butcher.

In a food processor, blend the walnuts, garlic, ¼ cup of the olive oil, the rosemary, and black pepper until a paste is formed. Spread the paste over the butterflied surfaces of the meat and roll each leg up. Tie securely with butcher's twine.

In a 10- to 12-inch sauté pan, heat the remaining ¼ cup oil until smoking. Add the stuffed rabbit legs and sauté on all sides. When fully browned, 10 to 12 minutes, add the onions, cherries, and apricots and sauté until softened, 6 to 7 minutes longer. Add the prosecco and bring to a boil, then lower the heat to a simmer and cover halfway. Cook the rabbit 50 to 60 minutes, until very tender, turning occasionally. If the liquid cooks down too much, add ¼ cup water as needed.

Remove the rabbit legs and cut the strings. Place on a platter, top with the fruit mixture, and serve.

Pork Shank with Garlic Cabbage

serves 4

Nineteen ninety-six was the year of the pork shank, and perhaps the very best rendition was the crispy behemoth created by my friend David Burke at New York's Maloney & Porcelli. This is a Friulian variation.

2 **PORK SHANKS** or shins

SALT and **PEPPER**

1 cup **LARD** or ½ cup virgin olive oil

½ medium Spanish **ONION**, cut into ½-inch dice

1 **CELERY** stalk, chopped into ½-inch pieces

1 medium **CARROT**, chopped into ¼-inch coins

6 **GARLIC** cloves, thinly sliced

1 sprig **ROSEMARY**

6 **JUNIPER BERRIES**

1 whole **CLOVE**

2 cups dry **WHITE WINE**

1 cup **VEAL STOCK** or chicken broth

2 tablespoons extra-virgin **OLIVE OIL**

1 medium white or purple **CABBAGE**, sliced ¼ inch thick (6 to 7 cups)

½ cup **RED WINE VINEGAR**

Rinse and dry the shanks and remove any hairs or hard skin; season with salt and pepper. In a heavy-bottomed Dutch oven, heat the lard or olive oil over medium heat. Add the shanks and sear until dark golden brown on all sides, about 10 to 12 minutes. Remove the shanks to a plate.

Drain all but 2 tablespoons of fat from the pan. Add the onion, celery, carrot, 2 cloves of sliced garlic, the rosemary, juniper berries, and clove. Cook until the vegetables are just softening, 4 to 5 minutes, then return the shanks to the pan, arranging them on top of the vegetables. Add the wine and stock and bring to a boil. Reduce the heat to a simmer and cover. Cook for 2 hours, turning every half hour; the meat will be falling off the bone.

Meanwhile, heat the olive oil in a 12- to 14-inch sauté pan until smoking.

Add the remaining garlic and cook until light golden brown, 1 to 2 minutes. Add the cabbage and vinegar and cook, stirring often, over medium-low heat until very tender, 20 to 25 minutes. Season with salt and pepper and set aside, covered, until the pork is ready.

Carve the pork off the bones into large chunks and serve with the cabbage.

Pork Scaloppina Perugina

serves 4

Perugia is a beautiful university town filled with gorgeous art, exquisite people, and some of the best Umbrian *trattoria* cooking you'll ever find, all at student prices. This pork dish is very popular with students and faculty alike.

4 tablespoons extra-virgin **OLIVE OIL**

4 scallops of boneless **PORK LOIN**, 1 inch thick

½ cup all-purpose **FLOUR**, seasoned with salt and pepper

4 ounces sliced **PROSCIUTTO**, cut into ¼-inch strips

2 **GARLIC** cloves, thinly sliced

2 tablespoons **CAPERS**, rinsed and drained

1½ cups **WHITE WINE**

4 **ANCHOVY** fillets, rinsed and chopped

zest of 2 **LEMONS**

6 **SAGE** leaves

1 cup **LENTILS**, cooked and kept warm (see page 65)

In a 12- to 14-inch sauté pan, heat the olive oil until smoking. Dredge the pork pieces in the seasoned flour and shake off excess. Sauté until golden brown on one side, 5 to 6 minutes. Turn and continue cooking 3 to 4 minutes. Remove to a plate and keep warm.

Drain the excess oil from the pan, then add the prosciutto, garlic, and capers and cook 2 minutes. Add the wine, anchovies, lemon zest, and sage. Stir well, then return the pork to the pan. Cook until heated through and the liquid is reduced by half, 8 to 10 minutes.

Place the pork pieces on a warm plate, cover with spoonfuls of sauce, and serve with warm lentils.

Pork Loin alla Porchetta

serves 6 to 8

A whole pig, with its bones removed and cavity stuffed with sausage and fennel, roasted slowly, is known as porchetta and is served at great parties, as well as from street carts along the highways outside of Florence. It's a bit laborious though, so often a boneless loin stands in for the pig, which makes a lot more sense for both home kitchens *and* mine at Pó. The leftovers make great sandwiches. Serve this with roasted potatoes and a simple salad.

4 pounds **PORK LOIN**

SALT and **PEPPER**

¼ cup extra-virgin **OLIVE OIL**

1 medium **ONION**, thinly sliced

1 **FENNEL** bulb, fronds chopped and reserved, bulb thinly sliced

2 pounds ground **PORK SHOULDER**

2 tablespoons **FENNEL SEEDS**

2 tablespoons freshly ground black **PEPPER**

2 tablespoons chopped fresh **ROSEMARY**

6 **GARLIC** cloves, thinly sliced

3 **EGGS**, beaten

4 **RED ONIONS**, halved

Preheat the oven to 425°F.

Have your butcher butterfly the pork loin to an even 1-inch thickness; you should have a flat piece of meat about 8 by 14 inches. Sprinkle with salt and pepper and set aside.

In a sauté pan, heat the olive oil until smoking. Add the onion and fennel bulb and sauté until softened and lightly browned, about 10 minutes. Add the ground pork, fennel seeds, black pepper, rosemary, and garlic and cook, stirring constantly, until the mixture takes on a light color, about 10 minutes. Allow to cool and drain any excess liquid. Mix in the chopped fennel fronds and eggs.

Spread the mixture over the pork loin and roll up like a jelly roll. Tie with butcher's twine and place in a roasting pan on top of the halved onions. Place in oven and roast 75 minutes, or until the interior temperature is 140°F.

Allow to rest for 10 minutes, then slice into 1-inch-thick pieces and serve.

Pork Loin with Caramelized Onions and Milk

Arista Toscana

serves 4

A Tuscan classic that translates well to the American kitchen, pork cooked in milk retains a rich moistness. The sauce looks like a broken mess when the pan comes out of the oven, but it achieves a fairly smooth texture in the blender. The leftovers, if there are any, make a great sandwich sliced paper-thin.

12 **GARLIC** cloves, peeled and left whole

2 large Spanish **ONIONS**, peeled

3-pound **PORK LOIN** with bone

SALT and **PEPPER**

3 cups whole **MILK**

Preheat the oven to 450° F.

Smash 4 of the garlic cloves to a paste and place in a roasting pan large enough to hold the pork loin. Slice the onions into 1-inch-thick rounds and arrange in the bottom of the pan in a single layer over the garlic. Season the roast all over with salt and pepper and make 4 deep incisions along the bone. Stuff 2 garlic cloves into each incision and place the pork loin on top of the onions and garlic. Pour 2 cups of the milk over the roast and place in the oven. After 65 minutes, add the remaining cup of milk and reduce the oven temperature to 425° F. Cook 30 minutes longer or until the onions are softened and an instant-read thermometer inserted in the thickest part of the roast reaches 160° F.

Remove the pan from the oven and transfer the pork roast to a warm platter. Place half the cooked onions and the pan juices in a blender and puree about 30 seconds or until smooth and thick. Arrange the remaining onions in a pile on the serving platter and cut the pork off the bone. Carve the meat into ½-inch-thick slices and arrange over the onions. Reheat the sauce if necessary, pour over the meat, and serve immediately.

Lamb Shanks with Artichokes and Olives

serves 4

In the early nineties, my good friend Tom Valenti single-handedly elevated the lamb shank to haute cuisine at a place called Alison on Dominick, in New York. Over the four years he was there, the price of these once economical shins doubled, as chef after chef copied his success in the tender and succulent meat department with both customers and critics. They qualify as a great dinner-party dish because they can sit in a warm oven for an hour with little loss of quality. Serve these with polenta.

12 **BABY ARTICHOKES**

4 large, meaty **LAMB SHANKS**

SALT and **PEPPER**

6 tablespoons extra-virgin **OLIVE OIL**

1 Spanish **ONION**, chopped into ¼-inch dice

12 **GARLIC** cloves, peeled and left whole

2 tablespoons chopped fresh **ROSEMARY** leaves

½ cup Gaeta **OLIVES**

1 cup dry **WHITE WINE**

1 cup **BASIC TOMATO SAUCE** (page 84)

1 cup **CHICKEN STOCK**

Preheat the oven to 375°F.

Trim off the tough outer leaves and stems from the artichokes and cut off the prickly leaf tips. Place in a bowl of acidulated water and set aside.

Rinse and dry the shanks and season liberally with salt and pepper. In a heavy-bottomed Dutch oven with a lid, heat the olive oil until smoking over medium-high heat. Sear the shanks until dark golden brown all over, 15 to 18 minutes. Remove the shanks and set aside.

Drain the artichokes and add to the pot along with the onion, garlic, and rosemary and cook until softened, 8 to 10 minutes. Add the olives, wine, tomato sauce, and stock and bring to a boil. Return the lamb shanks to the pan and bring back to a boil. Cover tightly, place in the oven, and cook for 1½ hours, until fork-tender. Remove and serve.

Grilled Lamb Chops Scottaditi with Pom-Pom Mushrooms, Garlic Confit, and Mint

serves 4

Scottaditi translates as "burn your fingers," meaning these chops look so good that you cannot resist picking them up the moment they come off the grill. Pom-pom mushrooms resemble little white sponges and are very susceptible to moisture. If you can't find them, substitute cremini, or even button mushrooms, which taste far better than usual when prepared this way.

5 tablespoons extra-virgin **OLIVE OIL**

20 **GARLIC** cloves, peeled and left whole

1 cup sweet **WHITE WINE**, such as Malvasia

2 cups dry **WHITE WINE**

8 rib **LAMB CHOPS**, 1¼ inches thick, trimmed

SALT and **PEPPER**

8 ounces **POM-POM** mushrooms, sliced ⅛ inch thick

4 **MINT** sprigs, leaves only

Prepare a charcoal fire or preheat the broiler.

In an 8- to 10-inch skillet, heat 2 tablespoons of the olive oil over medium heat. Add the garlic and sauté slowly until browned on all sides, shaking the pan to keep them moving, about 10 minutes. Add the sweet and dry wines and cook at a low boil until the liquid is reduced to ¼ cup, about 15 minutes. The garlic should be very soft at this point. Set aside.

Season the lamb chops with salt and pepper and grill or broil until medium rare, 4 to 5 minutes per side.

Heat the remaining 3 tablespoons olive oil in a 12- to 14-inch sauté pan over high heat. Add the mushrooms and sauté over high heat until brown and soft, 3 to 4 minutes. Add the garlic and wine reduction to the mushrooms and stir to coat. Stir in the mint leaves and remove from the heat.

Season the mushroom and garlic mixture with salt and pepper and spoon onto the centers of 4 serving plates. Lean 2 chops against the mushroom mix on each plate. Serve immediately.

Stracotto of Lamb with Olives and Orange

serves 4

Stracotto translates to "overcooked" in English. This melting dish is delicious for a cold winter night, when the delicate combination of olives and orange adds warming depth of flavor to the tangy gaminess of not-so-young lamb. Serve with cubes of sautéed pumpkin or butternut squash.

½ boneless **LEG OF LAMB** (about 5 pounds), butterflied

SALT and **PEPPER**

¼ cup extra-virgin **OLIVE OIL**

2 medium **RED ONIONS**, chopped into ½-inch dice

4 **GARLIC** cloves, peeled and left whole

2 **ANCHOVY** fillets, rinsed and dried

2 **ORANGES**, quartered, seeded, and sliced into ¼-inch quarter-moons

1 cup Tuscan green **OLIVES** or picholines

½ cup fresh **ORANGE JUICE**

1 cup Chianti or other dry **RED WINE**

1 cup **BASIC TOMATO SAUCE** (page 84)

Preheat the oven to 350° F.

Trim most of the fat from the lamb and season to taste with the salt and pepper. In a large, heavy-bottomed casserole, heat the oil until almost smoking. Brown the lamb on both sides until dark golden brown and remove to a side dish. Add the onions, garlic, anchovies, and orange pieces to the casserole and cook over medium heat until softened, 4 to 6 minutes, scraping the casserole bottom with a wooden spoon to loosen the brown bits. Add the olives, orange juice, wine, and tomato sauce and bring to a boil. Return the lamb to the casserole, lower the heat to a simmer, cover, and cook for 70 minutes, or until fork-tender. Remove the lid, raise the heat to medium high, and cook until the sauce is reduced to 3 cups. Slice and serve with the sauce.

Veal Shin with Marjoram

serves 4

Stinco, or veal shin, is made with precisely the same cut of meat as Osso Buco (page 202), but it is cooked whole and carved before serving. Marjoram is used frequently in Rome and points south, and to me is far more interesting than its blander, pizza-riding cousin, oregano. Serve this with broccoli or spinach.

1 whole **VEAL SHIN**, uncut (5 to 6 pounds)

SALT and **PEPPER**

6 tablespoons extra-virgin **OLIVE OIL**

1 medium **RED ONION**, chopped into ½-inch dice

1 **CARROT**, chopped in ¼-inch rounds

1 **CELERY** stalk, chopped into ½-inch pieces

6 **SAGE** leaves

1 bunch **MARJORAM**

1½ cups dry **WHITE WINE**

1 cup **BASIC TOMATO SAUCE** (page 84)

4 **ANCHOVY** fillets, rinsed and dried

Rinse and dry the veal shin. Season liberally with salt and pepper.

In a Dutch oven just large enough to hold the shin, heat the olive oil until just smoking. Place the meat in the pan and brown evenly on all sides, about 10 minutes. Remove to a plate. Add the onion, carrot, celery, sage, and marjoram to the pan. Cook until softened, about 10 minutes. Add the wine, tomato sauce, and anchovies and bring to a boil. Add the meat and return to a boil. Lower the heat to a simmer, cover tightly, and simmer for 2 hours (or bake at 350° F. for same amount of time, turning once), or until fork-tender.

Osso Buco with Toasted Pine Nut Gremolata

serves 4

Gremolata

¼ cup finely chopped Italian **PARSLEY**

¼ cup **PINE NUTS**, toasted under the
broiler until dark brown

zest of 1 **LEMON**

Mix the parsley, pine nuts, and lemon zest
loosely in a small bowl. Set aside until ready
to serve. Makes ½ cup.

This is the Pó rendition of the renowned braised veal
shanks served often with saffron-drenched "risotto
Milanese." The true trick to all braised dishes is the very
first step: carefully and comprehensively browning the
pieces to a deep golden brown. This not only makes for a
delicious, full-flavored piece of meat, but also contributes
to a rich and complex sauce. Contrary to popular belief,
you *can* overcook veal shanks and it is important that they
do not dry out, so pay careful attention to the final half
hour of cooking time. The meat must still offer a bit of
resistance when poked with a fork, but fall away from the
bone with a little firm pressure. As with all great dishes,
the more often you prepare them, the better your final
results will become.

4 **VEAL SHANKS**, cut 3 inches thick (about 3½ to 4 pounds)

SALT and **PEPPER**

6 tablespoons extra-virgin **OLIVE OIL**

1 medium **CARROT**, chopped into ¼-inch-thick coins

1 small Spanish **ONION**, chopped into ½-inch dice

1 **CELERY** stalk, chopped into ¼-inch slices

2 tablespoons chopped fresh **THYME** leaves

2 cups **BASIC TOMATO SAUCE** (page 84)

2 cups **CHICKEN STOCK**

2 cups dry **WHITE WINE**

1 recipe **RISOTTO MILANESE** (page 127)

1 recipe **GREMOLATA**

Preheat the oven to 375° F.

Season the shanks all over with salt and pepper. In a heavy-bottomed 6- to 8-
quart casserole, heat the olive oil until smoking. Place the shanks in the pan
and brown all over, turning to get every surface, 12 to 15 minutes. Remove

the shanks and set aside. Reduce the heat to medium, add the carrot, onion, celery, and thyme leaves and cook, stirring regularly, until golden brown and slightly softened, 8 to 10 minutes. Add the tomato sauce, chicken stock, and wine and bring to boil. Place shanks back into pan, making sure they are submerged at least halfway. If shanks are not covered halfway, add more stock. Cover the pan with tight-fitting lid or aluminum foil. Place in oven for 2 to 2½ hours and cook until meat is nearly falling off the bone.

Remove the casserole from the oven and let stand 10 minutes before serving with risotto Milanese and gremolata.

Stuffed Veal Rolls

Tomaxelle

serves 4

For my second appearance at the Degustibus Cooking School at Macy's, I prepared these brainlessly easy Ligurian rolls. I was a lot less nervous than on my previous appearance, but I still showed up with my full team an hour early. I take the same approach to restaurant cooking and home cooking: I'd rather start two hours early and relax until people arrive than be furiously prepping up to the last moment. These little rolls work just as well with pork loin.

4 **VEAL LOIN** scallops, ¾ inch thick (about 1 pound)

SALT and **PEPPER**

¼ cup extra-virgin **OLIVE OIL**

½ medium **RED ONION**, chopped into ¼-inch dice

4 **GARLIC** cloves, thinly sliced

1 tablespoon fresh **THYME** leaves

8 ounces **CHANTERELLES** or other wild mushrooms,
    sliced into ¼-inch pieces

¼ cup **PINE NUTS**

¼ cup chopped fresh **MARJORAM** leaves

½ cup finely chopped Italian **PARSLEY**

¼ cup freshly grated **PECORINO** cheese

2 **EGGS**

1 cup dry **WHITE WINE**

1 cup **BASIC TOMATO SAUCE** (page 84)

Preheat the oven to 425°F.

Using a meat mallet, pound the veal pieces between layers of oiled waxed paper until they are ⅛ inch thick. Season with salt and pepper and set aside.

In a 12- to 14-inch ovenproof sauté pan, heat the olive oil until just smoking over medium heat. Add the onion, garlic, and thyme and cook until light golden brown, about 3 minutes. Add the mushrooms and cook until softened, 8 to 10 minutes. Remove two-thirds of the mushroom mixture to a bowl and allow to cool, leaving the remaining third to cool in the pan.

To the cooled mushrooms in the bowl add the pine nuts, marjoram, parsley, grated cheese, and eggs and stir to mix well. Add the wine and tomato sauce to the mushrooms remaining in the pan and stir to mix.

Lay the 4 pounded veal pieces on a work surface and season with salt and pepper. Divide the pine nut mixture among them. Roll each piece jelly roll fashion and tie securely with butcher's twine. Place the rolls in the pan with the sauce and mushrooms and bake for 35 to 40 minutes. To serve, snip the strings off the veal rolls and place in the center of a platter. Spoon the sauce over the rolls and serve.

WILD MUSHROOMS

Wild mushrooms are truly wild in many parts of Italy. In the cool early autumn, particularly after a warm, late summer with just enough rain, Italian foragers tromp to their special spots amid great secrecy and excitement, searching out the truly luxurious riches of the forests and fields. Many restaurants in funghi-rich areas, including the lower Reno Valley (where La Volta was), prepare entire meals around a treasure trove of porcini, caesar's mushroom (*Amanita caesarea*), oyster, or chanterelle mushrooms. During the spring and fall seasons, funghi hunters gather in the cafés and bars, alternately bragging or complaining of the quantity of fungal comestibles they have unearthed, speculating about the proper conditions or the lack thereof.

When buying mushrooms, look for firm and relatively dry caps and stems. Bruised or obviously damaged mushrooms should be avoided except in the case of split porcini, which have been opened to show their lack of worm infestation. Store mushrooms in the coolest part of the house, wrapped in paper, not plastic, and use them quickly, as they do not age to any advantage. Mushrooms should be foraged in the wild only by experts, as there are several cognates, many of them poisonous, for each species. If ever in doubt, throw the mushrooms out; no one dies from mushrooms in the trash.

Rolled Flank Steak with Green Olives and Oregano

serves 4

This is my variation on the San-whomever-festival staple that is served across the United States wherever there are Italian-American communities. During New York's *festa di San Gennaro* tens of thousands of *paesanos* descend on Little Italy to consume mass quantities of food prepared in the Napolitano tradition. Having tasted the real things in Napoli, it's sad to see such poorly prepared food, because the originals are exemplars of Italian cooking.

3 cups **BASIC TOMATO SAUCE** (page 84)

1 cup green Italian **OLIVES**, preferably Ascolane

3 tablespoons chopped fresh **OREGANO** leaves

½ cup freshly grated **PARMIGIANO-REGGIANO** cheese

1 cup finely chopped Italian **PARSLEY**

¼ teaspoon freshly grated **NUTMEG**

1¾ pound beef **FLANK STEAK**, sliced into 8 thin scallops

SALT and **PEPPER**

FLOUR, for dusting

¼ cup extra-virgin **OLIVE OIL**

½ cup dry **RED WINE**

In a medium saucepan, combine the tomato sauce, olives, and 2 tablespoons of the oregano and bring to a boil. Reduce the heat and simmer while you assemble the braciole.

In a mixing bowl, mix the cheese, parsley, and nutmeg until well blended. Lay the pieces of steak out on a board and season with salt and pepper. Divide the cheese mixture evenly over the beef, spreading to form a thin layer on top of each piece. Roll up each piece like a jelly roll and tie securely with a piece of butcher's twine. Season with salt and pepper and roll in flour to coat lightly.

In a 12- to 14-inch skillet, heat the olive oil until smoking. Place 4 rolled steak pieces at a time in the skillet and brown evenly, rolling with tongs or a wooden spoon. Transfer to a plate and repeat with remaining 4 rolls. Pour off the cooking oil. Return the skillet to the heat and add the wine, stirring the bottom of the skillet with a wooden spoon to loosen the browned bits. Add the simmering tomato sauce and bring to a boil. Add the beef rolls and simmer uncovered 10 to 15 minutes, until the meat is cooked through. Remove the meat to a heated platter, pour the sauce over, and garnish with the remaining tablespoon of oregano.

Barbecued Veal Skewers Uccelli Scappati

"Escaped Birds"

serves 4

The title refers to birds that the hunter fails to bring home after a day's hunting in the fields and is the cook's response to a meal without the expected catch. Polenta flavored with tarragon suits the dish well.

8 pieces **VEAL LEG,** sliced thin by your butcher (about 1½ pounds)

8 thin slices **PROSCIUTTO** (about 4 ounces)

16 **SAGE** leaves

½ cup finely chopped Italian **PARSLEY**

8 1-inch cubes **PANCETTA** or slab bacon (8 ounces)

6 tablespoons (¾ stick) unsalted **BUTTER**

LEMON wedges

Soak 4 12-inch bamboo skewers in water for at least 30 minutes.

Pound the veal pieces to a ¼-inch thickness and spread out on a work surface. Place 1 prosciutto slice on each and top with 2 sage leaves and a sprinkling of parsley. Roll up each piece jelly roll fashion. Arrange 4 of the rolls side by side. Thread a cube of pancetta on a bamboo skewer, then thread through one end of all 4 rolls. Repeat with a second skewer and pancetta cube at the other end of the rolls. Place a second cube of pancetta on the end of each skewer and press so that the meat is pushed tightly together from both sides. Repeat with remaining rolls and skewers.

In a 10- to 12-inch sauté pan, heat the butter over medium heat until the foam subsides. Sauté the skewer sets for 10 minutes total, turning several times. Remove, cut in half between the skewers, and serve 1 hot skewer to each guest, with lemon wedges.

T-Bone Fiorentina with Sautéed Spinach and DaVero Olive Oil

serves 4

This recipe generated the largest number of recipe requests (and the most *oohs* and *aahs* from the production staff) of any dish I've ever demonstrated on *Molto Mario*. Traditionally cooked and simply presented, this is perhaps *the* definitive Tuscan dish.

1 T-bone **STEAK**, at least 3 inches thick (3 to 3½ pounds)

1 tablespoon chopped fresh **ROSEMARY** leaves

1 tablespoon chopped fresh **SAGE** leaves

1 tablespoon fresh **THYME** leaves

2 tablespoons freshly ground black **PEPPER**

2 tablespoons kosher **SALT**

1 cup plus 2 tablespoons best-quality extra-virgin **OLIVE OIL**

6 **GARLIC** cloves, thinly sliced

4 pounds **SPINACH**, washed, spun dry, stems removed

juice of 1 **LEMON**

SALT and **PEPPER**

Prepare a charcoal fire or preheat the grill to medium-high heat.

Pat the steak dry. In a small bowl, combine the rosemary, sage, thyme, black pepper, and kosher salt until well blended. Coat the entire steak with the spice mix and brush with 2 tablespoons of the olive oil. Place on the grill and cook until well charred, about 12 minutes on the first side and about 9 minutes on the second side. Let stand 5 minutes.

Meanwhile, in a 12- to 14-inch sauté pan, heat ¼ cup olive oil until smoking. Add the garlic and cook until light brown, 3 to 4 minutes. Add the spinach and stir quickly, cooking just until wilted. Remove from the heat, add the lemon juice and salt and pepper, and set aside.

Carve the fillet and strip steaks off the bone and slice. Divide the spinach and steak among 4 plates, giving each some of the fillet, and drizzle each serving with a few tablespoons of the remaining olive oil.

Beef Braised in Barolo

serves 6

This Piemontese classic is the perfect dish for showcasing a complex older wine. I find that I prefer to serve cellar selections with simple dishes, as opposed to pushing the envelope with many flavors and challenging preparations. With very complex dishes, conversely, I prefer a younger, more straightforward, less intense wine.

2 pounds beef **BRISKET**

SALT and **PEPPER**

6 tablespoons extra-virgin **OLIVE OIL**

1 medium **CARROT**, finely chopped

1 medium Spanish **ONION**, finely chopped

1 **CELERY** stalk, finely chopped

4 ounces **PANCETTA** or slab bacon, cut into ¼-inch dice

1 bottle Barolo or other full-bodied **RED WINE**

2 cups **BASIC TOMATO SAUCE** (page 84)

1 recipe **TURNIP "RISOTTO"** (page 241)

Season the brisket liberally with salt and pepper.

In a 6- to 8-quart heavy-bottomed casserole, heat the olive oil until smoking. Add the brisket and brown all over, turning repeatedly, until dark golden brown, 10 to 12 minutes. Remove the beef and set aside.

Pour the excess oil out of the pan and add the carrot, onion, celery, and pancetta and cook until light brown and starting to soften. Add the wine and tomato sauce and bring to a boil. Return the meat to the pan, lower heat to a simmer, and cook until the meat is very tender, 2½ to 3½ hours. Check the heat often; if the liquid is boiling hard, lower the heat.

Transfer the meat to a cutting board. Over high heat, reduce the cooking liquid to 2½ to 3 cups and season with salt and pepper.

Mound the turnip "risotto" in the center of a serving platter. Slice the meat and arrange over the turnips. Pour sauce over all and serve immediately.

Zampone with Potatoes and Balsamic Vinaigrette

serves 4

Zampone is the king of Emilian sausages and, along with the salama al sugo from Ferrara, it reigns over the Christmas table and the classic bollito misto. Similar to the cotecchino but stuffed into an entire pig's foot, hoof and all, zampone creates a dramatic and beautiful presentation for any celebration. At Pó, we accompany it with a balsamic vinaigrette because the truly traditional condiment of aged balsamic vinegar is too costly.

Balsamic Vinaigrette

¼ cup Dijon **MUSTARD**

¼ cup **BALSAMIC VINEGAR**

¾ cup extra-virgin **OLIVE OIL**

¼ cup freshly snipped **CHIVES**

SALT and **PEPPER**

In a medium mixing bowl, stir together the mustard and vinegar. Slowly add the olive oil in a thin stream to form an emulsion, stirring constantly until all the oil is added. Add the chives and check the seasoning. Makes 1½ cups.

1 small **ZAMPONE** sausage (4 to 5 pounds)

4 tablespoons (½ stick) unsalted **BUTTER**

2 pounds russet **POTATOES**, peeled and cut into ¾-inch cubes and placed in water

1 cup whole **MILK**

SALT and **PEPPER**

1 recipe **BALSAMIC VINAIGRETTE**

Wash and dry the zampone and prick it about 20 times all over with a needle. Place in a pot large enough to submerge the sausage in water. Fill the pot with warm water and bring just to a boil. Lower the heat slightly so the water remains almost boiling, cover, and cook for 1½ hours. Check the internal temperature of the sausage with a meat thermometer; an instant-read thermometer should read 150° F. Turn off the heat and let the sausage stand in the cooking water.

In a 12- to 14-inch nonstick sauté pan, melt the butter over medium heat. Add the potatoes and sauté slowly until lightly browned on all sides. Add the milk and simmer uncovered until the potatoes are soft, about 10 minutes. Season with salt and pepper and set aside in a warm place.

Remove the zampone from the water. Carefully slice half the sausage into ½-inch rounds. On a large serving platter, spread the potatoes around the base. Place the whole zampone piece and slices over the potatoes. Pour the balsamic vinaigrette into a serving pitcher, allowing each person to dress his or her own portion. Serve immediately.

SALUME

Salume, not to be confused with salami, refers to all cured and preserved pork and is produced at its apex in Emilia-Romagna. The undisputed king of cured meats is prosciutto di Parma—raw ham rubbed only with salt and hung for three to four hundred days in cool dark rooms by small artisanal producers. Quality is assured by the Consortium of Ham Producers, each ham tested by an inspector using a horse bone to probe and smell the meat nearest the bone. Those that pass are branded with the traditional five-point crown to be sold by the consortium in both local and interna-

tional markets. Artisan-made masterpieces of cotecchino and its elegant uncle, zampone, hang in the *salumerie* (I like to call them pork art galleries) next to coppa (cured pork shoulder), culatello (the heart of the prosciutto made in the plains around Parma), and mortadella and above ciccioli (pork rinds), strutto (lard for cooking), and salami (dried sausages in myriad variations). Although every region in Italy considers handmade salume an important part of its cooking heritage, the entire nation recognizes Emilia-Romagna as undisputed leader for the unerring consistency and quality of its cured meats.

OFFAL

Offal, also known as variety meats, is the edible nonmuscular parts of pigs, cows, and sheep. It has traditionally been highly prized in Italian cooking either as a delicacy, owing to scarceness, or as a necessity, to those whose consumption of meat may be limited to the animals they raise. Tending to be rich in iron and vitamin A, offal has a correspondingly higher cholesterol and fat content and should be eaten in moderation.

In the bovine department, tongue, liver, heart, kidneys, brains, tripe, tail, and sweetbreads are most widely consumed and usually preferred from a younger animal. In the ovine world, brains, kidneys, and sweetbreads are the most popular, with particular attention given to the thymus gland (sweetbreads). The best sweetbreads come from young animals, as age causes the hormone-producing gland to separate and atrophy.

When buying any offal, look for plump, shiny-skinned organs with a clean, meaty smell and a uniform light brown color devoid of dark spots or blemishes. It is generally best to prepare offal the day it is purchased, as all organs are highly perishable.

Sautéed Calf's Liver with Trumpet Mushrooms, Balsamic Vinegar, and Pancetta

serves 4

Liver and onions is a Venetian and American greasy spoon standard. Here it gets a Pó twist with trumpet mushrooms and a touch of balsamic vinegar. The pancetta adds great depth as well as a very cool textural contrast to the tender liver. I prefer liver cooked medium rare, but about half of our customers at Pó order it well done, and although it becomes slightly more firm, if cooked slowly at a simmer it does not have to dry out.

½ cup extra-virgin **OLIVE OIL**

2 large **ONIONS**, thinly sliced

4 ounces **PANCETTA** or slab bacon, cut into ¼-inch cubes

1 pound **CALF'S LIVER**, cut into 4 1-inch-thick slices

¼ cup **FLOUR** seasoned with **SALT** and **PEPPER**

¼ cup **BALSAMIC VINEGAR**

½ cup **BASIC TOMATO SAUCE** (page 84)

1 cup dry **WHITE WINE**

4 ounces **TRUMPET** or **OYSTER** mushrooms

¼ cup finely chopped Italian **PARSLEY**

In a large sauté pan, heat ¼ cup of the olive oil over medium heat. Add the onions and pancetta and cook slowly until onions are caramelized and pancetta is cooked through but not crisp, 8 to 12 minutes. Remove to a bowl.

Turn the heat up to medium-high and add the remaining ¼ cup oil. Dredge the liver in the seasoned flour and place all 4 pieces in the pan at once. Cook until quite dark brown on one side, 7 to 8 minutes, moving occasionally. Turn the liver over to the second side and add the vinegar, tomato sauce, onions, and pancetta. Bring to a boil, then reduce the heat, add the wine and mushrooms, and simmer 4 to 5 minutes, until the liver is medium-rare to medium, or a nice pink when cut in the center. Stir in the parsley.

Transfer the liver to a serving plate, pour sauce over, and serve.

Sweetbreads with Vin Santo, Shallots, and Napa Cabbage

serves 4

I had sweetbreads with Vin Santo at one of my favorite restaurants in all of Italy, La Tenda Rossa in Cerbaia, at the north end of Chianti. The richness of the delicate sweetbreads is perfectly balanced by the sweet acidity of a great Vin Santo such as the very dry one made by Monte Vertine or the delicately sweet one by Capezzana. If Vin Santo is unavailable, an acceptable substitute would be a fino or semi-dry sherry.

1½ pounds fresh **SWEETBREADS**

¼ cup distilled white **VINEGAR**

SALT and **PEPPER**

4 tablespoons extra-virgin **OLIVE OIL**

FLOUR, for dusting

12 **SHALLOTS**, peeled and halved crosswise

1 cup **VIN SANTO**

1 tablespoon **TOMATO PASTE**

1 tablespoon finely chopped fresh **ROSEMARY** leaves

1 cup **CHICKEN STOCK**

¼ head **NAPA CABBAGE**, thinly sliced (2 cups)

In a large saucepan, combine the sweetbreads with the vinegar, 1 teaspoon of salt, and cold water to cover. Bring to a boil, remove from the heat, and allow to stand 10 minutes. Drain the sweetbreads and cool in the refrigerator 30 minutes. Remove the center membrane, tough fibrous pieces, and connective tissue and cut into ³/₄-inch-thick slices.

In a 12- to 14-inch sauté pan, heat the olive oil until smoking. Season the sweetbreads with salt and pepper and dredge in flour. Sauté until dark golden brown on one side, 8 to 10 minutes. Turn, add the shallots, and cook until golden brown, 7 to 8 minutes. Add the wine, tomato paste, rosemary, and stock and bring to boil, stirring to distribute the tomato paste. Stir in the cabbage, cover, and simmer 2 minutes. Remove cover and simmer until quite thick, 3 to 4 more minutes. Remove the sweetbreads to a heated plate, pour the sauce over them, and serve.

Contorni

Vegetable

PUNTARELLE
ROMANE
£ 400
l.etto

and Side Dishes

CONTORNI

Near the end of a traditional *trattoria* menu you'll often find a section labeled *contorni*, or vegetable dishes. They can range from the incredibly simple, such as sliced tomatoes with oregano and Tuscan oil, to the complex, such as sformato of pumpkin. They can be chosen as simple *antipasto* or as a light main course, but are generally selected to augment the *secondo*, or main course. Unlike American restaurants where the main course is often accompanied by vegetables, a starch, or both, most Italian restaurants serve the *secondo* alone. This is because the traditional meal starts with an *antipasto*, often vegetables, and continues with a starch, the pasta, before reaching the *secondo*, which is usually meat, poultry, or fish. If you order veal scaloppine with porcini, that's exactly what you get on the plate. I learned this the hard way, after spending hours working on an elaborate vegetable terrine to accompany a duck dish I created for La Volta; each and every plate came back to the kitchen with everything eaten off of the plate except the vegetable terrine. The next day we put it on the *contorno* portion of the menu and we sold out.

When I had the good fortune to be invited to meals in Italian homes, however, I found most meals were served with vegetables. In modern homes, Italians, like their American counterparts, are limiting their fat intake and reducing their calories by eating meals composed of smaller dishes like the ones that follow in this chapter and avoiding large portions of meat. Seasonal variation as well as the pedigree of the produce are the keys to all of these recipes. Learn to inspect each thing you buy at the store carefully and thoughtfully. Buy produce at the farmer's market; support the local farmer. This is the way Italians shop; this is what makes even a simple plate of potatoes taste so good in Italy; this is the support you can give to *your* village.

Artichokes alla Giudea

serves 4

These artichokes typify the foods of the Jewish ghettoes of Rome and typify one of the greatest traditions in all Italian cooking, the art of frying. To impart the necessary flavor to the finished dish, it is essential to cook the artichokes in an excellent quality virgin olive oil. It helps to have a pair of professional-grade kitchen tongs to press down firmly on the chokes as they cook.

4 large **ARTICHOKES**

2 **LEMONS**, cut into wedges

juice of ½ **LEMON**

SALT and **PEPPER**

4 cups extra-virgin **OLIVE OIL**

Pull off the outer layers of deep green leaves from each artichoke and discard. Cut off the stems and set aside. Rub each cut with a lemon wedge. Place an artichoke on its side, cut off the top third, and discard. Using a pair of scissors, cut off any sharp pointed leaf tops that remain. Repeat for remaining artichokes. Soak the trimmed artichokes in about 2 quarts of cold water with about 2 tablespoons of lemon juice for 10 minutes.

Drain each artichoke on paper towels, shaking to remove all moisture. Open up the artichokes, gently prying the leaves with your fingers as if opening a flower, then press the opening facedown on the counter. Scrape out the choke with a grapefruit knife then season liberally with salt and pepper between the leaves and all over.

Heat the olive oil in a deep saucepan until just smoking. Add the artichokes and stems, and cook for 12 to 15 minutes, until golden all over. Adjust the heat as necessary to keep the oil at a simmer. As they cook, press the artichokes firmly against the bottom of the pan to help open the "flower." After 10 minutes of cooking, spritz the pan by shaking your wet hand over the artichokes to mist them. Be careful—this will cause the oil to sizzle and spatter somewhat. Cook 1 to 2 minutes longer.

When the artichokes are cooked, remove each one, and, holding the artichoke by skewering its base with a fork, press the flower side down to force it further open. Drain on paper towels, season with salt and pepper again, and serve with lemon wedges.

Fire-Roasted Artichokes with Almonds

serves 4

8 jumbo **ARTICHOKES**

12 **GARLIC** cloves, thinly sliced

1 cup thinly sliced **ALMONDS**

3 tablespoons **SEA SALT**

3 tablespoons freshly ground black **PEPPER**

2 **LEMONS**, peeled, seeded, and finely chopped

1½ cups fresh **OREGANO** leaves

1½ cups extra-virgin **OLIVE OIL**

Prepare a charcoal fire or preheat the grill.

Cut off 1½ inches of the pointy tops and tips of the artichokes.

In a medium mixing bowl, combine the garlic, almonds, salt, black pepper, lemons, and oregano until well blended. Using your fingers, spread the artichokes apart until they are open like flowers. Divide the oregano mixture among the artichokes, and stuff it down between the leaves. Drizzle 4 to 5 tablespoons olive oil over each artichoke and place directly into the coals or on top of the grill. Cook, turning occasionally, for 1 hour. The outer bases of the artichokes will char and become inedible, but the insides will be fully cooked and amazing.

ARTICHOKES

Italian artichokes are descendants of *Cynara cardunculus* and are considered the domesticated version of that wild and wooly thistle, the cardoon (see page 221). While both grow wild in many parts of southern Italy, it is the commercial cultivars that interest the artichoke aficionado the most. Artichokes grow successfully in warmer climates on plants that average four to six feet tall. It is the immature flower that is actually eaten, with the bracts perceived as the leaves, the base as its bottom, and the bud itself at the very center, the inedible choke. In America, the globe artichoke rules; a different species yet in the same genus, its leaves are barely edible but its gargantuan bottom is pure textural joy. You may also be able to find smaller artichokes that bear a great resemblance to the Ligurian or Provençal purple artichoke, which is characterized by a thinner overall base, leaves or bracts descending in size from the point to the heart, and the absence of an inedible choke in the smaller or baby sizes. In Italy, each region has its local favorites, with globes coming from Lazio, purple pointy ones from Toscana, golden green mid-sizers from Venice, and so on— at least a dozen varieties.

When buying artichokes, choose those with firm, tight green leaves that are still tender at the points. The presence of at least ¾ inch of stem without severe discoloration at the cut point is considered optimal in America, though I've seen them on a full foot of attached plant in markets in Florence and Rome. Store unwashed artichokes, cut ends trimmed and standing flowerlike, in a shallow vase of water in the fridge. If stemless, wrap in moist paper and store in the fridge in the vegetable drawer for up to four days.

FIRE ROASTING

Fire roasting refers to a method of cooking by direct or indirect exposure to an actual flame or coals. No doubt the earliest cooking technique, fire roasting is popular in Italy as a bonus by-product of cooking large pieces of meat or whole animals over a large fire. Often whole potatoes, beets, or onions are placed around the perimeter of a slow fire and left to roast in their own skins and juices.

Globe artichokes are a natural for this technique, as the inedible outer leaves char and burn away, leaving the tender inner leaves, which have essentially steamed in their own delicate juices. Another stellar example of fire roasting is the "dirty" steak served by Joanne Kileen and George Germon at Al Forno restaurant in Providence, which is literally cooked on the hot coals themselves. To protect more delicate vegetables such as new potatoes, corn, or fennel, wrap them in several layers of foil and place at the outer edge of your charcoal fire. After 30 to 40 minutes, they will have acquired an incredible, pure flavor that is indescribable. For variations on the theme, add a few leaves of rosemary, savory, or sage and a drop of fragrant oil to the packets with your favorite tender vegetable.

Artichokes with Mint and Garlic

serves 4

This artichoke recipe was first shown to me at Aimo and Nadia, a great Tuscan-inspired restaurant in a dreary suburb of Milan. They were served with a perfectly roasted squab glazed with chestnut honey that still dredges up memories and goosebumps every time I think about that meal. Aimo is a cool guy who walks around the fancy little dining room in a chef coat, and who does not seem to interrupt his wife, cooking in the kitchen.

20 **BABY ARTICHOKES**

¼ cup extra-virgin **OLIVE OIL**

12 **GARLIC** cloves, peeled and left whole

¾ cup dry **WHITE WINE**, preferably Frascati

1 tablespoon hot red **PEPPER FLAKES**

½ cup fresh **MINT** leaves

SALT and **PEPPER**

Peel and trim the artichokes, leaving the stems intact, and place in acidulated water.

Combine the olive oil and garlic in a 12-inch sauté pan and cook over medium-high heat until the garlic is light golden brown, 1 to 2 minutes. Drain the artichokes and add to the pan with the garlic. Cook until tender, spritzing occasionally with wine when necessary, to slow the cooking, about 10 minutes. Stir in the red pepper flakes and mint, season with salt and pepper, and serve.

Cardoons in the Oven

serves 4

My wife, Susi, grows cardoons for me every year. Blanched, they can be served in salads, in pastas dishes, or for dipping in the classic bagna cauda from the Piemonte. This is an appetizer or light lunch with grilled bread.

5 pounds **CARDOONS**

2 **LEMONS**

2 cups **BALSAMELLA** (page 229)

1 cup freshly grated **PARMIGIANO-REGGIANO** cheese

1 cup fresh **BREAD CRUMBS**

hot red **PEPPER FLAKES**

Trim the top leaves and fibrous strands off the cardoons until they resemble 14- to 16-inch heads of celery. Remove each stalk and peel off the fibrous outer ribs and hard green skin using a paring knife. Cut the cardoons into three 5- to 6-inch pieces.

Fill a stockpot or pasta pot three-quarters full with water. Halve the lemons and squeeze them into the water. Add the cardoons and bring to a boil over medium-high heat. Lower the heat to medium and cook at a rapid simmer for 1 hour. Drain, rinse, and allow to cool.

Preheat the oven to 400°F.

Arrange the cooled cardoon pieces in an ovenproof casserole and cover with the balsamella. Sprinkle with the grated cheese and bread crumbs and bake for 30 to 35 minutes, until dark golden brown and very bubbly. Serve immediately with red pepper flakes.

CARDOONS

Cardoons are members of the thistle family, *Cynara cardunculus* species, and grow both wild and cultivated throughout much of central and southern Italy. When mature, the fleshy silver-green stalks sprout a flower similar to its cousin the artichoke. In the cardoon's case, the stalk itself is the prize and is harvested before flowering to yield crisp spikes that are peeled and eaten either raw or cooked. In Italy, they are simply cooked in salted acidulated water and then baked or fried. Cardoons are generally available from November to January.

Seasonal variation and the pedigree of the produce are key.

Asparagus Sformato with Fonduta

serves 8

Sformato refers to the act of removing the edible from the structural, in this case the flan from the mold. Asparagus is a member of the lily family, and this preparation works just as well with many of its relatives; blanched leeks, caramelized onions, or finely chopped scallions will all produce a seductive and somewhat rich first course. To really push it, shave white or black truffles over the finished dish; it is quite traditional and truly delicious.

½ cup fresh **BREAD CRUMBS**, lightly toasted

1 pound fresh medium **ASPARAGUS** spears, tough ends removed

2 cups **BALSAMELLA** (page 229)

1 teaspoon **SALT**

pinch of freshly grated **NUTMEG**

¼ cup freshly grated **PARMIGIANO-REGGIANO** cheese

2 **EGGS** plus 2 **EGG YOLKS**

1 cup **FONDUTA** (page 233)

Preheat the oven to 400° F. Butter 8 ½-cup ramekins and coat with the crumbs. Bring about 4 quarts of water to a boil and add about 2 tablespoons salt. Have a bowl of ice water nearby.

Blanch the asparagus in the boiling water until just tender, 1 minute, and then drain and plunge into the ice water to stop the cooking. Drain again and pat dry.

Cut the asparagus spears in half crosswise. Slice the tops into ½-inch pieces and set aside. Place the bottoms in a food processor and blend until finely pureed. Transfer the pureed asparagus to a fine strainer to drain off any liquid, then place in a bowl.

Add the balsamella, salt, nutmeg, cheese, eggs, and egg yolks. Blend thoroughly. Add the sliced asparagus pieces and fold in gently. Pour into the prepared ramekins. Place in a 12-inch baking pan and fill two-thirds full with hot water. Bake for 25 to 30 minutes, or until golden brown and a toothpick inserted in the middle comes out clean. Remove and allow to cool 15 minutes.

Turn the sformatos out onto plates, spoon some of the fonduta on top, and serve.

Warm Asparagus with a
Black Pepper Zabaglione

serves 4

This elegant dish is a little fancy for a regular dinner, but works quite well for a special occasion in the spring. At La Volta, we served it only for Easter lunch, even though we made enough for both lunch and dinner. The staff meal occasionally had some of the best dishes . . . The zabaglione does not hold well, so prepare it right before serving.

2 pounds medium **ASPARAGUS** (30 to 34 spears)

6 extra-large **EGG YOLKS**

1 extra-large **EGG**

½ cup **VIN SANTO** or other dry fragrant wine

3 tablespoons unsalted **BUTTER**, melted

1 tablespoons heavy **CREAM**, warmed slightly

¼ cup freshly grated **PARMIGIANO-REGGIANO**

1 tablespoon freshly ground black **PEPPER**, plus

more to sprinkle on top

SALT

Wash the asparagus and snap off the stem ends. In the top of a double boiler large enough to hold the asparagus in the bottom half, combine the yolks, egg, and wine with a whisk, stirring vigorously over simmering water until frothy, about 10 minutes. Remove from the heat and set aside.

Drop the asparagus into the simmering water, bring to a boil, and cook 1 minute and 15 seconds.

Meanwhile, whisk the butter, cream, cheese, and black pepper into the egg mixture and season to taste with salt.

Drain the asparagus and divide among 4 plates. Spoon the sauce over the asparagus, sprinkle with fresh pepper, and serve.

ASPARAGUS

Asparagus is a member of the same lily family as leeks and onions, and has been cultivated in the eastern Mediterranean for two thousand years. The leaf-free plant more closely resembles thick grass than seedlings and is difficult to harvest, as each individual stem grows at its own pace and must be picked by hand. Asparagus is at its best in mid-spring in the Northern Hemisphere, though it can often be harvested from a second cut in California in the early fall, yielding slightly tougher stalks. As the plant matures during the summer, it eventually goes to seed, rendering the stalks woody with open, fernlike growth. White asparagus is achieved through the process of blanching, or covering the partially grown stalks with peat or loose soil for several days. Purple asparagus is an Italian cousin, highly prized particularly in Rome and only recently available in the United States.

When buying asparagus, look for firm, smooth bright green stalks with tightly closed, compact heads and smooth, light-colored butt ends. Avoid asparagus with dried-out bases or open flowering heads. Store wrapped in moist paper towels for two to three days maximum.

EGGPLANT

Owing in part to their incredible adaptability both as a cultivar and as an ingredient, there are nearly as many varieties of eggplant as there are ways to cook them. Originally a native of India, the eggplant was brought to western Europe through Moorish trade channels near the end of the Moors' domination of Spain in the fifteenth century. Like its relatives peppers and tomatoes, eggplant is a member of the nightshade family, and was considered poisonous or insanity provoking, and thus avoided in France until the eighteenth century.

Eggplant is often cooked in copious and unfortunate amounts of oil, as its spongy tissue is filled with air pockets that drink up liquids of all kinds. The best way to avoid this is to bake, grill, or roast the eggplant first and then add it to recipes calling for initial frying or sautéing. Choose firm, smooth-skinned fruit that is about half the size of the largest in the bin. Younger eggplant have fewer seeds and tend to be sweeter. Salting eggplant prior to cooking is an antiquated habit that dates back to times when eggplants were bitter, probably owing to the use of overripe fruit, as well as varietal variation. I find it a waste of time and do not recommend it. Like tomatoes, eggplant is best stored at room temperature, so it's best to buy several at a time but no more. If you find yourself faced with a spectacular harvest in your garden, I have only two words: caponata freezes—see page 226.

Caponata of Eggplant

serves 8

This eggplant preparation represents the lasting presence of outside influences on Sicily's exceptional cooking heritage. The inclusion of both sweet and sour elements is a trademark of many Sicilian dishes, typifying the importance of North African flavors in the melting pot of international cooking. Geographically, Sicily is much closer to Tunisia than to Milan, and the cooking reflects this quite convincingly.

1 cup extra-virgin **OLIVE OIL**

1 large Spanish **ONION**, cut into ½-inch dice

2 **GARLIC** cloves, thinly sliced

3 tablespoons **PINE NUTS**

3 tablespoons dried **CURRANTS**

1 teaspoon hot red **PEPPER FLAKES**

2 medium **EGGPLANTS**, cut into ½-inch cubes

1 tablespoon **SUGAR**

1 teaspoon ground **CINNAMON**

½ teaspoon unsweetened **COCOA POWDER**

2 teaspoons fresh **THYME** leaves or ½ teaspoon dried

¾ cup **BASIC TOMATO SAUCE** (page 84)

⅓ cup **BALSAMIC VINEGAR**

SALT and **PEPPER**

Heat ½ cup of the olive oil in a 12- to 14-inch sauté pan. Add the onion, garlic, pine nuts, currants, and red pepper flakes and sauté for 4 to 5 minutes over medium-high heat until softened. Add the eggplant, sugar, cinnamon, and cocoa and continue to cook 5 minutes, stirring often. Add the thyme, tomato sauce, and vinegar and bring to a boil. Lower the heat and simmer for 5 minutes. Season with salt and pepper. Cool and serve at room temperature.

Sautéed Japanese Eggplant with Scallions and Thyme

serves 4 to 6

Japanese eggplant more closely resembles the small eggplants that are common in Italy than do our American-size big guys, so I use these creamier, sweeter specimens often. The vinegar in this dish actually dissipates completely, leaving only a sweet hint of its presence.

6 medium Japanese **EGGPLANTS**

4 tablespoons extra-virgin **OLIVE OIL**

2 **SCALLIONS**, thinly sliced (about ½ cup)

2 tablespoons chopped fresh **THYME** leaves

2 tablespoons **BALSAMIC VINEGAR**

SALT and **PEPPER**

Trim the stem ends from the eggplants and cut each in half lengthwise. In a 12- to 14-inch skillet, heat the olive oil until smoking. Add the eggplant pieces and, stirring constantly, cook until softened, 6 to 8 minutes. Add the scallions, thyme leaves, and vinegar and continue cooking until the vinegar evaporates, about 30 seconds. Remove from the heat. Season with salt and pepper and serve immediately or allow to cool and serve at room temperature.

TOMATOES

Tomatoes are one of the most explosively flavorful, seasonally sensitive, and temperamental fruits of all. Unfortunately, the Evil Tomato Barons of America have spent years engineering tomatoes that can be harvested green, gassed red, shipped hard, and arrive intact, though quite nearly flavorless, at your local market year-round. A native of Central and South America, the tomato was introduced to Europe in the early sixteenth century by Spanish conquistadors. By the late seventeenth century, tomatoes were mentioned often in recipes, but not until the early twentieth century did the tomato and pasta tango become a permanent fixture on the culinary scene. Heirloom varieties, or seeds and tomatoes not yet squashed from existence by the above-mentioned ETBs, have become the darlings of American chefs and are justly sought out by cooks across the country. My wife, Susi, grows ten varieties every year, and our perennial favorites are Ruby Gold, Brandywine, and Green Zebra. Do not refrigerate tomatoes—ever. If they are ripening too quickly to eat, make sauce and freeze it for a nasty winter night.

Barbecued Endive in Tarragon Oil with Pepato

serves 4

The delicate bitterness of the endive is perfectly complemented by the tarragon and peppery sheep's milk cheese. This dish works quite well as an *antipasto* with a selection of two or three meatier vegetables such as eggplant or winter squash.

Tarragon Oil

½ cup extra-virgin **OLIVE OIL**

½ cup fresh **TARRAGON** leaves

Bring about 4 cups of water to a boil and have a bowl of ice water ready.

Drop the tarragon leaves into the boiling water and cook for 30 seconds. Drain the leaves and plunge immediately into the ice water to cool. Drain again and press to remove excess water. Place the blanched tarragon in a blender with the cup olive oil and blend until smooth. Makes ½ cup.

4 large **BELGIAN ENDIVE**

1 tablespoon extra-virgin **OLIVE OIL**

1 tablespoon **RED WINE VINEGAR**

1 tablespoon freshly ground black **PEPPER**

4 ounces **PECORINO PEPATO**, pecorino Romano, or cacio di Roma cheese

1 recipe **TARRAGON OIL**

Prepare a charcoal fire or preheat the grill.

Halve the endive lengthwise. In a shallow bowl, mix 1 tablespoon of the olive oil with the vinegar and black pepper. Dredge the endive in the vinegar mixture and place on the hot grill. Cook until slightly charred, 8 to 10 minutes, and remove to a serving platter.

Spoon the tarragon oil over the endive, shave cheese over each serving in long shards with a vegetable peeler, and serve at room temperature.

Fennel Gratin with Robiola

serves 4

I can eat fennel a thousand ways, but this is one of the most decadent. The robiola cheese comes both fresh and aged, and both work well, though with quite different results. The aged robiola is more intense and pungent and can overwhelm the fennel. The fresh is still very flavorful but softer and a little sweeter. It is important not to undercook the fennel in the first step; if it's too chewy, it won't be as sultry under its silken sheet of melted cheese.

2 **FENNEL** bulbs, trimmed of stalks, halved, and cut
 into ¼-inch slices

1 cup **BALSAMELLA**

4 ounces **FONTINA** cheese, grated

8 ounces **ROBIOLA** cheese, cut into 8 pieces

½ cup fresh **BREAD CRUMBS**, lightly toasted
 under broiler

Butter four 4-inch round gratin dishes or ramekins. Bring about 4 quarts of water to a boil and add about 2 tablespoons salt. Preheat the oven to 450°F.

Place the fennel bulbs in the boiling water and blanch 12 to 15 minutes, until tender. Drain and set aside until cool enough to handle.

In a mixing bowl, combine the fennel with the balsamella and fontina. Divide evenly among the 4 gratin dishes and pat down with the back of a spoon.

Bake in the top half of the oven for 25 minutes, until bubbling and hot. Remove from oven and place a square of robiola in the center of each dish, sprinkle with bread crumbs, and return to the oven for 5 to 6 more minutes, until the robiola is hot and soft and the crumbs have melted in. Allow to stand 3 minutes before serving.

Balsamella
Bechamel Sauce

5 tablespoons unsalted **BUTTER**

¼ cup **FLOUR**

3 cups **MILK**

2 teaspoons **SALT**

½ teaspoon freshly grated **NUTMEG**

In a medium saucepan, heat the butter until melted. Add the flour and whisk until smooth. Cook over medium heat until light golden brown, about 6 to 7 minutes.

Meanwhile, in a separate pan heat the milk until just about to boil. Add the milk to the butter mixture 1 cup at a time, whisking continuously until very smooth, and bring to a boil. Cook 30 seconds longer and remove from the heat. Season with salt and nutmeg. Makes 2 cups.

Sautéed Fennel with Anchovies, Garlic, and Sambuca

serves 4

This Roman-inspired *contorno* is a case of the dish being more than the sum of its parts. The incredible flavor combination of licorice two ways and anchovies might blow away some main courses, so choose a full-flavored *secondo*, such as a braised lamb shank, to go with it.

4 **FENNEL** bulbs, fronds reserved

4 tablespoons extra-virgin **OLIVE OIL**

4 **GARLIC** cloves, thinly sliced

6 **ANCHOVY** fillets, rinsed and patted dry

½ cup **SAMBUCA** or anise liqueur

Bring about 3 quarts of water to a boil in a large saucepan. Fill a large bowl with ice water and place nearby.

Blanch the fennel bulbs in the boiling water for 10 to 12 minutes or until fork-tender. Remove and refresh in the ice bath. Drain the bulbs well and cut each in half.

In a 14- to 16-inch nonstick sauté pan, heat the olive oil over medium heat until smoking. Add the fennel pieces, cut side down, and sauté slowly until golden brown, 8 to 10 minutes. Add the garlic to the pan and turn the bulbs over. Mash the anchovies to a paste and add to the pan with the liqueur. Swirl the pan and cook until the alcohol evaporates, about 1 minute. Remove the fennel bulbs to a serving dish. Chop the reserved fennel fronds, add to the liquid remaining in the pan, and pour over the fennel. Serve warm.

Scafata of Lima Beans and Escarole

serves 4

This simple vegetable stew is enlivened with pancetta and chiles, but could easily live without them. Fresh limas can be difficult to find out of season, but fava beans seem to be in season for half the year and are an excellent substitute. You can also use dried limas that have been soaked overnight and cooked until tender (see page 65). This dish is much better undercooked by two minutes than overcooked by one.

4 tablespoons extra-virgin **OLIVE OIL**

4 ounces **PANCETTA**, chopped into ⅛-inch dice

½ medium Spanish **ONION**, thinly sliced

1 teaspoon hot red **PEPPER FLAKES**

1 pound shelled fresh **LIMA BEANS** or 1½ cups soaked
   and cooked dried limas

½ head **ESCAROLE**, cut into ½-inch ribbons (about 2 cups)

½ cup **BASIC TOMATO SAUCE** (page 84)

1 tablespoon freshly ground black **PEPPER**

In a 12- to 14-inch sauté pan, heat the olive oil and pancetta until the pancetta is soft and translucent, 6 to 8 minutes. Add the onion, red pepper flakes, and lima beans and cook until the onion softens, 8 to 10 minutes. Add the escarole, tomato sauce, and black pepper and cook until wilted and soft, 4 to 5 minutes. Serve immediately.

Balsamic Glazed Onions

serves 4

These are great served just by themselves with a piece of crusty bread, or as a side dish with rich bollito misto, or something as simple as grilled birds. The sweetness of the onions is accentuated by the sweet and sour of the cooked vinegar. They combine well with leafy greens or even boiled potatoes as a simple appetizer.

2 large **RED ONIONS**

3 tablespoons extra-virgin **OLIVE OIL**

¾ cup **BALSAMIC VINEGAR**

Preheat the oven to 425°F.

Cut the onions in half lengthwise, leaving the skins on. In a 12-inch oven-proof skillet, heat the olive oil until smoking. Place 4 onion halves cut side down into the skillet and cook without moving them over medium heat until dark golden brown, 7 to 8 minutes. Add the vinegar, place the skillet in the oven, and bake until the onions are soft, 15 to 20 minutes.

Remove the onions from the pan immediately and place cut side up on a cool plate. Pour the syrup that has formed in the pan over the onions and cool to room temperature.

Onion Flans with Fonduta

serves 8

The velvet texture of these flans makes for a very delicate first course and is evocative of everything great about the Piemonte, where I first had this dish. Slow cooking is the key to achieving the right texture, free of bubbles, in the final result. You'll need 3-ounce ramekins or flan dishes for this recipe. To really push this into the supernal realm, shave black or white truffles over just before serving.

3 tablespoons unsalted **BUTTER**

2 medium Spanish **ONIONS** (about 1½ pounds), sliced ¼ inch thick

½ teaspoon freshly grated **NUTMEG**

½ teaspoon finely chopped fresh **ROSEMARY** leaves

¾ teaspoon **SALT**

2 cups **MILK**

3 **EGGS** plus 5 **EGG YOLKS**

¼ cup freshly grated **PARMIGIANO-REGGIANO** cheese

SALT and **PEPPER**

1 recipe **FONDUTA**

1 black or white **TRUFFLE** (optional)

Fonduta

4 ounces **FONTINA** cheese, freshly grated

¾ cup heavy **CREAM**

½ teaspoon **SALT**

PEPPER

In a small saucepan, combine the grated fontina, cream, salt, and pepper to taste and heat gently, stirring continuously, until smooth and creamy. Makes 1 cup.

In a 10- to 12-inch sauté pan, heat the butter over medium-low heat. When the foam subsides, add the onions and cook slowly until soft and golden brown, 12 to 15 minutes. Set aside to cool.

Preheat the oven to 350°F. and butter 8 3-ounce ramekins or flan molds.

Divide the sautéed onions among the prepared ramekins. In a bowl, whisk together the nutmeg, rosemary, salt, milk, eggs, yolks, and grated cheese. Season to taste with salt and pepper and ladle evenly into the ramekins. Place the ramekins in a baking dish and fill halfway with cool water.

Bake for 40 to 45 minutes, or until the flans are set and a toothpick inserted in the center comes out clean. Remove from the oven and allow to cool 5 minutes. Run a knife around each flan, unmold, and serve with fonduta and truffles, if desired.

Sautéed Pumpkin with Chiles, Mint, and Honey

serves 4

We serve this at Pó with slow-cooked oxtail; the pumpkin's sexy freshness stands up to the intense flavor of the rich braise. Served cold, this is also an excellent substitute for potato salad that will make your barbecue even hipper.

1 pound **SUGAR PUMPKIN** or acorn squash, peeled and seeded

4 tablespoons extra-virgin **OLIVE OIL**

4 **GARLIC** cloves, thinly sliced

1 teaspoon hot red **PEPPER FLAKES**

3 tablespoons **RED WINE VINEGAR**

3 tablespoons **HONEY**

3 tablespoons chopped fresh **MINT** leaves

Cut the pumpkin into 1-inch cubes.

In a 12- to 14-inch sauté pan, heat the olive oil until smoking. Add the pumpkin and garlic and cook, tossing frequently, until light golden brown, 4 to 5 minutes. Add the red pepper flakes, vinegar, and honey and bring to a boil. Cook until the liquid is reduced to a syrup around the pumpkin, about 1 minute. Remove from the heat, toss with the mint, and serve.

PUMPKINS AND WINTER SQUASH

Pumpkins, acorn squash, butternut, buttercup, hubbard, and turbans are all members of the winter squash genus *Curcurbita*, and are harvested at full ripeness from early autumn on through the first frost. Protected by a much harder skin than their batter-fried cousins from the summer, winter squash have dense deep golden- to orange-colored flesh that needs much more time to develop and yields much more wealth in the vitamin department, particularly A, C, iron, and potassium.

When buying winter squash, look for firm but dull-colored skin with moist stems that are still flexible in October and November and drier later into winter. The squash should be heavy for its size. Medium-size specimens are preferable to giants, as their liquid content is more consistent, making cooking them more predictable.

Pumpkin Sformato with Fonduta and Frisée

serves 8

This sformato is quite rich and full flavored. We often ate this and a large salad with some prosciutto as a family meal at La Volta before the dinner service on warm autumn nights.

1-pound wedge of **SUGAR PUMPKIN** or Hubbard squash

2 cups **BALSAMELLA** (page 229)

4 **EGG YOLKS**

2 **EGGS**

¼ cup freshly grated **PARMIGIANO-REGGIANO** cheese

1 teaspoon **KOSHER SALT**

¼ teaspoon **PEPPER**

¼ cup fresh **BREAD CRUMBS**

1 head **FRISÉE** lettuce, washed and spun dry

2 tablespoons extra-virgin **OLIVE OIL**

1 tablespoon **RED WINE VINEGAR**

1 recipe **FONDUTA** (page 233)

Preheat the oven to 375° F.

Wrap the pumpkin in foil and bake 1 hour. Remove, leaving the oven on, and allow to cool.

Peel the pumpkin and cut into 1-inch cubes and place in a mixing bowl. Fold in the balsamella, yolks, eggs, ¼ cup cheese, salt, and pepper and stir gently to combine.

Lightly butter a 6- to 8-inch tube pan and dust with bread crumbs. Pour the batter into the pan and set inside a larger baking pan. Fill halfway with warm tap water, place in the oven, and bake about 45 minutes, or until a toothpick stuck in the center comes out clean. Set aside to cool.

Toss the frisée together with the olive oil and vinegar and divide among 4 serving plates. Cut the sformato into 2-inch slices and arrange a slice on each plate. Drizzle with the fonduta and serve.

Radicchio di Treviso with Guanciale and Rosemary

serves 4

Guanciale is a very flavorful bacon made from the jowls of pigs, and it is often present in dishes from Rome. It adds such a great flavor to this dish. Pancetta is an acceptable substitute, however.

4 ounces **GUANCIALE**, pancetta, or slab bacon

4 long heads **RADICCHIO** di Treviso (see Note)

2 tablespoons chopped fresh **ROSEMARY** leaves

4 tablespoons white wine **VINEGAR**

SALT and **PEPPER**

Chop the guanciale into 1-inch strips and place a cold sauté pan over medium heat. Cook until the fat is rendered, 5 to 6 minutes.

Add the radicchio and sauté over lively heat until wilted, about 2 minutes. Add the rosemary and vinegar, season with salt and pepper, and toss to coat. Serve hot or at room temperature.

Note: If you cannot find the long heads of Radicchio di Treviso, substitute 2 heads of the more readily available Radicchio di Verona, cored and quartered.

RADICCHIO AND CHICORY COUSINS

Radicchio (both green and red), chicory, frisée, escarole, and endive are all members of the *Cichorium* genus and possess a somewhat bitter flavor that can be enjoyed raw or tamed with cooking. Red radicchio is a variety of red *Cichorium intybus* and is considered by many to be the quintessential Italian lettuce. When its leaves form balls or heads, it is called *radicchio di Verona*. When its leaves form upright, semi-open heads of long straight ribs, it is called *radicchio di Treviso*. Chicory, frisée, and escarole are close cousins, with saladlike dentated leaves that are dark green in the outer reaches and white, or even red-tinged, near the heart. When purchasing chicories, look for firm, light-colored hearts with plenty of vitality and crisp, shiny, smooth leaves. Brown coloration at the leaf end indicates infection, while a brown cut end implies an excessively long time out of the soil. Store chicories rinsed and spun dry for up to four days in a moistened kitchen towel, well protected from moving air. Store Belgian endive wrapped in towels, whole, away from a light source.

Radicchio Frittelle with Asiago

serves 6

These fritters are often served in wine bars in the Veneto, and generally serve to abate the appetite between meals rather than alongside an entrée.

2 medium heads **RADICCHIO**

9 large **EGGS**, beaten

½ cup fresh **BREAD CRUMBS**

¼ cup all-purpose **FLOUR**

2 tablespoons freshly grated **PARMIGIANO-REGGIANO** cheese

4 tablespoons extra-virgin **OLIVE OIL**

4 ounces **ASIAGO** cheese, coarsely grated

SALT and **PEPPER**

Core the radicchio, cut in half, and slice into ⅛-inch julienne. Place the radicchio in a large mixing bowl, add the eggs, bread crumbs, flour, and the Parmigiano-Reggiano and stir to mix.

In a 10- to 12-inch nonstick sauté pan, heat a tablespoon of the olive oil until just smoking. Cook the fritelle until golden brown, about 3 minutes per side. Adjust the heat as needed to cook the fritelle evenly. Drop the batter into the hot oil by heaping tablespoons, making 6 fritters at a time. Remove to a serving platter and repeat with remaining batter. Sprinkle with the Asiago and salt and pepper and serve.

Stuffed Peppers, Onions, and Tomatoes

serves 4

I love to eat these simple, peasant-inspired stuffed vegetables the day after they're made—if there are any left over. Always make your own fresh bread crumbs from fresh bread with the crusts on; simply cut in one- to two-inch cubes, toss in the food processor, and process until evenly and finely ground.

2 medium **RED ONIONS**, peeled with ends untrimmed, halved lengthwise

2 medium red **BELL PEPPERS**, halved, with seeds and ribs removed

2 large **TOMATOES**, halved crosswise, seeds and juice reserved

1 cup fresh **BREAD CRUMBS**, lightly toasted under broiler

½ cup freshly grated **PARMIGIANO-REGGIANO** cheese

½ cup finely chopped Italian **PARSLEY**

6 tablespoons extra-virgin **OLIVE OIL**

SALT and **PEPPER**

Preheat the oven to 450° F.

Bring about 2 quarts of water to a boil in a large saucepan. Drop the onion halves in the boiling water and blanch 2 minutes until pliable. Drain, and when cool enough to handle, remove the inner half of the onion using a paring knife, leaving the outer 3 or 4 layers intact.

Chop the inside layers of the onions and mix in a large bowl with the tomato seeds and juice, bread crumbs, grated cheese, parsley, and ¼ cup of the olive oil. Season with salt and pepper.

In an oiled shallow medium casserole, arrange the peppers, onions, and tomatoes cut side up. Stuff the vegetables loosely with the bread crumb mixture just to fill and drizzle the remaining oil over each in a thin stream. Bake uncovered for about 30 minutes, or until the bread crumbs on top of each are dark brown and crispy.

Serve hot or at room temperature.

Stuffed Zucchini Flowers

serves 4

Zucchini flowers have an amazing flavor and are a delicious partner for almost any kind of cheese or egg dish. Here the ricotta and pine nut stuffing is delicate enough to allow the actual flavor of the blossom to come through as it floats on a thin lake of watercress and yogurt.

4 tablespoons **PINE NUTS**, toasted under broiler until dark brown

8 ounces **RICOTTA** cheese

1 large **EGG**

¼ cup finely chopped Italian **PARSLEY**

pinch of grated **NUTMEG**

1 teaspoon **SALT**

12 large **ZUCCHINI BLOSSOMS**, rinsed and patted dry

1 bunch **WATERCRESS**, stems removed, washed, and spun dry

1 cup plain **YOGURT**

6 tablespoons extra-virgin **OLIVE OIL**

juice of 1 **LEMON**

In a large bowl, combine 2 tablespoons of the pine nuts, the ricotta, egg, parsley, nutmeg, and ½ teaspoon salt until the mixture is pastelike.

Gently open each flower and, using a small teaspoon, place 2 tablespoons of the ricotta mixture inside each. Close up again by twisting the ends of the flower like the ends of a mustache. Set aside.

In a blender, combine half the watercress with the yogurt and remaining ½ teaspoon salt until smooth and creamy, about 1 minute.

In a 10- to 12-inch nonstick pan, heat 4 tablespoons of the olive oil until just smoking and place 6 blossoms in the pan. Cook until golden brown, about 2 minutes. Turn once, and cook 1 minute more, then remove to a warm plate. Keep warm while you cook the remaining blossoms.

While the second batch of blossoms is cooking, toss the remaining watercress with the remaining 2 tablespoons oil and the lemon juice to coat. Mound in the center of 4 plates. Drizzle a puddle of yogurt sauce around the watercress and place 3 warm blossoms on top of the sauce. Sprinkle each plate with a few of the remaining toasted pine nuts.

Sautéed Spicy Peppers with Marjoram Vinaigrette

serves 4

Try this recipe at the end of the summer, when peppers are vibrantly colored and flavored, as well as inexpensive. When I make this dish at home, I add even more of the Mexican-style hot peppers and sometimes leave the peppers whole.

4 tablespoons extra-virgin **OLIVE OIL**

1 medium **RED ONION**, thinly sliced

1 **GARLIC** clove, peeled and left whole

4 Italian **FRYING PEPPERS** (banana shaped)

2 red **BELL PEPPERS**, cored, seeded, and cut into ½-inch strips

2 yellow **BELL PEPPERS**, cored, seeded, and cut into ½-inch strips

2 large **JALAPEÑO** peppers, cored, seeded, and cut into ½-inch strips

1 recipe **MARJORAM VINAIGRETTE**

In a 10- to 12-inch sauté pan, heat the olive oil over medium-high heat until smoking. Add the onion and garlic and sauté until softened, 4 to 5 minutes. Add all the peppers and, shaking regularly, cook until quite soft yet still retaining individual texture, 10 to 12 minutes. Transfer to a large mixing bowl and allow to cool.

Pour the marjoram vinaigrette over the cooled peppers and toss gently with your hands, being careful not to break up the peppers. Serve at room temperature.

Marjoram Vinaigrette

3 tablespoons **BALSAMIC VINEGAR**

2 tablespoons chopped fresh **MARJORAM** leaves

6 tablespoons extra-virgin **OLIVE OIL**

SALT and **PEPPER**

In a small mixing bowl, combine the vinegar, marjoram, and olive oil. Season with salt and pepper. Makes ½ cup.

Turnip "Risotto"

serves 4

I first tasted potato "risotto" in the late eighties, at Jeremiah Tower's phenomenal San Francisco restaurant, Stars. Mark Franz, perhaps the cook who has most profoundly influenced my career and a chef at Stars, served his version with poached sea scallops and a black truffle sauce that I can still remember as if it were yesterday. Here I give turnips the risotto treatment, complete with butter and Parmigiano. It's important to cut the turnips in uniform pieces so they will all be cooked through. This would also serve as an appetizer course.

6 tablespoons extra-virgin **OLIVE OIL**

1 medium **RED ONION**, cut into ⅛-inch dice

1½ pounds **TURNIPS**, cut into ⅛-inch dice

2 cups hot **CHICKEN STOCK**

SALT and **PEPPER**

2 tablespoons unsalted **BUTTER**

½ cup freshly grated **PARMIGIANO-REGGIANO** cheese

½ cup finely chopped Italian **PARSLEY**

In a 12- to 14-inch skillet, heat the olive oil over medium heat. Add the onion and cook until softened and light brown, about 10 minutes. Add the turnips and cook 2 minutes, stirring frequently, until opaque. Add 1 ladle of chicken stock and stir until the stock is absorbed. Continue adding stock a ladle at a time until the turnips are tender and fragrant, about 10 minutes. Season with salt and pepper and stir in the butter and grated cheese until rich and creamy, about 1 minute. Remove from the heat and stir in the parsley. Serve immediately.

Summer Vegetable Pickles

makes 3 quarts

Anyone with a garden knows that the bounty of even a small plot can overwhelm daily food needs. This is the quickest answer to a bumper crop
around. The whole recipe is really the brine, so feel free to substitute whatever vegetables you have in excess. Refrigerated, these will keep for a month.

6 cups **WHITE WINE VINEGAR**

4 cups **WATER**

3 tablespoons **SEA SALT**

15 black **PEPPERCORNS**

4 **GARLIC** cloves, peeled

1 tablespoon **FENNEL SEEDS**

½ cup **SUGAR**

3 **FENNEL** bulbs, cut into ½-inch wedges

3 small **ZUCCHINI**, cut into 5 × ½-inch batons

1 small **CAULIFLOWER**, cut into florets

10 small **RED ONIONS** with tops if possible, halved

½ cup extra-virgin **OLIVE OIL**

½ cup **BALSAMIC VINEGAR**

In a large nonreactive saucepan, stir together the vinegar, water, sea salt,
peppercorns, garlic, fennel seeds, and sugar and bring to a boil. Boil 2 minutes, then add the fennel. Cook the fennel until just tender, about 4 minutes,
and remove with a slotted spoon to a large bowl or platter.

Add the zucchini and cook until just tender, about 1 minute, then add to the
fennel. Add the cauliflower and cook until tender, about 3 minutes, and
remove to combine with the fennel and zucchini. Add the onions and cook
until tender, about 2 minutes, and combine with the other vegetables.

Return the cooking liquid to a boil and boil for 3 minutes. Remove the pan
from the heat and stir in the oil and vinegar.

Divide the vegetables among several 1-quart canning jars and cover them
with the cooking liquid. If there is not enough liquid, add a little white wine
vinegar to cover. Allow the jars to cool, cover with lids, and refrigerate.
Pickles will keep up to a month in the refrigerator.

Vegetable Fritto Misto

serves 4

In Italy, this would never be served as a *contorno*, but as the centerpiece of a meal. I like it as main course after a good plate of pasta with a lot of fresh hot peppers, but would also serve it as a flashy *antipasto* or a side dish.

6 cups extra-virgin **OLIVE OIL**, for frying, plus 3 tablespoons

½ cup unbleached all-purpose **FLOUR**

½ cup superfine **SEMOLINA** flour (see Glossary)

2 teaspoons **BAKING POWDER**

1 teaspoon **SALT**

1 cup cold **WATER**

8 ounces **CAULIFLOWER** florets, sliced ⅛ inch thick

8 ounces **BROCCOLI** florets, sliced ⅛ inch thick

6 medium cremini **MUSHROOMS**, halved

1 medium **ZUCCHINI**, cut into ¼-inch-thick rounds

6 baby **ARTICHOKES**, quartered and outer leaves removed

4 **LEMONS**, 2 cut into ⅛-inch-thick rounds and 2 in wedges

12 **ZUCCHINI FLOWERS**

kosher **SALT**, to sprinkle

Preheat the oven to 300°F. Place a large platter covered with a dish towel in the oven to warm. Heat 6 cups olive oil to 370°F. in a 6-inch-tall deep-fryer with a basket.

Make the batter. Stir together the flour, semolina, baking powder, and salt. Slowly add the water, stirring until smooth. Mix in 3 tablespoons olive oil and combine thoroughly.

Dip the vegetables and lemon slices in the batter in the order listed, using as little batter as possible, and deep-fry, just a few at a time, until golden brown and crisp. The time will vary depending on the vegetable, 3 to 4 minutes at most. Drain after frying on paper towels.

Arrange the vegetables on a large platter. Sprinkle the whole platter with kosher salt and serve immediately with lemon wedges.

Soft Polenta with Asparagus, Prosciutto, Garlic, and Ramps

serves 4

Ramps and asparagus show up at farmer's markets around the same time every year and hit a particularly harmonious high note when combined with prosciutto and lemon in this simple one-course meal. It is best served when the spring has not quite succeeded in banishing winter's chilly presence.

1 pound thick **ASPARAGUS**, trimmed

1 cup quick-cooking **POLENTA** or yellow cornmeal

1 cup **MASCARPONE** cheese

6 tablespoons (¾ stick) unsalted **BUTTER**

3 **GARLIC** cloves, thinly sliced

3 slices **PROSCIUTTO**, cut into julienne

12 **RAMPS**, cleaned and root ends removed

juice and zest of 1 **LEMON**

½ cup dry **WHITE WINE**

SALT

Set up an ice bath. Bring about 5 cups of water to boil in a 4-quart saucepan. Drop the asparagus into the boiling water and cook until tender, about 1½ minutes. Use tongs to remove the asparagus and refresh in the ice bath.

Return the same water to a boil and, whisking constantly, add the polenta in a thin stream until all is incorporated. Stir with a wooden spoon until as thick and dense as Cream of Wheat and remove from the heat. Fold in the mascarpone and let stand.

In a 12- to 14-inch sauté pan, heat 4 tablespoons of the butter over medium heat until foaming. Add the garlic, prosciutto, and ramps and sauté until the ramps are wilted, 6 to 7 minutes. Add the asparagus, lemon juice and zest, and wine and bring to a boil. Add the remaining 2 tablespoons butter, shake pan to emulsify, and season with salt.

Divide the polenta among 4 bowls, top each with the asparagus-ramp mixture, and serve immediately.

Grilled Polenta with Sautéed Spinach and Robiola

serves 4

Because this is somewhat labor-intensive, it is best served with a plain dish such as grilled lamb chops or steak. The complex flavors of the cheese create a lot of action on an otherwise austere plate.

3 cups **WATER**

1 cup quick-cooking **POLENTA** or yellow cornmeal

1 teaspoon **SALT**

3 tablespoons extra-virgin **OLIVE OIL**

2 **GARLIC** cloves, thinly sliced

1 pound fresh young **SPINACH**, washed, stems removed, and spun dry

SALT and **PEPPER**

4 ounces **ROBIOLA** cheese

In a medium saucepan, bring the water to a boil. Add the polenta in a thin stream, stirring constantly. Lower the heat to a simmer, season with salt, and cook 5 to 7 minutes, until the consistency of thick oatmeal. Pour the polenta into a clean but not greased 9 × 13-inch baking dish and allow to cool 30 minutes.

Preheat the grill or broiler. Cut the polenta into quarters, then halve each quarter diagonally to make 8 wedges. Brush the wedges with 1 tablespoon olive oil, set over the grill, and cook until slightly charred and crispy, about 10 minutes.

Meanwhile, heat the remaining 2 tablespoons oil in a 12- to 14-inch skillet. Add the garlic and cook 45 seconds to 1 minute, until light brown. Add all the spinach at once and cook quickly, about 30 seconds, until just wilted. Season with salt and pepper and set aside.

Remove the polenta from the grill and spread 1 tablespoon robiola over each hot piece. Spoon some warm spinach on top of each and serve.

Caciotta
Dolce
₤ 16.00
etto

Formaggi and Dolci

Cheese and Sweets

FORMAGGI and DOLCI

Italians, by and large, have very little interest in desserts, and in many *trattorie* the only courses available after the *secondo* might be local cheese, seasonal fruit, and maybe gelato or sorbet. In Italy, it is common to have a small piece of cheese after the *secondo*. This is because Italians are often still a little hungry for something savory as they finish their wine. Massive cheese boards and even huge wobbling carts in the French style have become quite popular in the last ten years in American restaurants, leading people to believe that all Europeans enjoy a wide selection of cheeses near the end of their meal. Although this may occur in some fancier *ristoranti* in the Piemonte or Lombardia areas, it is by no means the norm. Most restaurants in Italy offer just two or three cheeses—more than likely including Parmigiano-Reggiano, local aged or fresh sheep's milk cheese, and maybe a soft cheese such as Taleggio or Gorgonzola. Each region, of course, will have several cheeses specific to that region, and they will probably be featured throughout the meal, as well as at the end.

This is not to imply that Italians do not eat dessert; Sicily's greatest gifts to Italian cooking are its sweets and pastries. And Italians eat gelato, Italy's true contribution to the world of dessert, all day long, even on their way home to dinner. But many restaurants, including La Volta, offer a modest assortment of sweets. Hence, a lot of the desserts that I make have been developed at Pó or elsewhere along my travels. My favorite desserts to eat and make are generally based on seasonal fruit and shine in their simplicity, as opposed to reveling in rich chocolate or elaborate pastry technique. (This is most likely sour grapes, owing to my general ineptitude and lack of experience in the pastry kitchen.) Nonetheless, as in all aspects of Italian cooking: simpler is very often better.

Here I offer a list of Italian cheeses suitable to follow the *secondo*, and you'll find some nontraditional cheese course recipes I've developed at Pó on pages 250 to 253.

- **Robiola**—soft, fresh, and creamy—ripened five to fourteen days, made of cow's, sheep's, or goat's milk and combinations of the three. My favorite producer is Roccaverano.

- **Taleggio**—washed rind cow's milk cheese from Lombardy with a creamy soft interior, a soft edible rind that turns dark golden as it ages, and huge luscious flavor. My favorite producer is Mauri.

- **Gorgonzola**—soft, mildly sweet and slightly pungent blue cheese, at its best six to eight weeks after release. More intense with age, this is a cow's dream date. Try those produced by Lodigiani.

- **Asiago**—a firm cow's milk cheese from Veneto. Choose vecchio, aged four months or more to produce an amber color and caramel flavor. Montegrappa is my preferred producer.

- **Parmigiano-Reggiano**—undisputed king of Italian cheese. Huge spicy flavor with nut and mineral components, rich, complex, and intense. All producers are excellent.

- **Pecorino Toscano**—sheep's milk cheese from Tuscany. Soft and creamy when young, harder and more nutty when older. The best producers are in and around Sienna and Arezzo, so check the label for origin.

- **Pecorino Sardo**—unlike pecorino Romano, which is too salty for after dinner, this Sardegnan sheep's milk cheese is often spectacular. It is somewhat inconsistent, so taste each time you buy.

- **Stracchino**—a fresh cheese that comes from Lombardy, this cow's milk cheese is very creamy and mild flavored.

Robiola in Chestnuts with Persimmon Sauce

serves 4

8 ounces **ROBIOLA** cheese

½ cup finely chopped roasted **CHESTNUTS** (see page 17)

1 very ripe **PERSIMMON**

¼ cup **ORANGE JUICE**

2 tablespoons **SUGAR**

Remove the robiola from its package and drain. Cut each cube into 2 equal pieces. Gently press each piece into the ground chestnuts, so that the nuts adhere. Set aside at room temperature.

Peel and seed the persimmon and place in a food processor with the orange juice and sugar. Blend until smooth, about 30 seconds.

Divide the cheese among 4 plates, drizzle with persimmon sauce, and serve.

Sautéed Apples in Amarone with Asiago

serves 4

2 tablespoons plus 2 teaspoons unsalted **BUTTER**

4 medium **MCINTOSH APPLES**, peeled, cored, and quartered

4 tablespoons **SUGAR**

pinch of grated **NUTMEG**

1 cup Amarone di Valpolicello or other light, dry **RED WINE**

4 ounces **ASIAGO** cheese, the youngest possible

Heat 2 tablespoons of the butter in a 12-inch sauté pan over medium heat. When the butter begins to brown, add the apples and cook until soft and light golden brown, 3 to 4 minutes. Add the sugar, nutmeg, and wine and cook 1 minute, until the wine is reduced by half.

Add the remaining 2 teaspoons butter and swirl the pan to emulsify the sauce. Pour the apples and sauce into a shallow serving dish. Use a peeler to shave thin shards of Asiago over the apples, and serve warm.

Aged Goat Cheese with Dried Fruit–Moscato Compote

serves 4

¼ cup dried **APRICOTS**, cut into ⅛-inch strips

¼ cup dried **CRANBERRIES**

¼ cup dried **CHERRIES**

¼ cup dried **CURRANTS**

¼ cup **DRIED QUINCE**, sliced

1 cup Moscato d'Asti or other **SPARKLING DESSERT WINE**, plus remainder of bottle to serve

8 ounces aged semi-dry **GOAT CHEESE**, such as the Coach Farm stick

In a medium saucepan over low heat, stir together the apricots, cranberries, cherries, currants, quince, and Moscato. Bring to a boil, turn off the heat, and let stand 30 minutes.

Divide the fruit among 4 martini glasses, shave shards of the aged goat cheese over, and serve with a glass of chilled Moscato.

Gorgonzola with Spiced Walnuts and Port Wine Syrup

serves 4

3 cups inexpensive **PORT** wine

1 tablespoon unsalted **BUTTER**

½ cup **WALNUT** halves

½ teaspoon **CAYENNE** pepper

½ teaspoon freshly ground black **PEPPER**

½ teaspoon **SALT**

2 teaspoons **SUGAR**

8 ounces sweet **GORGONZOLA** cheese

In a 2-quart saucepan, bring the wine to a boil. Cook over medium heat until reduced to ½ cup, about 12 minutes, and allow to cool.

In an 8-inch sauté pan, melt the butter over medium heat. When the butter starts to sizzle, add the walnuts, cayenne, black pepper, salt, and sugar and sauté until well coated and lightly toasted, 2 to 3 minutes. Set aside to cool.

Divide the Gorgonzola into 4 portions and spoon the nuts over each portion. Drizzle the wine syrup over in a pretty pattern and serve with crusty bread.

Sautéed Stracchino with Pine Nuts, Cinnamon, and Amaretto

serves 4

12 ounces **STRACCHINO** cheese, well refrigerated

½ cup **PINE NUTS**, spread out on a flat plate

2 tablespoons plus 2 teaspoons unsalted **BUTTER**

½ teaspoon ground **CINNAMON**

¾ cup **AMARETTO**

Cut the cheese into 4-inch square pieces about ½ inch thick. Press into the pine nuts so that they adhere on one side and set aside.

Heat a 10-inch nonstick pan over medium heat and add the 2 tablespoons butter. When the butter is sizzling, place the cheese pieces in the pan nut side down and cook until golden brown on the nut side, about 3 minutes.

Remove and place each piece on a separate plate, nut side up. Add the cinnamon, Amaretto, and remaining 2 teaspoons butter to the pan and reduce by half over high heat, about 2 minutes. Pour the sauce over the cheese and serve immediately.

Strawberries with Balsamic Vinegar and Black Pepper

serves 4

This seemingly strange combination of sweet fresh fruit and tangy aged vinegar is by no means nouvelle cuisine. In Modena, home of Pavarotti, Lamborghini, and balsamic vinegar, desserts utilize the best fruit and a touch of the local magic potion, enlivened with a spritz of freshly ground pepper to create an unusually refreshing dessert. This is equally good with peaches, melons, or small citrus fruits, like clementines.

2 pints **STRAWBERRIES**

2 tablespoons best-quality **BALSAMIC VINEGAR**

1 teaspoon **SUGAR**

freshly ground black **PEPPER**

In a medium mixing bowl, toss the strawberries, vinegar, and sugar together well. Divide among 4 martini glasses, drizzling all the vinegar over the fruit. Grind fresh black pepper over each portion and serve.

Cheese is milk's leap to immortality; dessert revives a slowing appetite.

Peaches in Primitivo Syrup

serves 4

Primitivo di Gioia is a dry red wine from Puglia, where this dessert originates. A Primitivo is not really all that essential to this dish, but any substitute should share the characteristics of this full-bodied, rough red—or even a simple cabernet or merlot. The syrup can be used for a plethora of fruits, as well as for any dessert that needs just a touch of sweetness or juice to bring it around, ice cream included.

1 whole **CLOVE**

2 cups **SUGAR**

2 cups **PRIMITIVO DI GIOIA** or other dry red wine

4 **PEACHES**

In a medium saucepan, combine the clove, sugar, and wine and heat together until the sugar is dissolved, about 10 minutes. Cool and keep covered.

Bring about 2 quarts of water to a boil in a medium saucepan. Drop the peaches in the boiling water for 10 seconds to loosen the skins. Peel and slice the peaches and divide among 4 wineglasses. Pour ¼ cup of the cooled wine syrup over each serving and serve immediately with biscotti.

Fresh Watermelon with Cool Citrus Mascarpone

serves 4

This cool dessert is on the summer menu at Pó, but you'd never find it in Italy, where they are smart enough to leave perfect fruit alone. But I could not resist gilding the alleged lily.

1 **ORANGE**

2 **LEMONS**

1 **GRAPEFRUIT**

1 pound **WATERMELON**

1 cup **MASCARPONE** cheese

2 tablespoons **SUGAR**

Zest the orange, lemons, and grapefruit, then use a sharp knife to cut off any remaining peel and pith. Cut between the membranes to free the individual segments, working over a bowl to catch the juices. Reserve the segments and juice separately.

Halve the watermelon lengthwise. Using a melon baller, cut the melon into balls and place in a shallow serving bowl. Add the reserved fruit juices and set aside.

In a blender, mix the mascarpone, fruit zests, and the sugar until smooth. The mixture should be as thick as yogurt; if necessary, thin with a little water. Drizzle the macarpone over the watermelon balls and sprinkle the fruit segments over and serve cool.

Ciambella with Summer Berry Compote

serves 8

In Italy, you'd find this cake served as a mild afternoon snack, though some fancy restaurants tend to gussy it up with elaborate presentations and extra sauces. It's often important in Italian cooking to remember where a dish came from before putting it on a really expensive plate.

1 pint **BLUEBERRIES**

1 pint **BLACKBERRIES**

1 pint **RASPBERRIES**

juice of ½ **LEMON**

½ cup plus 3 tablespoons **SUGAR**

2 cups all-purpose **FLOUR**

½ teaspoon **BAKING POWDER**

½ cup (1 stick) cold unsalted **BUTTER**, cut into ½-inch cubes

1 large **EGG**

1 teaspoon **ALMOND** extract

¼ cup cold **MILK**

In a large saucepan, combine the berries, lemon juice, and 3 tablespoons sugar. Place over medium heat and heat just to the boiling point, 5 to 6 minutes. Remove from the heat and allow to cool.

Preheat the oven to 375° F. Butter a cookie sheet.

Combine the flour, remaining ½ cup sugar, and the baking powder in a food processor and pulse quickly to blend. Add the cold butter and pulse quickly until the mixture resembles fine bread crumbs.

In a separate bowl, beat the egg, almond extract, and milk until smooth. With the food processor running, add the liquid all at once and blend 10 to 15 seconds, until the dough just forms a ball.

Transfer the dough to a well-floured cutting board and shape into a log about 14 inches long and 1½ inches thick. Form the log into a ring in the center of the cookie sheet. Bake for 30 to 35 minutes, until light golden brown. Remove, transfer to a rack, and cool to room temperature.

Cut the cake into slices about 1 inch thick, top with 2 tablespoons of berry compote, and serve.

Rhubarb Compote with Crushed Biscotti and Honey-Scented Yogurt

serves 4

I've always loved the tangy sweet taste of rhubarb in pies, on ice cream, and even raw with a sprinkling of salt. We serve this as a layered parfait at Pó with the cookies sprinkled on top, but the compote can become filling for pies, syrup for pancakes, or a sauce for any simple, warm cake.

4 pounds **RHUBARB**, leaves discarded, cut into ½-inch pieces

juice and zest of 2 **LEMONS**

1½ cups **SUGAR**

4 plain **BISCOTTI** (storebought is fine)

2 cups goat's or cow's milk **YOGURT**

4 tablespoons **HONEY**

4 scoops vanilla **GELATO** or best-quality ice cream

In a nonreactive 6-quart pot, combine the rhubarb, lemon zest, lemon juice, and sugar and cook over medium heat until the mixture has a jamlike consistency, 20 to 30 minutes. Set aside to cool.

In a blender, process the biscotti until they are reduced to crumbs. Pour out and set aside. In the same blender, combine the yogurt and honey and blend until frothy, about 1 minute.

In each of 4 large goblets, place half a cup of the rhubarb mixture, 4 tablespoons of the yogurt mixture, and 2 tablespoons biscotti crumbs. Add a scoop of gelato, sprinkle with the remaining biscotti crumbs, and serve immediately.

Roasted Pears with Chestnut Honey and Pecorino Toscano

serves 4

To my mind, this is one of the most perfect desserts of all time. It has everything that an Italian could want after dinner: fruit, cheese, honey—even wine. It was quite popular at La Volta, but the American taste for dessert tends to chocolate or the elaborate sweet thing, and it simply does not sell at Pó, so this dessert is more often on the staff menu.

4 large **PEARS**, Bosc or Anjou, not quite ripe

1 cup **CHIANTI** or other dry red wine

1 cup **SUGAR**

¼ cup chestnut or orange blossom **HONEY**

8 ounces **PECORINO TOSCANO**

Preheat the oven to 400° F.

Trim the bottoms of the pears so they'll stand up. Arrange them upright in a small baking dish just large enough to hold them. Pour the wine and sugar into the pan around the pears. Place in the oven and cook until soft, about 40 minutes. Remove and allow to cool. Strain the liquid in the bottom of the pan and set aside.

To serve, place each pear in the center of a dessert plate. Drizzle with chestnut honey and spoon the wine sauce around the base of each. Using a peeler, shave pieces of pecorino over the pears and serve.

Chocolate Biscotti

makes 30

Grandma's biscotti recipe, which was the genesis of this variation, is quite simple to make. The name comes from *bis*, or "twice," and *cotti*, the past participle of the verb "to cook." The second cooking is the most important step in the whole recipe. Too often biscotti are soft or crumbly when they should be crisp and relatively hard, the better to stand up to the heinous crime (vilified on *Seinfeld*) of double dipping in wine left over from dinner, the appreciation of which is an important step in the passage from youth to adulthood.

2¼ cups all-purpose **FLOUR**

½ cup unsweetened **COCOA POWDER**

1⅔ cups **SUGAR**

1 teaspoon **BAKING POWDER**

3 large **EGGS**

4 **EGG YOLKS**

1 tablespoon **AMARETTO**

¾ cup **HAZELNUTS**, skin on

½ cup mini **CHOCOLATE CHIPS**

Preheat the oven to 350°F.

In a large mixing bowl, stir together the flour, cocoa, sugar, and baking powder. In a separate bowl, whisk together the eggs, yolks, and Amaretto. Add the wet ingredients to the dry ingredients and stir just until the dough comes together, about 1 minute. Add the hazelnuts and chocolate chips and mix until just incorporated.

Roll the dough into 3 logs about 10 inches by 2 inches and place on an ungreased baking sheet. Bake 20 minutes until light golden brown and remove from the oven. As soon as they are cool enough to handle, cut the logs on a slight diagonal into pieces ⅓ inch thick and arrange cut side down on the sheets. Lower the heat to 275°F., return the pieces to the oven, and bake 20 minutes longer, until crisp and dry. Allow to cool.

Bones of the Dead

Ossi di Morti

makes 40 to 50

Humorously named because of their strange appearance when baked, bones of the dead are a little tricky because they need to sit out over night rolled out. The step is well worth it, so however you need to rig the place, try it. Cook them until they're just firm; they will become rather crunchy once they've set.

3 large **EGGS**

2 cups **CONFECTIONERS' SUGAR**

2 cups all-purpose **FLOUR**

1 teaspoon **BAKING POWDER**

In a large mixing bowl, beat the eggs at high speed for 5 to 6 minutes. Add the confectioners' sugar and mix 6 minutes more, starting at low speed and gradually increasing to medium. Mix the flour and baking powder together and add one-third at a time to the egg mixture. The batter will look like firm meringue.

On a floured work surface, roll the dough into 4 logs about 3 inches wide by ½-inch thick and as long as a cookie sheet. Cover with a clean towel and let sit overnight.

Preheat the oven to 375°F.

Remove the dough logs from the cookie sheet and lay on a floured surface. Cut into 1½-inch lengths and replace on the cookie sheet. Bake 20 minutes or until light golden brown. Remove from the sheet and allow to cool. Cookies can be stored for up to one month in an airtight container.

Apostle's Fingers

Diti di Apostoli

serves 4

Trying to demonstrate these simple egg white omelets on TV gave me the hardest time. I was using a plastic spatula to flip the eggs out of an extremely hot nonstick pan and the spatula kept melting to the pan. At home, I recommend using a thin-edged wooden spoon to turn these puppies—it will make your life a lot easier. Italians serve these after dessert, with coffee.

¾ cup fresh **RICOTTA** cheese

¼ cup **SUGAR**

4 tablespoons unsweetened **COCOA POWDER**

¼ cup **AMARETTO**

zest of 1 **ORANGE**

4 large **EGG WHITES**

2 tablespoons extra-virgin **OLIVE OIL**

In a medium mixing bowl, stir together the ricotta, sugar, 2 tablespoons of the cocoa, the Amaretto, and orange zest. In a separate bowl, beat the egg whites till foamy and light peaks barely form.

In a 6- to 8-inch nonstick pan, heat about ½ teaspoon of the olive oil over medium heat. Pour 2 heaping tablespoons of the eggs whites into the pan and quickly spread into a 6-inch circle. Cook 1 minute on first side, then turn and cook 20 seconds more. Continue until all the egg whites are used up; you should have 8 "crepes." Add more oil to the pan as needed and adjust the heat if the pan gets too hot.

To assemble, place 2 tablespoons of the ricotta mixture in center of each crepe. Fold both sides over the filling to form an omelet shape. Place on each dessert plate, sprinkle with some of the remaining 2 tablespoons cocoa, and serve.

Pinoccate

makes about 3 dozen cookies

With the essential help of a candy thermometer, these no-bake pine nut cookies are even easier to make than they seem.

3 cups **SUGAR**

¾ cup **WATER**

2 cups **CANDIED CITRON** or candied orange peel

2 cups **PINE NUTS**

zest of 4 **ORANGES**

Line 2 cookie sheets with waxed paper or parchment.

In a 3-quart saucepan, heat the sugar and water until the sugar is completely dissolved and the liquid is clear. Continue to cook the sugar syrup until it reaches 240°F.

Remove the saucepan from the heat and whisk the syrup until it cools and begins to turn opaque. Working quickly, add the citron, pine nuts, and orange zest and combine thoroughly, placing over low heat briefly if the mixture becomes too stiff. Using a small soup spoon, drop irregular shapes onto the cookie sheets and allow to cool and harden. Store in an airtight container.

Sciumette

serves 6

These cooked meringues are much simpler to make than floating island and hold up quite well for as long as a day, so you can make them early in the afternoon and keep them cool till after the cheese course at dinner. Any citrus fruit, or cooked fruit puree for that matter, can be substituted for the blood orange. I often use cooked apples or quince, or even pureed figs in the summer. If using fruit other than citrus, delete the cocoa.

4 cups **MILK**

1 cup heavy **CREAM**

juice and zest of 1 small **BLOOD ORANGE**

1½ cups **CONFECTIONERS' SUGAR**

5 extra-large **EGGS**, separated

2 tablespoons unsweetened **COCOA POWDER**

Bring the milk and cream to a boil in a 12- to 14-inch sauté pan. Stir in the orange zest and ¼ cup of the sugar and lower the heat to a simmer.

Whisk the egg whites to form soft peaks. Add ¼ cup of the sugar and the orange juice, and whisk until stiff peaks form. Scoop up large tablespoonfuls of the egg white mixture and drop them carefully into the barely simmering milk, cooking 3 or 4 at a time. Cook for 2 minutes per side, flipping carefully with a large kitchen spoon. Do *not* allow the milk to boil. Use a slotted spoon to transfer the cooked *sciumette* to a shallow bowl.

Fill a large bowl with ice cubes and set a smaller bowl inside.

In a heavy enameled saucepan, whisk the egg yolks with the remaining 1 cup sugar until the mixture forms a pale ribbon as it runs off the whisk. Add the warm poaching milk to the yolk mixture and cook *carefully* over low heat, whisking constantly, until very hot and thickened, 5 to 6 minutes. When the mixture is as thick as heavy cream, transfer to the smaller bowl over the ice bath and whisk until cool.

Pour some of the cooked custard into each serving dish and top with *sciumette*. Dust with cocoa and serve.

Sfince with Honey

serves 4

These little doughnuts are originally from Sicily, but we served them at La Volta, especially on religious holidays, though I am not clear what the association was. These are not on the menu at Pó, as we do not have the space to fry safely, and I recommend that you always undertake deep-frying with caution and in a spot a little removed from the kitchen action.

These can be cooked in advance and served room temperature, but they are twice as good if served right out of the oil. In French cooking, this dough is called *pâte à choux* and it is used for profiteroles and Paris-Brest.

VEGETABLE OIL, for frying

½ cup(1 stick) unsalted **BUTTER**

1 cup **WATER**

pinch of **SALT**

1 cup all-purpose **FLOUR**

4 **EGGS**

1 cup **HONEY**, preferably chestnut (available at specialty stores)

CONFECTIONERS' SUGAR, for dusting

In a 6-inch-deep saucepan, heat 3 to 4 inches of oil to 375° F.

In a 2- to 3-quart saucepan, melt the butter in the salted water and bring to a boil. Stir in the flour and cook until the mixture pulls away from the sides of the pan. Transfer the batter to a mixing bowl and allow to cool. When cool, beat in the eggs, one at a time.

Place the honey in a small saucepan and heat over low heat.

Using 2 tablespoons, form almond-size balls of dough and drop into the hot oil. Fry 3 or 4 at a time (don't crowd the pan—they will double or triple in size) until golden brown on all sides, about 8 minutes. Remove and drain on paper towels. Continue until all the dough is fried.

Sprinkle *sfince* with confectioners' sugar, drizzle with the warm honey, and serve.

Frittelle di Mele

serves 4

Apple fritters are a terrific way to warm up chilly autumn nights, and in Borgo Capanne there were plenty of those. We often made these in the afternoon on our days off, just to relax around the empty restaurant and sip a grappa with our espresso.

6 green **APPLES**, peeled and cored

2 quarts **CANOLA OIL**, for frying

2 large **EGGS**

¼ cup **MILK**

1 cup all-purpose **FLOUR**

¼ cup **SUGAR**

2 tablespoons **KIRSCH**

2 cups vanilla **GELATO** or best-quality vanilla ice cream

ground **CINNAMON**, for dusting

Slice the apples crosswise into ½-inch-thick rounds and set aside.

Heat the canola oil in a deep-fryer to 375°F.

In a medium mixing bowl, whisk together the eggs and milk. Slowly add the flour to the mixture, 3 tablespoons at a time, until all is incorporated. Stir in the sugar and kirsch. Allow to stand for 10 minutes.

Dip the apple slices in the batter and carefully place in the hot oil, 3 or 4 at a time. Cook until golden brown, then drain on a plate lined with paper towels. Keep warm while you cook the remaining apples slices.

Place 5 fritters on each plate in an overlapping circle. Place a scoop of vanilla gelato in the center, sprinkle with cinnamon, and serve.

Cannoli

makes 16

The all-time number one dessert in Little Italy, this Sicilian classic is often ruined if filled more than twenty minutes before serving, allowing the shell to become leaden and soggy. When cannoli are properly prepared, the crisp shell is an essential textural contrast to the dense, soft filling.

To make this dessert, it is essential to have metal cannoli tubes.

PASTRY SHELLS

1½ cups all-purpose **FLOUR**

¼ teaspoon ground **CINNAMON**

1 teaspoon **GRANULATED SUGAR**

1 teaspoon unsweetened **COCOA POWDER**

4 tablespoons (½ stick) unsalted **BUTTER**

½ cup **MARSALA** wine

FILLING

1 pound sheep's or cow's milk **RICOTTA** cheese

½ cup **SUPERFINE SUGAR**

1 tablespoon **VANILLA** extract

4 tablespoons grated **ORANGE ZEST**

¼ cup mini **CHOCOLATE CHIPS**

2 quarts canola **OIL**, for frying

1 **EGG WHITE**, lightly beaten

CONFECTIONERS' SUGAR, for dusting

Make the pastry. Mix the dry ingredients in a the mixing bowl. Cut in the butter with 2 knives until the butter is the size of peas. Add the Marsala and shape the dough into a ball. Wrap in plastic and refrigerate until firm, 1 hour.

Make the filling. In a large mixing bowl, stir together the ricotta, sugar, vanilla, orange zest, and chocolate chips until well combined. Spoon into a pastry bag with a large round tip and refrigerate for 30 minutes.

Heat the canola oil in a deep 3½-quart pot to 350° F.

Remove the dough from the refrigerator and divide into 4 pieces. Roll 1 piece on a flat surface with rolling pin until $1/16$ inch thick. Cut into a 4-inch circle and, using a rolling pin, elongate the circle into an oval. Wrap the oval lengthwise around a metal form and seal the edge with egg white. Flare the ends open with your fingers. Repeat for remaining dough pieces.

Place the dough forms in the hot oil and fry until golden brown, 2 to 3 minutes. Drain on paper towels. When cool enough to touch, twist the shells off of the molds. Shells may be made 1 day in advance and left unfilled and uncovered.

Just before serving, pipe the ricotta cream into the shells. Dust with confectioners' sugar and serve immediately.

Tangerine, Grapefruit, Lemon, and Orange Digestivi

makes 8 quarts

Digestivi are drinks served after a meal to help digest a many-course meal. This is usually accomplished—especially when using grappa-based *digestivi*—by actually burning a hole right through to the lower intestine.

10 cups **SUGAR**

10 cups **WATER**

zest of 5 **TANGERINES** cut in wide strips

zest of 5 **GRAPEFRUIT** cut in wide strips

zest of 5 **LEMONS** cut in wide strips

zest of 5 **ORANGES** cut in wide strips

3 bottles **GRAPPA**, such as Nadini

Make a simple syrup by combining the sugar and water in a saucepan. Heat them together until the sugar has dissolved and the syrup is clear. Allow to cool.

Arrange 8 quart bottles and divide each type of zest equally between 2 bottles to yield 2 quarts each of tangerine-, grapefruit-, lemon-, and orange-flavored liqueur. Pour an equal amount of the sugar syrup into each bottle, using it all, and top each with grappa.

Brutti ma Buoni

makes 4 dozen cookies

This translates as "ugly but good" and is an especially useful dish for restaurants that use a lot of egg yolks and thus have a lot of egg whites left over. When cooked properly, these cookies should have a slightly chewy, flexible texture.

4 **EGG WHITES**, at room temperature

¾ cup **SUGAR**

3 tablespoons all-purpose **FLOUR**

1 tablespoon **VANILLA** extract

1 tablespoon **AMARETTO**

1 tablespoon unsweetened **COCOA POWDER**

zest of 1 **ORANGE**, finely grated

½ cup chopped **HAZELNUTS**

¼ cup chopped **ALMONDS**

¼ cup **PINE NUTS**

Preheat the oven to 325°F. Butter a cookie sheet and dust with flour.

Place the egg whites in the bowl of an electric mixer and whip to soft peaks. Gradually add the sugar and beat 2 minutes. Stop the machine and add the flour, vanilla, Amaretto, cocoa, and zest all at once. Mix 1 minute and stop the machine. Quickly stir in the nuts by hand.

Place the batter in 2-inch blobs on the cookie sheet 2 inches apart. Bake about 30 minutes, checking after 25 minutes, until crisp. Transfer the cookies to wire racks to cool completely, then store in an airtight container.

Panettone

serves 8

Here is my variation on the holiday classic, a recipe I learned in the course of a day spent at the Disney World of gourmet stores—Peck, in Milano. I had hoped to spend a week there, watching and observing, but the kitchen was crowded with other extras from all over the world, so after one day I was sent packing. Coming away with this recipe lessened my disappointment. You will need a heavy-duty standing mixer and a special panettone pan for this recipe.

½ cup (1 stick) unsalted **BUTTER**, softened to room temperature

2 large **EGGS**

3 large **EGG YOLKS**

3½ cups all-purpose **FLOUR**

1 cup **MILK**

1 cup **SUGAR**

½ cup dried **CURRANTS**, soaked 1 hour in warm water and drained

zest of 2 **ORANGES**

2 teaspoons **CREAM OF TARTAR**

1½ teaspoons **BAKING SODA**

Preheat the oven to 425° F. Butter and flour a tall-sided 8-inch round cake pan.

In a mixer, cream the butter with the eggs and yolks until pale yellow, 3 to 4 minutes (small bits of butter will still be visible). Switch to the dough hook attachment and, with the mixer running, add half of the flour. Add half of the milk and mix 1 minute. Add the remainder of the flour followed by the remainder of the milk and all of the sugar; the dough will be quite sticky. Mix 10 minutes.

Turn the dough out onto a floured surface and sprinkle with the currants, orange zest, cream of tartar, and baking soda. Knead for 8 to 10 minutes, form into a ball, and place into pan.

Bake for 35 to 45 minutes, or until an inserted toothpick comes out clean. The top should be quite cracked. Invert onto a rack and allow to cool. Serve in wedges.

Olive Oil and Orange Cake

serves 8

This recipe is very similar to the cake I enjoyed for breakfast while taking part in one of Faith Willinger and Beatrice Contini's seminars at the Capezzana winery in Carmignano. It is best served with a drizzle of new oil and a smear of the local berry preserves, or dipped simply in yogurt. It is most successful when made with a high-gluten flour, such as bread flour.

6 medium **ORANGES**

2¼ cups **BREAD FLOUR**

1 tablespoon **BAKING SODA**

4 large **EGGS**

½ teaspoon **SALT**

1 cup **SUGAR**

½ cup extra-virgin **OLIVE OIL**

Preheat the oven to 350° F. Oil a 9-inch round cake pan.

Remove the zest from the oranges and juice one of them. Set fruit aside for another use. Sift the flour and baking soda together onto a piece of waxed paper.

In a large mixing bowl, beat the eggs and salt together with an electric mixer until frothy and light, about 2 minutes. Slowly add the sugar, continuing to mix 2 minutes longer. Add the flour and baking soda gradually to the egg mixture, then mix 1 more minute.

In another bowl, combine the olive oil, orange zest, and juice. Using a spoon, stir it into the egg mixture, folding just until combined. Pour the batter into the prepared pan and bake 50 minutes, or until a toothpick inserted in the center of the cake comes out clean. Invert onto a wire rack.

Cool to room temperature, cut into wedges, and serve.

Torta della Nonna

serves 6

This is my variation on a classic Tuscan dessert served in simple and fancy places alike all over Italy. Here the freshness of the ricotta is very evident, so be certain to buy the best you can find. Serve with a glass of Vin Santo.

PASTRY

2 cups all-purpose **FLOUR**

1 large **EGG**, beaten

2 large **EGG YOLKS**, beaten

½ cup **SUGAR**

3 tablespoons unsalted **BUTTER**, melted with 3 tablespoons extra-virgin **OLIVE OIL** and cooled

½ teaspoon **VANILLA** extract

FILLING

2 cups fresh **RICOTTA** cheese, preferably sheep's milk

½ cup **PINE NUTS**

½ cup **SUGAR**

juice and finely grated zest of 1 **LEMON**

3 large **EGGS**, beaten

Preheat the oven to 375° F.

Make the pastry. Mound the flour on a pastry board. Make a well in the flour and place the egg, yolks, sugar, butter and olive oil mixture, and the vanilla in the center. Proceed as you would with fresh pasta, bringing the flour in bit by bit from the sides. When the dough comes together, knead until smooth, then allow to rest 10 minutes. The dough will be very soft; chill if necessary.

Combine the filling ingredients in a large bowl and mix until creamy.

Divide the dough into 2 portions, one slightly larger than the other. On a floured board, roll the larger piece to a 6-inch circle. Transfer to a 10-inch tart pan with a removable bottom and press into the bottom and up the sides. Spoon the filling into the tart, then roll the second piece of dough to a 10-inch circle. Carefully place over the filling and pinch to seal. Bake 35 to 40 minutes until just golden. Serve warm or at room temperature.

Castagnaccio with Red Grape Sauce

serves 6–8

During the First and Second World Wars, supply lines between Borgo Capanne and the rest of Italy were completely cut off, forcing the locals to eat what they could find. Chestnuts still grow everywhere and this dessert, along with the *necci* recipe that follows, represent the resourcefulness of the mountain-dwelling locals during most difficult times.

2 tablespoons extra-virgin **OLIVE OIL**

2 cups **CHESTNUT FLOUR** (available at specialty stores)

1 cup plus 2 tablespoons **SUGAR**

¼ cup **WALNUT** pieces

2 cups cold **MILK**

1 tablespoon chopped fresh **ROSEMARY** leaves

2 cups seedless red **GRAPES**

Preheat the oven to 375°F. Grease a 12-inch springform pan, preferably non-stick, with 1 tablespoon of the olive oil.

In a large mixing bowl, combine the flour, 2 tablespoons sugar, and the walnuts. Stir in ½ cup cold milk, then slowly add the remaining milk, stirring constantly to prevent lumps from forming. Pour the batter into the prepared pan and drizzle the top with the remaining tablespoon oil. Distribute the rosemary evenly over the top. Bake for 25 minutes, or until a toothpick inserted in the center comes out clean.

Place the grapes and remaining 1 cup sugar in a small saucepan over medium heat. Add 2 or 3 tablespoons of water and cook until quite soft and bubbly, about 10 minutes.

Cut the cake into wedges and serve either warm or cool, with the grape sauce spooned over.

Chestnut Flour Crepes *(Necci)* with Ricotta and Honey

serves 4

These crepes were quite challenging when I first tasted them, but after a couple they became truly addictive. Chestnut honey is available at specialty stores and subtly enhances the flavor, but any mild-flavored honey is acceptable.

1 cup **CHESTNUT FLOUR** (available in specialty stores)

2 extra-large **EGGS**

1¼ cups **WATER**

2 cups fresh sheep's or cow's milk **RICOTTA** cheese

½ cup chestnut or orange blossom **HONEY**

2 tablespoons extra-virgin **OLIVE OIL**

Sift the flour into a mixing bowl and beat in the eggs, one by one. Add half the water and whisk until smooth. Add the remaining water and whisk until smooth. Allow to stand 15 minutes.

Place the ricotta in a mixing bowl and stir in half the honey.

Heat a 6- to 8-inch cast-iron skillet or nonstick crepe pan over medium heat and brush with some of the olive oil. Add 2 tablespoons crepe batter and roll pan to distribute evenly and thinly. Cook until the crepe is firm on the underside and is curling up at the edges, about 1 minute; turn and continue cooking for 1 more minute. Slide the crepe onto a plate and continue making crepes until all the batter is finished, stacking each finished crepe on top of the previous one to keep them warm. You may want to use two skillets to speed up the crepe-making process.

To serve, place 2 tablespoons of the ricotta-honey mixture in the center of each crepe, fold in half, drizzle with 1 teaspoon of the remaining honey, and serve warm.

Spumone di Zabaglione

serves 4

Spuma refers to foam and spumone, although considered a variation on tutti-frutti ice cream by many Italian-Americans, is actually a wisp of big, rich foam. The addition of the whipped cream just before freezing gives the dessert a lighter texture than gelato, and it is often poured into a loaf pan and sliced. I prefer to serve it scooped, along with the Amaretti cookies.

6 extra-large **EGGS**, at room temperature

½ cup **SUGAR**

½ teaspoon grated **NUTMEG**

½ cup **MARSALA** wine

3 tablespoons **DARK RUM**

1½ cups heavy **CREAM**

12 Amaretti **COOKIES**, crushed

Fill a large mixing bowl with ice cubes and set aside.

Separate the eggs and place the yolks in the top of a double boiler. Place the whites in a stainless steel bowl and set aside. Add the sugar and nutmeg to the egg yolks and beat, off the heat with a hand-held mixer, until they form a ribbon. Stir in the Marsala and rum, place over barely simmering water, and beat until frothy, foamy, and quite firm, 3 to 5 minutes. Remove to the ice bath and whisk until cooled.

Beat the egg whites to soft peaks and set aside. Beat the cream to soft peaks and fold all 3 mixtures together gently. Pour into an ice cream maker and chill according to the manufacturer's instructions. Place in the freezer, well covered. When ready to serve, scoop into balls and roll in the cookie crumbs.

Black Grape Foam

serves 10

This simple dessert requires an ice cream or gelato maker, a valuable addition to any kitchen equipment list, though a pricey one. You could easily substitute 1½ cups pureed fruit for the black grapes in this recipe.

2 pounds black **GRAPES** or any wine grape, coarsely chopped
   by hand or in a food processor

½ cup **SUGAR**

½ cup **WATER**

juice and zest of 1 **LEMON**

1 cup heavy **CREAM**

additional **CREAM** and **GRAPES** for garnish

Wash and stem the grapes. Pass the grapes through a food mill, discarding the seeds but including all pieces of pulp or skin that come through. Refrigerate until well chilled.

Make a simple syrup by heating the sugar and water in a small saucepan over medium heat until clear and slightly thickened, 5 to 6 minutes. Refrigerate until quite cold.

Add the simple syrup to the grape pulp. Add the lemon juice and zest and stir to mix well. Whip the cream to soft peaks and fold into the cold grape mixture. Place in an ice cream machine and follow manufacturer's instructions. Pour the chilled mixture into 4-ounce Dixie cups. Cover with plastic wrap and freeze.

To serve, remove cups from the freezer and allow to stand 10 minutes. Unmold into martini glasses and garnish with fresh cream and whole grapes.

This is best eaten the day it is made.

Index

Conversion Chart
Equivalent Imperial and Metric Measurements

American cooks use standard containers, the 8-ounce cup and a table-spoon that takes exactly 16 level fillings to fill that cup level. Measuring by cup makes it very difficult to give weight equivalents, as a cup of densely packed butter will weigh considerably more than a cup of flour. The easiest way therefore to deal with cup measurements in recipes is to take the amount by volume rather than by weight. Thus the equation reads:

1 cup = 240 ml = 8 fl. oz.   ½ cup = 120 ml = 4 fl. oz.

It is possible to buy a set of American cup measures in major stores around the world.

In the States, butter is often measured in sticks. One stick is the equivalent of 8 tablespoons. One tablespoon of butter is therefore the equivalent to ½ ounce/15 grams.

Liquid Measures

Fluid Ounces	U.S.	Imperial	Milliliters
	1 teaspoon	1 teaspoon	5
¼	2 teaspoons	1 dessertspoon	10
½	1 tablespoon	1 tablespoon	14
1	2 tablespoons	2 tablespoons	28
2	¼ cup	4 tablespoons	56
4	½ cup		110
5		¼ pint or 1 gill	140
6	¾ cup		170
8	1 cup		225
9			250, ¼ liter
10	1¼ cups	½ pint	280
12	1½ cups		340
15		¾ pint	420
16	2 cups		450
18	2¼ cups		500, ½ liter
20	2½ cups	1 pint	560
24	3 cups		675
25		1¼ pints	700
27	3½ cups		750
30	3¾ cups	1½ pints	840
32	4 cups or 1 quart		900
35		1¾ pints	980
36	4½ cups		1000, 1 liter
40	5 cups	2 pints or 1 quart	1120

Solid Measures

U.S. and Imperial Measures		Metric Measures	
Ounces	Pounds	Grams	Kilos
1		28	
2		56	
3½		100	
4	¼	112	
5		140	
6		168	
8	½	225	
9		250	¼
12	¾	340	
16	1	450	
18		500	½
20	1¼	560	
24	1½	675	
27		750	¾
28	1¾	780	
32	2	900	
36	2¼	1000	1
40	2½	1100	
48	3	1350	
54		1500	1½

Oven Temperature Equivalents

Fahrenheit	Celsius	Gas Mark	Description
225	110	¼	Cool
250	130	½	
275	140	1	Very Slow
300	150	2	
325	170	3	Slow
350	180	4	Moderate
375	190	5	
400	200	6	Moderately Hot
425	220	7	Fairly Hot
450	230	8	Hot
475	240	9	Very Hot
500	250	10	Extremely Hot

Any broiling recipes can be used with the grill of the oven, but beware of high-temperature grills.

Equivalents for Ingredients

all-purpose flour—plain flour
coarse salt—kitchen salt
cornstarch—cornflour
eggplant—aubergine

half and half—12% fat milk
heavy cream—double cream
light cream—single cream
lima beans—broad beans

scallion—spring onion
unbleached flour—strong, white flour
zest—rind
zucchini—courgettes or marrow